D1241410

THE CONSTITUTIONS OF ABRAHAM LINCOLN AND JEFFERSON DAVIS

THE CONSTITUTIONS OF ABRAHAM LINCOLN AND JEFFERSON DAVIS

A HISTORICAL AND BIOGRAPHICAL STUDY IN CONTRASTS

by

Russell Hoover Quynn

An Exposition–Banner Book

EXPOSITION PRESS NEW YORK

An earlier version of Part Three of this book was issued separately at Danville, Virginia, in 1956 under the title *A Comparative Study of the United States Constitution and the Constitution of the Confederate States of America.*

Exposition Press Inc., 386 Fourth Avenue, New York 16, N. Y.

FIRST EDITION

To the memory of my grandfather,

JOHN HENRY SKINNER QUYNN

Born 1846, Nottingham, Maryland,

Trumpeter 1861–65, First Maryland Cavalry, Company C,
Army of the Confederate States of America,
Battles of Monocacy, Antietam, and Gettysburg,
Prisoner 1865, Fort Delaware,
Pardoned by President Andrew Johnson,

Died 1916, Confederate Home, Pikesville, Maryland,

Buried in Loudon Park, Baltimore, Maryland.

Introduction

JEFFERSON DAVIS AND ABRAHAM LINCOLN were born in the same Kentucky county within a year of each other, Davis in 1808 and Lincoln in 1809. It would appear that Fate, or Providence, had destined them to head the two new "revolutions" that were to break out in 1861 with the inauguration of Lincoln as President of the United States and of Davis as the first, and only, President of the Confederate States of America. Their native state, which had been part of old Virginia until it became a separate territory in 1790, had been admitted in 1792 as the fifteenth state of the Union—Vermont, the fourteenth, having been the first to join the original thirteen colonies.

The adjective "great," when applied to persons—their work, character, achievements, etc.—means "eminent, distinguished." Any man who attains to the Presidency to become Chief Executive of the United States of America is without question considered great. Therefore we can indeed say that two great Americans were born at the dawn of the nineteenth century in the same Kentucky county, and lived to achieve fame, or notoriety, as one chooses, in the annals of their country. Abraham Lincoln became known as "Honest Abe," the Great Emancipator, patron of the Negro race in North America. Jefferson Davis, on the other hand, came to be called Jeff Davis the rebel and traitor, and was even imprisoned, for a time in irons, in a strong fortress of the great republic to await trial on a number of charges—murder, maltreatment of prisoners; of war and of treason. That he was never brought to trial in a court of justice to answer them seems not to have weighed in his favor toward wiping out the stigmas of crime and wrongdoing invoked against him by his enemies and captors. Lincoln, at the summit of his public career on the pinnacle of American political success, was suddenly shot down amid the supposed security and protection of a theater in the national capital not far from the White House.

With Mrs. Lincoln and some friends and staff members, he had put aside for the moment the pressures and responsibilities of his office, seemingly weightier at the close of the war than in the heat of it.

As Presidents, each of his section of a vast country, these two men in their separate characters personified the visions, the hopes, the trusts, and the desires of their peoples. Lincoln represented them perhaps less than Davis did, because Davis had been the unanimous choice of his countrymen, while Lincoln, according to the returns from the national election of November 6, 1860, was not a nation-wide popular choice. Of a total of 303 electoral votes he received 180, his opponents 123; and his election in itself was one of the causes of the break between the North and the South. The open breach, long in the making, was realized when a number of states of the South withdrew from the Union to form their own Union, under its own Constitution and laws, in 1861.

Jefferson Davis had long stood for the equality of the states within the Union in accordance with the guarantees of the Constitution of the United States of America. But Abraham Lincoln, after much seesawing and looking both ways before his selection as leader of the new Republican Party, had boldly stated that the states could not remain in union as they had originally agreed and as had been stipulated in the Constitution. In contradiction to the opinions and the covenants of the great men who had achieved our independence and had adopted the Constitution, which had created the Union, Lincoln and the administration that came to office with him under the forms of that Constitution decided that the states could not remain politically united "half slave and half free." This was emphatically denied at the beginning (see his first Inaugural Address); it was dragged in near the end to justify events by maintaining that an "irrepressible conflict" existed which had to go on until that "relic of barbarism"—that is, slavery—should be forever eradicated from the Constitution and the laws.

The Union was divided into fixed, hostile cultural and geographical parties, or regions, strongly distinguished by institutions, opinions, products, and pursuits. The stronger section, the North, by the misuse of constitutional forms through the "simple" majorities in the Congress, was struggling, and in the popular opinion licensed, to enlarge its powers: the weaker section, the South, was striving to preserve its rights, guarantees, and equalities provided under the Declaration of Independence and under the original Constitution by the founding fathers of the Republic.

The South's stand can be called a "rebellion" only if we agree to use that doubtful word to describe opposition to a sectional government interpreting the Constitution to its own selfish ends, ignoring its provisions, and, in all but empty *forms,* trampling it underfoot. It can be said that the North's position also constituted a rebellion, in a very real sense, against a Constitution that in its opinion had outlived its usefulness to those who were now very strong. Some of its provisions had even come to be considered of the nature of "a pact with Hell." A new political party had emerged, about which Wendell Philips had said that there was "merit in the Republican Party, the first sectional party ever organized in the country. . . . It was not national, it was sectional; it was the North arrayed against the South." There was much similar agitation in the northern states and by their representatives and senators in the Congress. There, necessary legislation was often delayed, and tempers roused on the floor, by the continual interjection of extreme Abolitionist propaganda that grew in volume and vituperation. The South was told that if they would not get out of the Union, those of the North would.

"The times demanded that we must have an anti-slavery Constitution, an anti-slavery Bible, an anti-slavery God." It seems that it was not so much that the times demanded, or needed, them but that the demanders had no answer to such claims as John C. Calhoun, then at the graveside in 1850, had Mr. Mason of Virginia read for him before the Senate concerning the state of the Union, slavery, and the agitations disturbing and threatening the land. Although submerged by the outcome of the war, his essay is nevertheless one of the great and important documents of American history, and it must be studied if one would resurrect the atmosphere of that hour. That it was not heeded reflects no credit upon the statesmanship or the patriotism of the North at that critical time. Their ignoring it helped to bring on the great storm that came near to swamping the Ship of State in the mid-nineteenth century.

CONTENTS

THE CONSTITUTIONS OF ABRAHAM LINCOLN AND JEFFERSON DAVIS

☆☆

PART ONE

The Republican Attack Against Constitutional Government

☆☆

CHAPTER 1

Lincoln and the Abolition Amendments

ABRAHAM LINCOLN IN 1860, at the request of a friend who was preparing a campaign biography, wrote a brief picture of himself. It is a compact, bird's-eye view of his career as he saw it. He was born, he wrote,

> . . . in Hardin County, Kentucky, February 12, 1809, of parents both born in Virginia of undistinguished families, second families perhaps I should say. . . . My mother, who died in my tenth year, was of a family of the name of Hanks; paternal grandfather, Abraham Lincoln, emigrated from Rockingham County, Virginia, to Kentucky about 1781 or '82, where a year or so later he was killed by Indians, not in battle but by stealth when he was laboring to open a farm in the forest. My father was six then, and he grew up literally without education, going from Kentucky to Indiana in my tenth year. It was a wild region, many bears and other wild animals in the woods; there I grew up. Though few schools, there were no qualifications required of a teacher beyond reading, writing, and ciphering to the rule of 3. There was nothing to excite ambition for education; when I came to age I did not know much, but learned to read, write, cipher; I have not been to school since, doing farm work until 22, a store clerk at New Salem, Illinois, a captain of volunteers in the Black Hawk war, a member of the Illinois legislature for eight years [during which he studied law], a member of the House of Representatives one term in Washington, and law practice at Springfield, Illinois.

In this letter he made no mention of family or wife, and closed with a note that "if any personal description of me is desired, I am six feet, four, in height, lean in flesh, weighing 180 lbs., dark complexion, with coarse black hair and grey eyes, no other marks or brands recollected."

The first photograph of Lincoln was apparently taken with Mary Todd (whom he had married in 1842) while he was a congressman in 1846 at the age of thirty-seven. Research has shown that he was descended, through his father Thomas Lincoln, an illiterate pioneer farmer, in the sixth generation from Samuel Lincoln, who had emigrated from Norwich, England, to Massachusetts about 1638. From there his offspring had moved south as far as Virginia and the backwoods of Kentucky.

This "little biography" is found in Lincoln's two-volume *Complete Works* (Century Company), compiled and edited by Nicolay and Hay, who also wrote a ten-volume *Life of Lincoln* (Century), which is considered an indispensable reference and is also available in a more manageable one-volume condensation. Lincoln's law partner wrote a two-volume account (Putnam), and Miss Tarbell also wrote two volumes (McClure Company). There are a number of others, and the list continues to grow—a number of short "lives," essays by Lowell, Carl Schurz, Emerson (and a commemorative address), poems by Holmes, Bryant, Stedman, Gilder, and some works about him for young people by Coffin, Thayer, Stoddard (who wrote juvenile stories as only a juvenile could). There is an intimate account of life in the White House, his private life, by Frank B. Carpender—*Six Months at the White House.* Three novels of interest by Honoré Wiltsie Morrow—*With Malice Toward None* and two companion volumes making a sort of trilogy—about complete the list of the more important and memorable *littera* on the Patron of the Negroes, the Great Emancipator who alone by one intemperate act forced upon the country a far greater racial issue than the one that he (as it is made to appear) tried to solve on January 1, 1863.

There is no doubt that the greatest achievement of his administration, at least according to his admirers, was the Emancipation Proclamation and the later attempt to justify it and to make it legal by the unconstitutional Thirteenth Amendment, supposedly ratified December 18, 1865, in the 38th Congress, which reported to the nation that it was "ratified by 27, of 36, States." Among those twenty-seven were listed states of the

South whose electorates were disfranchised, kept from the polls by federal troops, while voting in their place were Negroes, alien troopers in blue, local riffraff, and criminals. Can such a ratification affecting the people of a certain section, made valid only by the votes of non-citizens coming from afar and unaffected by the ratification, be considered constitutional? Of course it cannot.

The Emancipation Proclamation, an incredible act, must be laid wholly to Lincoln and the small group of fanatic Abolitionists and radicals whose hatred of the South and of southern people seems to have known no bounds. It disgusted the great majority of northern citizens and was out of favor even with the troops who were fighting Lincoln's war at the hearthstones of the South. It was characterized in northern thought as the act of "an absolute, irresponsible monarch." Justice Curtis of the United States Supreme Court, who had dissented in the Dred Scott case, publicly called it an unconstitutional act issued without legal right by the President. North and West it was denounced. In a speech against conscription and arbitrary arrests, Governor Horatio Seymour of New York declared it "a proposal for the butchery of women and children, for arson and murder, for lust and rapine." Truly, it was not something that could have emanated from a "great" man. Governor Seymour reminded Lincoln that the war was supposedly being fought solely to suppress "rebellion," not to change the social system of the United States.

In the Confederacy it was received with evidences of a just indignation and was to bring forth sterner purpose in the conduct of the war. Jefferson Davis thought:

> We may well leave it to the instinct of that common humanity which a beneficent Creator has implanted in the breast of our fellowmen of all countries to pass judgment on a measure by which several millions of human beings of an inferior race—peaceful and contented laborers in their sphere—are doomed to extermination, while at the same time they are encouraged to a general assassination of their masters by the insidious

> recommendation "to abstain from violence unless in necessary self-defence." . . . Our own detestation of those who have attempted the most execrable measure recorded in the history of guilty man, is tempered by profound contempt for the impotent rage it discloses.

The South was remembering Haiti, and San Domingo; others recalled other outbreaks of the horror of racial conflict.

Nevertheless, Union generals ordered freedom wherever they marched, and enlisted and armed the blacks as soldiers. And a vengeful group in December, 1865, forced the Thirteenth Amendment through the Congress, to ensure the final abolition of slavery throughout the United States and all its territories, three years after the American President, in violation of the oath of his office and the provisions of the Constitution that he had sworn to uphold, had officially issued the Proclamation. Among his own adherents, even amid the distress of a great war, it was recognized as unconstitutional; therefore the new amendment was proposed at the end of the war to correct the highhanded procedure by drawing it under the Constitution by means of the amendment methods laid down in Article V.

An amendment to the Constitution refers either to some particular article so as to add to it, to alter or change it, or to repeal it, or provides a new and independent subject complete in itself. There can therefore be proposed amendments so inconsistent with the spirit and purpose of the original Constitution that grave questions immediately arise as to the authority of Congress to propose them or of the states to ratify them. The method employed by Congress is a joint resolution of the two houses, "whenever two-thirds of both Houses shall deem it necessary." That two-thirds vote in each house is of two-thirds of the members present (assuming the presence of a quorum), not necessarily a "yes" vote of two-thirds of the entire membership. Further, the joint resolution proposing an amendment need not contain a declaration that those voting for its adoption regard it "as necessary"—its adoption being regarded as sufficiently indicating that as fact. Already having a two-thirds vote, an accepted resolution does not need the President's signature before it is sent to the state legislatures. If there has been irregularity or insufficiency in the action of Congress, the proposal cannot be attacked in the courts on such grounds until after it has been adopted by the legislatures, when it is made effective by appropriate legislation. The states, in ratifying the proposed amendment, act not in a strictly legislative capacity but rather in a political capacity as the representatives of their people; here they exercise a federal, not a state, function.

The Secretary of State of the United States is required to issue a proclamation upon receipt of notices certifying ratification from the necessary number of states. It would seem that he has no discretion to enquire into the truth of statements in the notices, other than the requirements of his oath of office and the moral obligation and duty to know about the circumstances before his signature makes the amendment conclusive in the courts.

The technique of amendment is peculiar to the American basic instrument of government. That basic charter, the Constitution, came from an attempt to amend the old Articles of Confederation, of which George Washington in 1786 had said that he "could not conceive we would last long as a nation without having lodged somewhere a power which would pervade the whole of the Union in as energetic a manner as the authority the States' governments extends over the several States." Two years earlier Jefferson had written to Madison of a conviction that "nothing can preserve our confederacy unless the bond of Union, their common council, is strengthened." At the beginning of the struggle in 1776 Tom Paine in *Common Sense* had suggested a "Continental Charter" on grounds that "our strength is continental not provincial." There were many others—some names illustrious, some mediocre, some now lost—all with ideas of a *new* kind of government for the former colonies that were now thirteen new nations loosely allied.

From these various ideas grew the United States Constitution. A widely read work of the time was Montesquieu's *Spirit of Laws,* from which undoubtedly was taken the proposed "checks and balances"—his ideal form of government of three powers, Legislative, Executive, Judicial, each to function freely in its own sphere without encroachment on the powers conferred upon the other two. And this was achieved, the founding fathers thought.

The Constitution has been praised, pondered, cursed—from "the greatest work of man" to "a compact with Hell." It is the "agent" contract of the sovereignties, the states; it is a swallowing-up of them with all power centralized at Washington, D.C. Yet it is federative. The Supreme Court was to pass on *all* constitutional questions; it was the Legislature's duty to interpret constitutionality. The Supreme Court was something wholly new in government; it was but a descendant of the British Privy Council. Therefore, arguments *ad infinitum.* We have the notes of James Madison, last surviving convention member, bought by Congress for $30,000 and published by the Library of Congress; we have Publius' eighty-five *Federalist* pamphlets. We have full, stacked shelves of "authorities" on every aspect of the Constitution of our country. We still have arguments: this is one of them. In demonstration, we touch a few high spots—of famous names, authoritative works, opinions, well- and long-known arguments, but without pretense of exhausting any of them here . . . pro or con.

What Abraham Lincoln stood for, what Jefferson Davis stood for, culminated in a terrible civil war, an Emancipation, a "Reconstruction," and three unconstitutional so-called amendments forced upon the Constitution and upon the American people along with an exasperating race problem—all by perversion of the form of the government; by dictatorship and armed might, lawless and utterly ruthless, bringing ruin and desolation to half the country of that day, initiated by "reformers" and intermeddlers. These are blunt facts, some never before openly stated and faced, in our history. They are being presented here to the best of our ability, judgment, belief.

It is perhaps not out of place in the beginning to state that the Civil War grew out of a long-disputed question: whether the central government in Washington was supreme, or the states had inalienable "rights." The second was the view of Jefferson Davis, the first of Abraham Lincoln. Who was in error?

It was Daniel Webster who said:

> The sovereignty of government is an idea belonging to the other side of the Atlantic. No such thing is known in North America. Our governments are all limited. In Europe sovereignty is of feudal origin, and imports no more than the state of the sovereign, his rights, duties, exemptions, prerogatives, and powers. But with us all power is with the people; they alone are sovereign; they erect what governments they please and confer on them such powers as they please. None of these governments are sovereign in the European sense of the word; all being restrained by written Constitutions. [*Congressional Debates,* Vol IX, p. 565.]

"The people" here, their governments, are the states. The people do not speak, never have, never can, speak in their sovereign capacity, without a subversion of our whole system, otherwise than as *people of the states.*

In the beginning of this statement, Webster merely stated truth and elemental fact. Then, oddly, he proceeded to demolish his own presentation when, in hostility to state sovereignty, he fell into the very error by confounding the people of the states with their governments. He seems, like his disciples, who included Lincoln, unable to comprehend that sovereignty is *not* of the state governments but of the people who endow them. Jefferson Davis pointed this out: "It is merest self-stultification to admit the sovereignty of the people and deny it to the *States* in which alone they have community existence." A fratricidal war was fought over that.

It is not the *government* of the United States that is declared supreme but the *Constitution* and the laws and the treaties made in accordance with it. A proposal to endow and organize a government of "supreme Legislative, Executive, and Judicial powers" was not adopted at the 1787 conventions, but was *deliberately rejected*; and that rejection is more significant than would be the fact that it had never been proposed. This is a fact that no student of constitutional law, no lawyer, legislator, or judge, can overlook or pass by as inconsequential—if he remembers that the intention of the lawmaker is the law, surely here it is.

It should also be remembered that all officers, civil and judicial, state and federal, swear to support, not the government, but the Constitution of the United States. This is another fact that cannot be overlooked, ignored, or not recognized. All support a Constitution according to which laws, acts, decisions, are to be legally made.

Prohibition of exercise by the states of some of the functions of sovereignty—such as making treaties, declaring war, coining money, etc.—are seized upon as evidence against state sovereignty. But as Jefferson Davis pointed out (*The Rise and Fall of the Confederate Government,* Vol I, Ch. 7–10), these are not denials, but are merely agreements among the states to exercise certain powers of sovereignty in concert, not separated and apart.

Another constitutional provision generally pointed to by friends of centralism is the second clause of Article VI: "This Constitution, and the Laws of the United States which shall be made in Pursuance thereof . . . shall be the supreme Law of the Land. . . ." This has been magnified and perverted to a meaning and purpose entirely foreign to its intention: it is only the enunciation of a principle which, even if it had not been expressly stated, would be a necessary deduction from the very acceptance of the Constitution itself. From the documents of the *Rebellion Record* (Vol I, p. 213) even the historian Motley mistakenly claims state sovereignty to be "completely disposed of at a word, could language be more imperial?" It is this kind of specious United States "history" and twisted theory that we here seek to expose to light of day. Motley's error lies in not perceiving that the states which ordained and established the Constitution accepted nothing besides what they themselves prescribed; they acknowledged no superior. The supremacy, both in degree and in extent, is only that which they were delegating in the agreement between themselves—to which agreement the general government was not a party but was the result created by it.

Each existing state already had its own constitution and code of statute laws; it was undoubtedly primarily with reference to these that the provision was inserted—not in the expectation, as Davis says, of future conflicts and discrepancies. It was in this light that Madison, in the *Federalist,* No. XLIV, considered it, in explanation and vindication. Hamilton similarly pointed out, ". . . the laws of the Confederacy [that is, the United States] as to the *enumerated* and *legitimate* objects of its jurisdiction, will become the supreme law of the land"—the state functionaries co-operating in their observance and enforcement with the general government *"as far as its just and constitutional authority extends."* (Italics are Hamilton's.) Indeed, so crude and confused seem most of the ideas about the Constitution that lawyers, even judges (not to mention the present justices of the United States Supreme Court), and particularly legislators might profit, and the country with them, by attendance once more at law school to refresh their minds on aspects of constitutional law and the Constitution.

The federal Constitution and its successive amendments are to be read together as a single enactment that makes no further change in the established order than is necessary and is reconciled to the original order as far as possible. All conflicts are to be avoided by construction, wherever possible.

The Twelfth Amendment to the Constitution, on regulation of the Electoral College, was adopted by the 8th Congress and ratified, and was made part of the organic law September 25, 1804. Sixty-one years were to pass before another was ratified. In that time only two Acts of Congress had been declared unconstitutional by the Supreme Court—those reviewed in the cases of *Marbury* v. *Madison* (1803), and the Dred Scott decision (1857): a remarkable record.

Constitutional provisions are mandatory, almost invariably,

not merely directive; they are prospective, not retrospective, their operation being looked to, its meaning assumed not to change with changing conditions. Therefore there would be no way of preventing contractual obligations or vested rights; those obligations should not be impaired nor the rights divested.

The first ten amendments to the Constitution were accepted under the original ratification of the Constitution. After that there were two more, then no more until the close of the Civil War. The first ten seem to have given rise since then to persistent popular misconceptions because they do not explicitly state that the things enjoined or prohibited therein are enjoined and prohibited to the United States, not to the several states. Similar misconceptions exist concerning the effect of many provisions of these amendments. It is to be regretted that the first ten were ever treated as amendments, and were not declared to be part of and incorporated in the original body and substance of the Constitution.

This was later done in drawing up the Confederate Constitution, in which the first eight were incorporated as the last part of Article I, Section 9, with the necessary addition "Every law, or resolution having the force of law, shall relate to but one subject, and that shall be expressed in the title." In drawing up the Confederate Constitution, the convention closely followed the Constitution of the United States throughout, with those changes that experience had suggested for better practical working or, as was said, for greater "perspicuity." That Constitution expired with the Cause; and what it attempted to prevent being foisted upon its citizens was now to be written into the other, in revenge and war hatred and to secure political perpetuity in office for a new party, the Republicans.

Though the postwar amendments were written into the charter and by force and coercion imposed upon the states, and are today a supposedly valid part of our fundamental law, we insist that they are *null and void,* of no effect, because they are against the spirit and letter of the United States Constitution. No one but advocates of national supremacy, of destroying states' rights and moving all powers to Washington, D.C., favors their retention or looks with any approval on those acts of a recalcitrant Congress immediately after the Civil War. We urge upon all the states of the Union the earliest consideration of their total repeal and removal, through Article V, to return us to the true form of American government.

The Confederate Constitution (reprinted in full beside the United States Constitution in Chapter 13, below) contained some distinguishing features:

1. Additional and less disputable guarantees against anti-slavery

2. Prevention of the enlargement of the powers and jurisdiction of the general government

That very important part, the Bill of Rights, was from the first added to the original federal Constitution. But later the Ninth, Tenth, and Eleventh Amendments were and have been continually derogated by the Thirteenth, Fourteenth, and Fifteenth so-called Amendments. Dr. Jabez Lamar Monroe Curry tells how Garfield, when a candidate for the Presidency in 1880, said, "The powers do and ought to gravitate more and more towards the central government." It was this very gravitation that the Confederate States feared and had tried to arrest. The pretensions of George III and the British Parliament, which the founding fathers resisted in 1776, concerned Parliament's claim to omnipotence in legislation over the Colonies. It would seem that the Lincoln-Garfield-Webster types of asserted government would only put us back into the very web we fought the Revolutionary War to disentangle ourselves from, spun now not in London, but in Washington, D. C.

3. Limitations on the power of taxation of the general government

The Confederates dreaded the abuse of the taxing power; it menaced the purity of government and the liberties of the people. Preference of partial over general interest is the greatest of all public evils. Of all the powers conferred upon government, that of taxation is the most liable to abuse. Among the limitations of powers which the North had so grossly abused, to the injury of the South, had been the matter of taxation. As Judge Miller had pointed out (20 Wall. 655):

> To lay with one hand the power of government on the property of the citizen, and with the other to bestow it upon favored individuals, to aid private enterprises, build up private fortunes, was none the less robbery because done under the forms of law and called taxation. It was not legislation; it was a decree under legislative forms.

Immediately after the Civil War, three radical changes, by maneuvers undefinable except by using the terms "lawless" and "unconstitutional," were fastened upon the organic law, changing the constituency and revolutionizing the whole theory of our form of government. The Thirteenth Amendment provided for the abolition of the "peculiar institution" of slavery of the South, for so long a bitter target of rabid reformers of the North. It added to the Proclamation that Lincoln had pretended was a necessary war measure, and was meant to be a constitutional inhibition in the United States, with similar inhibitions to the organic laws of the states that had seceded. It was proposed in Congress and ratified while none of the seceding States was represented, although the validity of ratification depended on the approval of the states thus barred from having any voice in ratification. In the Thirteenth Amendment the word "slavery" appears, *eo nomine,* for the first time in the Constitution—in the article abolishing it! Of the twenty-seven states certified to have "ratified" it were Virginia, Louisiana, Arkansas, North and South Carolina, Georgia, and Tennessee, though all except Tennessee were then under governments that were to be declared illegal under the Reconstruction Act of March 2, 1867, and its supplements.

The same objection holds for the other two amendments: their ratification was coerced, forced upon helpless, unrepresented states by being made a condition of readmission to their ordinary rights in the Union. Among the states "ratifying" the Fourteenth Amendment were listed Georgia, North and South Carolina, Louisiana, Alabama, and Florida; the acceptance of the Amendment had been made a prerequisite to the readmission of each of them to the Union—of their emergence from the condition of "provinces" to states. Arkansas was declared readmitted because of her antecedent ratification. Virginia, Mississippi, and Texas, under the Reconstruction Act, which was passed because of their refusal to ratify the proposed Fourteenth Amendment, were placed under military rule.

The Thirteenth and Fifteenth Amendments pertain wholly to the Negro slaves. The Fourteenth concerns the slaves for the most part, with the addition of bills of attainder (constitutionally forbidden) against the Confederates *ex post facto*. In 1870 a congratulatory message from President Grant called the Fifteenth a "measure which makes at once four millions of people voters who were heretofore declared by the highest tribunal not citizens, nor eligible to become so." A whole race had suddenly been incorporated into the body politic. They had already voted under the Reconstruction Act, while citizens had been disfranchised. It is to be noted that the red race, former owners of America, had not so been taken into citizenship, but only one by one, each man on proving his competency, dissolving tribal relations, and taking land in severalty, were Indians accepted.

Under the Constitution of the United States the states, in respect to the powers not delegated or named or implied, are sovereign and have rights that are as incapable of violation without a violation of the Constitution as are the rights delegated to the general government. Now, consider a hypothetical case: say that a constitutional right of a state is invaded or is about to be invaded by the federal power; some unquestioned attribute of state sovereignty is about to be assailed in a manner incontestably in derogation of the Constitution. (The 1957 Arkansas school incident?) A judicial solution *may* be practicable. But there may be others, especially when the usurpation scheme is sudden and forcible (Maryland, 1861), and any delay would put an end to possible defense or remedy. Suppose a usurping President, under the direction of a usurping Congress or ignoring the remonstrances of a faithful one, is about to overthrow a state government by force of arms and appropriate its territory to his own or federal use in acknowledged violation and contempt of the fundamental law (Maryland, West Virginia, 1861 *et seq.*). Liberty they are seeking to crush. Is it to be disputed that a state has no right to resist such aggression by force, mustering its militia and manpower and defending its people by all possible means? Or that sister states have no right to join in the resistance, or no duty to maintain inviolability of rights? The question in its harshest aspects was first presented in 1861 at the culmination of long disputes.

Hamilton, in the *Federalist,* No. XXVIII, believed it to be

> . . . an axiom in our political system that State governments, in all possible contingencies, afford complete security against invasions of public liberty by the national authority. . . . Possessing the organs of civil power and confidence of the people, they can adopt a regular plan of opposition in which they can combine all the resources of the community, readily communicate with each other in the different States, and unite their common forces for the protection of their common liberty.

Madison, in the *Federalist,* No. LVI, said the same when he endeavored to allay apprehensions of danger from federal power, indicating how its scheme or usurpation would be readily defeated by the state governments, which the people would support. He denounced indignantly those who would "insult the free and gallant citizens of America by the suspicion they would hesitate about defending their liberties." Today? Presidents, Congresses, courts—so attempting—presume to substitute themselves—men —in place of laws and Constitutions. We have not "grown" to the point where oaths to support the law become mere mockeries or absurdities, mere "paths" to office.

Two men were leaders at a fateful hour. Abraham Lincoln

was not a learned man, even by the scanty standards of his day and environment. He played to the political gallery and endorsed the vapid theories of the new party he had been chosen to lead. Study of the events of 1861 shows that they followed the old, familiar course. It is hardly to be expected that even Lincoln-worshipers class his letters and other writings with those of Cicero, Pliny, Lord Chesterfield—certainly not those rewritten, recast, and edited by a professional secretariat (of whom more later). The mysterious and secret doings which they rationalized for him, his Cabinet, and others in the administration for which he was responsible would be better known from another kind of *lettres* or missives—i.e., *lettres de cachet*. Once laws, the rights of men, become suspended under the fog of tyranny and dictatorship, *lettres de cachet* can most readily become commonplace and widespread—call them by what name, designate them under what term, one will. They are the ominous portents accompanying revolution and tyranny throughout the ages. In such times come strange goings-on, and 1861 was no exception.

The type and form of government that had grown out of the successful end of the Revolutionary War, brought to fruition by the convention of 1787, was meant to end tyranny, the possible rule of men. In written and precise form, a new type of government created a Union, under a Constitution to be amended as the need arose. Note the Eighteenth Amendment prohibiting the manufacture, sale, transportation of intoxicating liquors; adopted by the 65th Congress and ratified by three-fourths of the states, it was made part of the Constitution January 29, 1919, and was repealed by the Twenty-first Amendment in 1933, Section 1 of which states: "The eighteenth article of Amendment to the Constitution of The United States is hereby repealed." There can be no mistake: the Eighteenth is *out*. But it is to be noted that there is no mention of "repeal" in the Thirteenth, Fourteenth, or Fifteenth Amendments, or any explicit reference of any kind to the Constitution or to other amendments. They are only simple, flat, lawless alterations of the American government, robbing the American people of their liberties and the states of authority, and transferring the whole of governmental powers to the Congress at Washington, D.C. Each of them ends with the clause "the Congress shall have power to enforce this article by appropriate legislation" or its variation. There is no mention that the Ninth and Tenth Amendments are *repealed*, though the Thirteen–Fifteen construe away the rights retained by the people and disparage the powers reserved to the states, or to the people. A Supreme Court evaded the issue by calling them "political."

These so-called Abolition Amendments therefore were and are unconstitutional because they attempt to alter the form of the American government; and that can be done, lawfully and properly, only in the manner laid down in Article V of the Constitution of the United States. The Thirteenth Amendment attempted to "force" the sovereign states, change their constituency, and invade the functions and prerogatives of their governors and legislatures and the private and domestic rights of their citizens. At the time it was declared ratified, the only citizens of the United States were those of individual states; it would be two more years (1868) before another unconstitutional amendment, the Fourteenth, attempted another violation, making alterations and again invading the prerogatives of the sovereign states in its Section 1: "All persons born or naturalized in the United States, and subject to the jurisdiction thereof, are citizens of the United States and of the States wherein they reside," etc. With the Fifteenth, the Negro Suffrage Amendment, in March, 1870, came another equally unconstitutional invasion of the states.

All three were, and still are, unconstitutional because they unlawfully altered the form of American government, forced the states, and were—none of them—properly and constitutionally ratified by three-fourths of the states, as the Constitution requires. This is a mere outline of their unconstitutionality. Under the excuse that they were "political," like the Reconstruction Acts, and therefore "outside" its jurisdiction, the United States Supreme Court has never formally passed upon them fully. They remain today, equivocations upon the instrument of organic law, in opposition to and in defiance of the Ninth and Tenth Amendments and of Article V of the Constitution of the United States. They were the result of war, of dictatorship, of tyranny; they are against the form of the American government and should be removed from the books, even as the Prohibition Amendment was.

CHAPTER 2

The Amendments Before the Supreme Court

UNDER THE UNITED STATES CONSTITUTION the states cannot be forced, invaded, their republican form of government changed; nor can the Constitution itself be changed until three-fourths of the states ratify the change or changes. The three "abolition amendments" have never been properly ratified, and in early court cases in which the enabling clause at the end of each was invoked (notably the slaughterhouse cases, 1873), the Supreme Court declared the efforts unconstitutional and void. About the civil-rights and some other cases the Court said, "It is repugnant to the Tenth Amendment," in upholding the states' reserved powers in a dozen cases (1870–1926). Some of the decisions were bitterly attacked by those who felt that the gains to liberty won by the Civil War had been sacrificed, but they were defended by others able to see farther than the ends of their own noses and, like the majority of justices on the Court, foresaw the inconceivable amount of litigation that the Supreme Court would have been called upon to hear if state legislation involving every possible civil right of a state citizen could be brought before it under the "privilege and immunity" clauses. (So important are these decisions that the student would do well to compare them with the view of the meaning and scope of the Fourteenth Amendment taken by the Congress that formulated it, a discussion of which can be found in Guthrie, *Lectures*; Flack, *Adoption,* Chapter V; and Cooley's edition of *Story's Commentaries,* Vol. II, pages 632–92).

On the first section of the Fourteenth Amendment the Court made some comments that we shall summarize:

> It opened with a definition of citizenship, not only of the United States but of the states. No such definition was previously found in the Constitution, nor had any attempt been made to define it by act of Congress; it had been the occasion of much discussion in the courts, by executive departments, and in the public journals. It had been said by eminent judges that no man was a citizen of the United States except as he was a citizen of one of the states composing the Union. Those therefore who had been born and resided always in the District of Columbia, or in the territories, though within the United States, were *not* citizens. . . . Whether sound or not had never been judicially decided, but it had been held by the Supreme Court in the celebrated Dred Scott decision only a few years before the outbreak of the Civil War that a man of African descent, whether a slave or not, was not and could not be a citizen of a state of the United States.

That decision, while it met with the condemnation of some of the ablest statesmen and constitutional lawyers in the country, had never been overruled, and if it was to be accepted as a constitutional limitation of the right of citizenship, then all of the Negro race who had recently been made "freedmen" were not only not citizens but were incapable of becoming citizens by anything short of an amendment to the Constitution, on which *all* states must properly act, according to Article V. Instead, the amendment to do this was "forced" through a partisan Congress and, supposedly, became part of the organic law after the South had surrendered, been disarmed, and lay prostrate and helpless—the one section of the nation most vitally and immediately and intimately affected by it.

"Had its sections changed the structure of our government?" Justice Hughes asked (1927 *Lectures* at Columbia University). "There were not wanting opinions that they had; the argument was that a citizen of a state was now only a citizen of the United States residing in that state." But the Fourteenth Amendment had not attempted to confer any new privileges and immunities, or to enumerate or define those already existing. It was *not* intended to have Congress take over *all* the constitutional prerogatives of the states; and that is what the Court had felt obliged to find.

Sections 2–4 of the fantastic Fourteenth Amendment form another riddle of intolerable interference in each state's prerogative to decide who shall be its citizens and who shall exercise the franchise. The question involved in the amendment is the admission to citizenship and the ballot of the Negroes in those states, and Section 2 even acknowledges that the authority to determine this resides in the states severally and nowhere else. In plain words, it recognizes the state's authority to grant or to withhold the elective franchise as existing in the state government; then it attempts to control it.

The plan of President Andrew Johnson to restore the recently Confederate States to all rights and privileges as co-equal states of the Union was approved by both the Judicial and the Executive branches, but the Legislative—Congress—withheld assent during the 1866 session. It required, as a condition prerequisite to recognition of any one of those states and admission of its representatives and senators to seats, adoption by its legislature of the Fourteenth Amendment—that is, *compelled* its acceptance.

Adopted by Congress June, 1866, by March, 1867, thirty-three of the then thirty-seven states (Nebraska admitted March 1, 1867) had voted on the Fourteenth Amendment, twenty for ratification and thirteen not: the constitutional requirement had *not* been met. When it was seen that no advance had been made in extending the franchise to the recent slaves, the Congress then adopted by "Act"—a method wholly new to Americans—a new administrative system dividing what it termed "the Rebel States" into five military districts to be held by armed force, the sovereignty of the people extinct and the states becoming conquered territories. The fifth section (and others) of this "Act" is a fantastic concoction of attainders, *ex post facto*'s, impairments, divestments, denials; that caused President Johnson to veto it, but it passed over his veto to become "law."

The new Congress supplemented it with another concoction

that the President also vetoed, only to be overridden again. It contemplated two governments in each of the southern states—one military, the other civil. When the next supplemental "Act" was sent to Johnson, he vetoed it in scorching terms: "It were impossible to conceive any state of society more intolerable than this, and yet it is to this condition that twelve millions of American citizens are reduced by the Congress of the United States. . . . They are denied every one of the Constitution's sacred guarantees." So the crushing wheels of a juggernaut of subjugation rolled forward, to threaten the vetoing President himself by seeking his impeachment. Is there any question of our using here the mild term "unconstitutional"?

In Virginia the commanding Union general thought that no government was possible under these regulations. Thousands fled the country; they were guilty of defending the Constitution—were "states' rights" advocates.

It would appear that when the Fourteenth Amendment was proposed in a one-sided Congress as a guarantee of protection of *all* citizens, adopted by the 39th Congress (1866), declared to be ratified by "more than three-fourths of the states" (although no Confederate state was properly represented), then made part of the United States Constitution on July 28, 1868, there was but little discussion on the floors of the "due process" clause. The wide scope of federal jurisdiction it authorized seems not then to have been appreciated. The question came up in the slaughterhouse cases but seems to have been dismissed with only a brief statement. In 1878 Justice Miller observed that the "constitutional meaning or value of the phrase 'due process of law' remains without that satisfactory precision of definition which judicial decisions have given to nearly all the other guarantees of personal rights found in the constitutions of the several States and of the United States." In 1868 there had been an attempt to place in the Constitution the declaration that "no State shall deprive any person of life, liberty, or property without due process of law." But can a state make anything due process which, by its own legislature, it chooses to declare to be such?

To affirm it would be to hold the prohibition to the states of no avail, or of no application where the invasion of private rights is affected under the forms of state legislation. From many cases before his court, Justice Miller felt that there was "some strange misconception of the scope of the provision; it seems a means of bringing to that court the abstract opinions of every unsuccessful litigant in a State court, of the justice of the decision there against him, and of the merits of the legislation on which such a decision was founded." The Supreme Court was learning of the burden placed upon it by attempts to "force" the sovereign states, laying upon them prohibitions to the organic law not known before 1868; and their thought was "that if it were possible to define what it is for a State to deprive a person of life, liberty, or property without due process of law, in terms which would cover every exercise of power thus forbidden to the State" (remember that to that time all prohibitions of the amendments had been *not* to the states but to the federal government) "and exclude those which are not, no more useful construction could be furnished by this or any other court to any part of the fundamental law." How true!

"Forcing" the states involved difficulties, though the "nation" must grow. And this was but one clause of startling changes that the three amendments were to force on the land. Sovereignty must be replaced, the Ninth and Tenth Amendments repealed, even Article V overhauled? How so? In the slaughterhouse decisions, those others saw the maintenance of the due authority of the states. It had been noted that, had the decisions been otherwise, the states would by judicial decree have largely lost their autonomy and would have become, as political entities, only of historical interest: the boundary lines between the "national" government and the states' would have been practically abolished. America, not the United States, would have been born. That court used "restraint."

The confusion and chaos among the victors of 1865 were the direct result of President Abraham Lincoln's seizure of dictatorial powers. On July 22, 1861, the House of Representatives denied any intention of conquest or subjugation in pursuing the war, affirming "that the war is waged to preserve the Union with all the dignity, equality, and the rights of the States unimpaired, and as soon as those objects have been accomplished, the war ought to cease." Nothing about "slavery." The evasion by the general government and by the administration of Lincoln is made obvious when we see how, with a perverse inconsistency, a conflict to prevent secession on the battlefield was followed, under a policy of "peace," by depriving the states that had seceded of their autonomy and consigning them to the status of subjugated provinces, conquered territory ruled arbitrarily as military districts by armed forces under Lincoln-appointed generals. With the social structure turned upside down by the proscription of white inhabitants, particularly those who had taken any part in the secession movement, the states of the South were without any genuine governments to represent their own sovereigns, their people. In them was now a vacuum. Yet at the same time that it was asserted they could legally ratify constitutional amendments, they were kept out of the Union as long as the Congress wished, and were admitted only on the arbitrary terms the conquerors chose to dictate. Does that make sense?

If we look at some Supreme Court decisions of that time we shall find ourselves in still greater confusion and wonder. The Court had the impossible job of reconciling situations that could not possibly be held to conform in justice to American constitutional government or to make right what to Americans was patently wrong. This no court could do. The South was right—but the South was defeated. Force had triumphed but, as always, only so long as passion raged. In the light of the declared congressional purpose "to preserve the Union with all the dignity, equality, and the rights of the States unimpaired," what now, after the war was over?

It is said that President Truman once remarked that he never opened the Constitution without finding something therein he had not noticed before. Turn to Article I, Section 9, and note the clauses about the writ of habeas corpus, bills of attainder, *ex post facto* laws, and, further along, the clause concerning the drawing of money from the Treasury: ". . . but in Consequence of Appropriations made by Law." These are among the powers denied the federal government; another, under Article IV, Section 3, is ". . . no new State shall be formed or erected within the Jurisdiction of any other State; nor any State be formed by the Junction of two or more States, or Parts of States, without the Consent of the Legislature of the States concerned as well as of the Congress." (We note the case of West Virginia.) Section 3 ends with the rule-making power of the Congress concerning territories and other property of the United States: ". . . nothing in this Constitution shall be so construed as to Prejudice any Claims of the United States, or of any particular State." The next section concerns federal protection of the states:

> SECTION 4. The United States shall guarantee to every State in this Union a Republican Form of Government, and shall protect each of them against Invasion, and on Application of the Legislature, or of the Executive (when the Legislature cannot be convened), against domestic violence.
>
> (NOTE: "Legislature" or "Executive" of the state–nothing about mayors!)

The states are also denied power to pass any bill of attainder or *ex post facto* law or to "engage in War, unless actually invaded, or in such imminent Danger as will not admit of Delay" (Art. I, § 10). Now examine again Sections 2–4 of the Fourteenth Amendment and note the denials, attainders, *ex post facto*'s, the assumptions, pensions, bounties, debts, the words "rebellion." We ask, "What rebellion?" (It was 1898 before some of the "disabilities" were removed.)

The border states, by blood, affinity, political agreement, slavery, tradition, and material interests as well as unwillingness to be buffers between hostile communities, in 1861 were still in full sympathy with the Confederacy, but had varying Union sentiments also. Conservatism finally restrained them from immediate affiliation. Their disposition was "to bear the ills they had, rather than fly to the unknown"—which gave Lincoln a sentence of his first Inaugural Address. Among northerners in favor of letting the South depart were Sumner, Horace Greeley, Chase, Seward, and other Cabinet members. They considered that, let alone, the seceding states, "finding the position untenable, will be forced ignominiously back into the Union." Indeed, Seward was saying, as a substitute bring on war with France and Spain; that "would revolt good men of the South."

An experienced, long-in-the-public-eye professional politician of the old school and former governor of New York, Senator William H. Seward had no good opinion of the man in the White House, whose Secretary of State he had now become. Many others of the Cabinet, other Republicans, and prominent and patriotic men on both sides across the country were much in agreement. It would appear fully possible that, with almost any other man than Lincoln as President, war could have been averted. Seward may have thought that—somewhat as in the apochryphal description of Jefferson Davis in Pierce's Cabinet as being the real President of the United States, though Pierce had the title: he might fill a similar role with Lincoln. But Lincoln was not long in disillusioning him.

In private conversation and in official papers Seward repudiated the right, even the wish, to use armed force against the will of a majority of people in the southern states; and he tried in an astonishing way to promote the belief that the President accepted as true, and willingly, the cardinal doctrine that the federal government could not reduce the seceders to obedience by conquest. That of course is true enough: four years of war, and defeat, did not do it, nor has it yet been accomplished in the century that has followed. Trying to confine the break to South Carolina, Seward played a subtle and intricate game for delay, apparently misled by mistaken belief in the transient nature, the "passing mania," he labeled it, of the southern wish and determination to secede. As early as March and until May, 1861, according to Sir William Russell, correspondent of *The Times*

(London), the Secretary of State asserted that if a majority of the people of the seceding states really desired secession, he would let them have it, but that he was unable to believe in anything "so monstrous." Seward and the Cabinet wanted no civil war, and thought it could be averted.

The English correspondent's visit to the South, however, revealed plainly to him the real sentiments—that the people there "were of one mind . . . There was *no* Union sentiment"—and he wrote for London the startling statement of his belief that "assuredly Mr. Seward cannot know anything of the South or he would not be so confident that all will blow over. . . . Because of the hallucination he is prepared to precipitate a general war, confident the United States will emerge from it victorious and more than ever consolidated. . . . The mad scheme, not consistent with sanity of judgment, as a substitute for domestic war, was two or more foreign ones." (France was violating the Monroe Doctrine by conquering Mexico, and Spain was creating a situation in San Domingo.)

Was it inevitable that—as the country grew, the main political parties changed, and new leaders came forward—the form of government must also change? If so, *must* it change back into consolidation, rather than adjust itself to new conditions under home rule? We see how, under the political parties and their leaders between 1804 and 1865 (the no-amendment period), slow but sure changes were coming over the country. There were the Democratic-Republican Party of Jefferson and the Federalist Party of Hamilton up to about 1815 and President Monroe's so-called "era of good feeling"; then the first-named party became the Democratic Party of 1830–50, led by Jackson and Calhoun, against the Whigs (no longer the Federalists) under Clay and Webster. Then the Whigs merged slowly by 1860 into the new Republican Party under Lincoln, to be pitted against a divided Democratic Party with several leaders until it split, with Jefferson Davis leading the southern states. In the North the Democrats were too much divided and too weak for several decades after the war to oppose the Republicans effectively—during the "nationalist" period, when "states' rights" had supposedly been scratched off the books forever and the organic law maimed by three postwar amendments.

Yet questions kept coming up concerning "usurpation." A king, a Parliament, a Lord Jeffreys, was not acceptable: the question was *who* would make redress, prevent further wrongs, when the reservations and the rights still retained were invaded. It could not be the federal government: that hope would only be looking at the source of the evil; it would be to expect power to tie its own hands, to relinquish its own claims. It would seem to fall to the invaded states to take steps; vicious legislation would have to be remedied by the people who suffer from its effects, and not by those who enjoy its benefits—to put the case succinctly.

It was but the old impasse—interposition by the states. Calhoun believed that

> . . . its general recognition would of itself, in great measure, if not altogether, supersede the necessity of its exercise, by impressing on the movements of the [United States] government that moderation and justice so essential to harmony and the peace, in a country of such vast extent as ours, and would if controversy should come, turn the resentment of the aggrieved from the system to those who had abused its powers [a point all-important] and cause them to seek redress not in revolution or overthrow, but in reformation.

In short, to remove the abusers and violators, the would-be dictators. The question was, How? Surely not as with Lincoln: assassination?

The war over, some modicum of reason, sanity, returned and uneasiness grew over what had been done precipitously in the fervor, hatred, excitement of war; and revulsion began to set in. The Thirteenth Amendment was declared in force by the Secretary of State December 18, 1865, the Fourteenth July 28, 1868, and the Fifteenth March 30, 1870. (There were to be no more until 1913.) New Jersey had ratified the Fourteenth Amendment September 11, 1866; then on March 27, 1868, it had tried to rescind its action. The preceding January Ohio had attempted also to rescind its ratification. In announcing ratification in July, the Secretary of State mentioned their efforts; the Congress then passed a concurrent resolution declaring the amendment to be part of the Constitution. That that was going too far is obvious today; both Oregon and New York undertook to withdraw their ratifications of the Fourteenth and Fifteenth Amendments, respectively. Lacking a Supreme Court ruling at that time, the government accepted the principle that when a state legislature has ratified, it has exercised its constitutional authority but has exhausted its power to act further. This was highly questionable, for it was not an adjudication; it was not until 1920, in cases concerning the Eighteenth Amendment, that the Supreme Court held, concerning the referendum provisions of some states, the requirement to be that the legislature or a convention, *not* the voters, must ratify or reject an amendment.

A former Secretary of State,* in a speech before the House of Representatives during Congressional debate on the proposed Income Tax Amendment (the Sixteenth, adopted by the 61st Congress in 1909, properly ratified, and made a part of the United States Constitution on February 25, 1913), and while he was yet a State judge, outlined to the lawmakers a brief history of Constitutional amendments. "The three wartime amendments," he declared, "were ratified by methods or steps so arbitrary, unusual, and irregular as not to be considered reliable precedents to follow in attempting to amend the Constitution. . . . Singular circumstances attended the adoption of the 14th. . . . The sole function of Congress is to propose to the States such amendments as two-thirds of both Houses see fit—to be ratified or rejected then by State legislatures or conventions; yet in this instance Congress did *not* permit all the States so to act. . . . The Reconstruction Acts operated in ten States, though President Andrew Johnson had held them to be unconstitutional while a hurried act of Congress intercepted and prevented a consideration by the United States Supreme Court of the constitutional validity of these Acts. . . . Under them existing State

---

* Cordell Hull

governments were abolished; and new governments created by a convention of delegates made up largely of Negroes were substituted. . . . Under this regime if a *de jure* government was about to reject the proposed amendment, it was promptly deposed, and one of these new Negro 'governments' at once installed whose action would insure immediate ratification . . . a course at direct variance with the Constitutional provision directing that only 'legislatures' or 'conventions' in the states are given authority to ratify or reject the proposals of Congress." The bicameral body can only direct a State to act on an amendment by its legislature or a convention, *and with this the power of Congress terminates!* Even with the absurd, fraudulent, largely Negro government of ten Southern States "ratifying" under instruction of their carpetbag leaders, Ohio and New Jersey withdrew their ratifications, while others had qualms, before the requisite number of States had replied, and with Secretary Seward's first Proclamation these recissions were noted, whereon Senator John Sherman of Ohio introduced a concurrent Resolution in the Senate declaring the ratifications "sufficient," which passed both Houses of that partisan Congress, *after* which Mr. Seward issued a second Proclamation declaring that the Fourteenth Amendment was ratified. It was a power that no Congress has; and it was, as the speaker stated, "*Ultra vires* and void." *Ipso facto,* the Fourteenth Amendment is unconstitutional.

No comparative act in the history of any civilized nation of the world is to be found which is on a par with the results brought about by the wartime amendments and the Reconstruction Acts. It all grew out of results a new party in power initiated when, about 1858, the old regime of Southern hold upon the Congress gave way to Northern newcomers. Senator Hammond of South Carolina in a speech on the Kansas Bill then used words of solemn and historical accuracy when he said, "You have complained of the rule of the South; that has been another cause that has preserved you. . . . We have kept the government conservative to the great purposes of the government. We have placed her and kept her upon the Constitution, and that has been the cause of your prosperity. The Senator from New York (Mr. Seward) says that is about to end; that you intend to take the government from us; that it will pass from our hands. Perhaps what he says is true, but do not forget—it cannot be forgotten—it is written on the brightest page of human history that we took our country in her infancy, and after ruling her for sixty out of seventy years of her existence, we shall surrender her to you without a stain upon her honor, boundless in her prosperity, incalculable in her strength, the wonder and admiration of the world. . . . Time will show what you will make of her; but no time can diminish our glory or your responsibility."

Time had indeed shown—a mere decade of it, from 1858 to 1868—a Civil War and an attempted overturn of the American form of government. The South had been charged, she would "rule or ruin"; but it is shown that the North, "taking over the government," as the Southern senator stated, did "rule *and* ruin" nigh half a great nation. As the truths of 1861-65 emerge, we see but the barren Pyrrhic victory won on false pretenses, and memorialized on labored perversions and obscurities, a Lincoln of fabulous creation and facultative dimensions, the false god of idolatrous devotees, an "Olympian" that never was!

And as for that disingenuous claim so vigorously asserted "the Union never would have been formed had it been supposed a State, any State, might withdraw at its pleasure," we turn the medal to its obverse, and ask, as Southerners long have asked, "On the other hand can it be supposed that any State, Virginia say, back in the day of the Charter's creation, would have adopted it and gone into the Union, even donated a great Empire to help found it, if she had imagined that in so doing she would be giving her sister States the right to invade her soil, to divide her territory, scorch her farms and plantations and valleys, devastate her fields, overturn her government, bombard her towns, slay her sons, rob and degrade their survivors and descendants?" If Fourteenth-Amendment-enthusiasts may ask the first question, surely Southerners may demand answer to the second. For, simply, it was a matter where the North must give up their prejudices, or the South must give up her constitutional rights. It was not Negro slavery, nor conservation of the Union, but against their own subjugation and enslavement the Confederacy was created to guard and defend. Was that "insurrection" or "rebellion"? Were "traitors" engaged four years in *that*?

In his last Address Washington had cautioned against

> . . . any spirit of innovation upon the principles of the Constitution, however specious the pretexts. . . . Facility in changes upon the credit of mere hypothesis and opinion exposes to perpetual change from the endless variety of hypothesis and opinion; and, in any event, should a modification of the Constitutional powers be necessary, it is to be made in the way the Constitution designates . . . but no change by usurpation."

What but "usurpation" of the rights of three-fourths of the states by making such changes were those three postwar amendments? Eleven states had no say whatever, except the raw pretenses of seizure of power, about their own ratifications; and these states were those most intimately and immediately affected. It would seem indeed as if efforts to abolish republican forms of government or to destroy equality (e.g., in the Senate) should not be subject to deliberation.

What, after all, had come out of that cruel, needless war, brought on by defying and ignoring and perverting the forms of government? True, slavery, so called, had been abolished. Then by the Supreme Court decision in the famous case *Texas* v. *White* (1869) the indestructibility of the Union was supposedly established: The Confederate States had never been out, nor could they go out, of the Union! The Union is perpetual, because the Constitution looks to an indestructible Union of states. Three of seven justices dissented in various ways to this decision. Were four justices, then, the final power over the states, their peoples, and their indubitable rights and prerogatives —over their constitutions and sovereignty? It could hardly be.

Three unconstitutional amendments, incorporating the final

results of the so-called "Rebellion," are in summary the treaty between the belligerents—a duress. In them are the trophies of the victors, but no mention of the cause, the real cause, of the conflict—states' rights. One observer commented that ". . . of the war waged ostensibly to maintain the integrity of the Union, and in denial of the dogma of State sovereignty, the future historian will not fail to note that the three amendments are silent on this subject, and that two of them relate exclusively, and the other principally, to the freedom, citizenship, and suffrage of the Negro race"—the only race in the history of the world that has ever been given *gratis* the priceless privileges of freedom and liberty and attempted equality. All others have had to fight and die, sacrifice and suffer, for eons to gain the highest prizes and achievements mankind can attain or rise to.

What was to be the government and who were to comprise the constituency—hence the sovereignty—in 1866, of eleven American states? Was it proposed to take these endowments away and to install the tyrant's whim and rule? No wonder chaos reigned in all departments of the federal government in 1865! Nothing was said then about the right of secession; if that right existed, it exists now, so far as any declaration in the organic law is concerned. It has not been renounced, and the supremacy of the "nation" has not been affirmed in the Constitution. Truth crushed to earth *will* rise again. . . .

Determination of such a constitutional question as the permanence of the Union can never be decided by four justices of the Supreme Court, leaving unheard about forty million citizens. We note Justice Grier's dissent. (Justices Swayne and Miller also dissented, in less degree.) His dissent presents a puzzle, and the student should compare it with the delivered opinion. (See 7 Wall. 700, *Texas* v. *White,* 1869, etc.)

The first dissent is on all points raised and decided—with the first question in order, the jurisdiction of the Court: Could it entertain the bill in behalf of Texas? The original jurisdiction was to be invoked by *one* of the United States. Was Texas a state, at the time the bill was filed, or since? That was to be decided as a political fact, not as a legal fiction. The Court was bound to know the public history of the country, to take "judicial notice." Now, in the realm of proof, that kind of notice is a subject that, while not properly a part of the law of evidence, yet embraces the rules determining what facts a court will recognize as true without evidence, and are largely found in the principles of common sense. What is of common, accepted knowledge does not require formal proof. The rules of evidence derive from the principle that life is too short to allow admission of everything relevant; they are rules of exclusion. Judicial notice is founded in part on the same regard for time limitations.

To Justice Grier, Texas for at least eight years had *not* been one of the United States. He wrote:

> Is she represented by members chosen by her people, and received on the floor of Congress? Has she two senators to represent her in the Senate? Has her voice been heard in the election of a President? Is she not now held and governed as a conquered province by military force? The Act of Congress March 2, 1867, declared Texas to be a "Rebel State," and provided for its government until a legal and republican State government could be legally established; it constituted Louisiana and Texas the Fifth Military District and made it subject, *not* to civil authority, but to the military authorities of the United States.

All of which could scarcely be controverted. Justice Grier therefore did not consider himself bound to express an opinion "as to the Constitutional right of Texas to exercise the rights and privileges of a State of the Union, or the power of Congress to govern her as a conquered province, to subject her to military domination, and keep her in pupilage." He submitted only to the fact as decided by the political position of the government, and was not disposed "to join in any essay to prove Texas to be a State of the Union when Congress decided that she was not." It was a question of fact only. Politically Texas was not a state of the Union: whether rightfully out of it or not was not a question before the Court, the dissenting justice affirmed.

But the Court had decided—not as in other cases it had declined—nevertheless to take jurisdiction of a "political" question.

It took an absolute power never granted.

By the Constitution, seven men could *not* abolish the States of the Union, but three-fourths of those States *could* abolish that court and all its judges. And, along with it, all the Lincolns that ever sat in the White House and all the Sumners and Stevenses that ever sat in the House or Senate.

Associate Justices Miller and Swayne did not wholly join, though Swayne said that he had concurred "with my brother Grier as to the incapacity of the State of Texas, in her present condition, to maintain an original suit in this court. The question in my judgment is one in relation to which this court is bound by the action of the legislative department of the government. Upon the merits of the case, I agree with the majority of my brethren. I am authorized to say that my brother Miller unites with me in these views."

So difficult and so embarrassing was the status of the ex-Confederate States during "Reconstruction," the student should consult Charles Warren, *The Supreme Court in United States History* (Chapter XXX), who gives a survey of the political background of the decisions. Texas was but one of the hard-nut cases that court had to crack.

The Confederate State of Texas had held out long after Johnston and Durham Station. I was once informed by a "Union Defender" that "it did not matter *who* fired the *first* shot of the war; it was the *last* shot that counted," and smilingly he asked *who* it was that fired *that*. Smiling myself, I was able to inform him that the Confederates did, in Texas, quite some time after Appomattox, in an engagement which, oddly enough, they won, driving the Union forces in headlong flight, with heavy losses, back to their seacoast gunboat protection.

The aforementioned case of Texas is usually the first one given a law student in casebook work in Constitutional Law, in an attempt to fix the "permanence" of the Union and the Constitution.

Some remarkable statements have been made by those who should have known better on how the Constitution was made. For instance, Motley wrote to the London *Times* in 1861 on the "Causes of the War," saying, "The name of no State is mentioned in the whole document," and that it was not ratified by the States but by the people of the whole land in their aggregate capacity acting through conventions. This statement was made in the face of the express provision of Article VII that the ratification of the conventions of nine States shall be sufficient for the establishment of the Constitution between the States ratifying the same. Edward Everett, in an address at the Academy of Music, July 4, 1861, made the incredible assertion that "the States are not named in the Federal Constitution." It is obvious he either had never looked at the second clause of Article I and was heedless or ignorant that each of the thirteen States (including two that did not immediately come in, Rhode Island and North Carolina) *were* named, providing for representation until an enumeration or census could be made, *or*, he deliberately uttered a complete falsehood.

Other writers have made assertions that "one people, or a nation *de facto,* formed the Constitution, but we know that the committee reporting the first draft, August 6, 1787, recited in the preamble, "We the people of the States of New Hampshire, Massachusetts, . . . (naming all the states in order) do ordain, declare and establish the following Constitution." No change was made in the preamble until September 8, when a committee was appointed "to revise the style of the articles (not change their meaning). On September 12, the committee made its report, using the present language: "We the people of the United States," a change accepted without comment, and irresistibly seeming to regard the two forms as substantially the same. The omissions of the State names had a conclusive reason behind it, for, unlike the Articles of Confederation, which the Constitution was to replace, unanimity was not required for the adoption or validity of the Constitution. It became obligatory on the States adopting when nine had ratified; no human prescience could forecast the action of the States in their free and separate deliberations. How different that action was from one supposedly done by thirteen States of peoples compounded into a mass body, whom the above writers so blatantly asserted made the Constitution. The form of expression was devised, necessarily, to apply to and to cover the States which should become members of the government. All thirteen had taken active parts in the Revolution; it was hoped all thirteen would combine, and would ratify the new charter of government; so the expressions "the people of His Majesty's Colonies," "the people of the United Colonies," "the people of the United States" occurred frequently without any intention to deny or surrender the separateness of the several Colonies or States. The people of the several Colonies were never a unit in a political sense, neither before nor after the Declaration of Independence, were never a nation, nor an entire community contradistinguished from the people of the several States, having, as such, community rights and powers of a political character. The Revolutionary Government emphatically was a government of the States, through Congress as their agent with very limited powers. The preamble phrase was thus falsely relied upon as lodging in the government all powers. If a collective people acted, when, where, was it done? We know it never was and never can be done without a revolutionary change.

In 1798 the Virginia House of Delegates complained of the efforts of the Federalists in "establishing by successive precedents such a mode of construing the Constitution as would rapidly remove every restraint upon Federal power." They were a powerful and compact group of men, the Federalists, hostile to popular rights and honestly inclined to a strong central government. They resisted those who held that no power should be conceded to exist unless conveyed in unmistakable terms.

The sectional feeling which disturbed and hindered the efforts to agree upon a common government is shown as early as during Washington's administration, a jealousy that manifested itself so painfully in resisting and defeating the admission of Kentucky in the Union as a State until Vermont was ready to enter as a counterpoise and counterbalance.

Henry Cabot Lodge, speaking on Webster, thought it was "probably necessary, at all events Mr. Webster felt it to be so, to argue that the Constitution at the outset was not a compact between the States, but a national instrument, and to distinguish the cases of Virginia and Kentucky in 1799 and of New England in 1814 from that of South Carolina in 1830." Fortunately, the facts are against him in both instances. When the Constitution was adopted by the votes of the States at Philadelphia, and accepted by the votes of the States in popular conventions, it is safe to say that there was not a man in the country, from Washington and Hamilton on one side to George Mason and George Clinton on the other, who regarded the new system as anything but an experiment entered upon by the States, and from which each and every State had the right peaceably to withdraw, "a right which was very likely to be exercised." Ohio, in 1859, declared the Constitution a compact to which each State acceded as a State and was an integral party, and that each State had the right to judge for itself of infractions, and of the mode and measure of redress, and to such a declaration men like Chase, Giddings, Wade, Denison, and others assented. There seems little doubt many men of America viewed the form of government under the Constitution as a doubtful experiment, we knew it was regarded with aversion and hostility by the rulers and governments of the Old World of Europe.

CHAPTER 3

Regional Inequality and Secession

As a matter of history, the wrongs that precipitated the Civil War had their origin long before 1861, when they merely came to a point of crisis at the advent of Lincoln and the new political party. In the beginning the states antedated the Union; they were, by separate actions, a sufficient number concurring, the creators of the Union and stood each upon a plane of absolute equality. Having conquered or otherwise acquired them (Virginia especially), they owned outright vast tracts of land to the west, to the Mississippi, half of a great, undeveloped continent to which they indubitably were heirs. In the course of time new states were carved out of the common territories that had their territorial organizations, enabling acts, school funds, admission to the Union, through the will of the central government at Washington, D.C. They became new states of the Union under the Constitution, as the others had, with the same rights and guarantees; and their entry had not changed the Constitution an iota in sixty years.

It would seem that these new states were hesitant about considering themselves on the same plane and equal to the Virginia or the Massachusetts of the days of '76—the origin from which they had sprung and come to statehood—although each had its representative or representatives and two senators in the Congress. It would seem that they reasoned: In 1789 the original thirteen states were the creators of the federal government; in 1861 it was the federal government that was the creator or sponsor of a large majority of the states. In 1789 that federal government had derived *all* the powers delegated to it in the Constitution from the original thirteen states; by 1861 a majority of the states had derived all their powers and some attributes as states from the federal Congress under the Constitution. In 1789 the people of the United States were severally the citizens of originally independent and wholly sovereign states. The peace treaty with Britain after the Revolution had acknowledged all of them to be "independent and sovereign States," with all the attributes and the powers of sovereigns, who later at the formation of the Union delegated *part* of their powers to a federal tripartite government of limited powers as laid down in the organic instrument which could be altered only in the manner and by the methods prescribed therein in Article V (which has never been repealed and cannot be repealed until three-fourths of the states agree to). In 1861 a vast majority of the people of the United States were citizens of states that had originally been mere dependencies of the federal government, which they considered the author of their political being. For this reason, they were both slow and hesitant to believe that they existed on a plane in perfect equality with the original thirteen.

It does not seem to be generally understood that the people do *not* derive their rights from the government. The situation was different in Europe, where, through the Magna Carta in England and other franchises that kings or emperors had granted, residuary rights remained in and with the government. In the United States ungranted rights remain with the grantors; these are the people *of the states*. In the Old World of monarchies, nobility, aristocracy, and privileged classes, the king—*parens patriae*—was naturally the father of his country. In America, however, it was the state—that is, the people of each state—who was *parens patriae*. The people would give; they could take away.

It was to get away from the old and worn, often tyrannical European autocratic forms that the United States was founded and the Constitution adopted to form a Union of a self-governing type new to the world. It differed essentially from all others—as definite and positive a political and social system as had ever been developed on earth. It was founded upon a particular conception of the art of self-government of which *decentralized,* local responsibility was the base. It was conceived that only through ordered liberty, freedom, and equal opportunity to the individual citizen would there arise incentive and enterprise on his part toward progress that would yet advance the system beyond any then known. The founding fathers were rare men and wise, men who had "come to themselves," men who measured their words. They knew history; they knew law and government; they knew the ancient classics; they knew the ancient failures; they knew the Bible. But theirs was a wisdom which, as always, can be misunderstood by lesser mortals. It can be misinterpreted; it can be misapplied through ignorance; it can be misused and perverted through ambition, interest, even plain human cussedness. Like gravity, the wisdom is there: the rules have been made and laid down, and they are not violated but are demonstrated when violation is attempted. They are inexorably, inevitably there, and are best consulted and obeyed.

The future no man can foresee. To allow for changes and normal evolution, the organic law was provided with means for changing and altering it as the occasion arose. Liberty was never to be license.

But as growth occurred, the influx of millions of immigrants from the Old World, from different backgrounds, settled north and west in established communities and crowded the cities. They knew little of a constitution, and cared less. This was the land of liberty; men were "free and equal"; the majority ruled—the "American" way, their Carl-Schurz-like leaders told them while ordering their votes, urging war on the South, and anathematizing slavery. They knew nothing of the South's acute problems. This was the beginning of a false premise, wholly without foundation in the Constitution, of "an aggregate people," of unrestricted democracy, of the absolute right of a popular majority—even a "simple" majority—whenever it exists and however ascertained, to rule without check or restraint, independent of constitutional limitations or of state interposition. This absurd proposition that the will of a mere majority for the time being becomes *vox Dei* was held by numerous leaders of the

North and the West, not least among them Abraham Lincoln. The southerners opposed, opposed strenuously, and fought it to the end.

Imposition of the theory of an aggregate people who rule by simple majorities in the Congress and in interpreting the Constitution to their own ends began when population and industrial growth transferred leadership of the Congress to the northern states from the men of the South who had long dominated it. Calhoun attempted ameliorations by such proposals as vetoes, nullifications, interposition, and "concurrent" majorities, all of which at one time or another were rejected, leaving the South, as he said in 1850, helpless to retain equality in the Union and relegated to a position hardly different from that which the Revolutionary fathers rejected in 1776. In answer to these efforts to obtain justice, Northern leaders undertook an attack on the domestic institutions of the South. "At first harmless and scarcely noticed movements" of small, so-called humanitarian groups in the North were seized upon by those who saw political possibilities in them, and the agitations spread from isolated spots to the halls of Congress. Abolitionists began to attack the South at every opportunity and demanded an end to the labor arrangements of the region and the emancipation of the African Negro "slaves" who worked mostly upon the great plantations.

Abolitionists' fathers and grandfathers had brought those poor black creatures—often savages, sometimes cannibals—from the Guinea coasts of West Africa and had sold them to the planters, much of whose capital was invested in them. Now the sons, not to mention some of the same fathers and grandfathers, were to raise "Ned" because the Negroes were there? That seemed to be it. "Slavery" then was available and lawful in all the states, but had largely died out in the North because of the climate, inclement and incapable of the agricultural returns of the lusher South, where two crops were raised to one northern crop and where the Negro fitted well into the established social order and regional economy. Moreover, there he was well treated and was protected under state laws to an extent unknown to the northern white laborer. The long-accepted stories about mistreatment of Negroes were many, but they were generally sheer nonsense and may be dismissed as examples of the misrepresentations and childish poppycock perpetrated to injure the people of the South and their way of life by engendering prejudice. Such ignorant and contemptible efforts helped bring on the war of 1861, and ashamed as one must be to say it, it was the Abe Lincoln—John Brown type of "martyr" and "saint" who were at the bottom of it, along with the fatuous writer of *Uncle Tom's Cabin,* down to the sadistic author of the recent *Mandingo.*

We still teach these falsehoods to children by slanted history textbooks that parrot the clichés, though it is surely time to make some changes and tell the truth. Listen to what the Hon. Clement C. Clay of Alabama had to say when he left his seat in the United States Senate when his state withdrew from the Union in 1861:

> There has not been a decade, nor scarce a lustrum, since Alabama became a State that has not become strongly marked by proofs of the growth and power of that anti-slavery spirit of the Northern people, which seeks the overthrow of that domestic institution of the South, which is not only the chief source of her prosperity but the very basis of her social order and State polity. It is today the master spirit of the Northern States, and, before our secession, had severed most of the bonds of the Union. It denied us Christian communion because it could not endure what it called "the moral leprosy of slaveholding"; it refused us permission to sojourn, or even to pass through, the North with our property. It claimed freedom for the slave if brought into a Northern State; it violated the Constitution and treaties, and laws of Congress; refused us any share of lands acquired mainly by our diplomacy; . . . it murdered Southern men when seeking their property on Northern soil; it invaded the borders of Southern States, poisoned their wells, burned their dwellings, murdered their

> people . . . exerted all the moral and physical agencies that human ingenuity can devise, or diabolical malice can employ, to heap odium and infamy upon us, and make us a by-word of hissing and scorn throughout the civilized world.

It was true. Is there any wonder that, year after year of propaganda like that (all of which is easily and readily proved in the records and archives of the nation), southerners came to believe that no nation on earth could be more hostile or alien to them than that northern section with which they were allied under the same flag and the same Constitution and theory of government?

Under the dangerous theory of an aggregate people a simple majority in the Congress could interpret such an expression in the Constitution as "the general welfare" to mean anything and everything their own immediate interests dictated, and no pointing to the constitutional provisions by the southern minority had the least effect. The North was getting the benefits and the South the burdens. How was the power of the majority to be checked? For no government based on the naked principle that the "majority" ought to rule can preserve its liberty for even a single generation. Further, when and where had an aggregate American people, separate from their states, ever assembled, debated, voted, legislated, acted, executed, adjudicated, ratified, or resolved any other act in the aggregate? To ask the question is to answer it: they never did, never could, never will—without a complete revolution in the American system.

So much for the "aggregate people" theory, by which three-fourths of the United States population living, say, in the northeastern corner of the land—New England—could by their three-fourths vote alter at will the Constitution or any of its provisions. *That* can only be done by *three-fourths of the states*—an entirely different proposition, as will be obvious to anyone.

In his first Inaugural Address Abraham Lincoln spoke of the constitutional questions: ". . . we divide upon them into majorities and minorities. If the minority will not acquiesce, the majority must, or the government must cease. There is no other alternative; for continuing the government is acquiescence on one side or the other." Whoever rejects must of necessity fly to anarchy or despotism; the rule of a minority as a permanent arrangement (unanimity being impossible) would be wholly inadmissible, so that rejecting the majority principle leaves one with only anarchy or despotism in some form.

"Simple" majorities, of course, are easiest and more convenient, and they always leave matters in the hands of such a majority. But what can be wrong with the idea of "increased" majorities, such as the constitutional requirements of Article V for the concurrence of two-thirds of Congress and of three-fourths of the states? John C. Calhoun had early suggested "concurrent majorities," but they were never put into effect, probably because they meant possible loss of what had become the North's sweeping power. He conceived of their use as giving any substantial minority the power of self-protection; they would impose neither minority rule nor minority control but would introduce "a principle of consent" into any Union of political units having, as he put it, "definite self-consciousness and awareness of divergent interests." Though he was thrust aside, there was both sense and justice to the proposal. When opportunity for exploitation arises—human nature being what it is—a majority will undoubtedly use it; but if an increased, or concurrent, majority is required, exploitation may be prevented. For instance, he argued, "an association of four shoemakers and three tanners would give rise to economic exploitation of the minority if all decisions of the association or partnership were made by a 'simple' majority." But suppose the association could act only when a majority of shoemakers and a majority of tanners agreed? "Surely," it seemed to Calhoun, "seven rational men could act by concurrent majority." Why not a union of states, by their representatives in Congress, on questions of diverse interests? Why not indeed?

We have here one of the simplest keys to the causes underlying the American Civil War and the reasons for states' seceding. It pertained to "the burdens and the benefits of Union." What had the Negro to do with it, any more than a Massachusetts bond servant, black, white, or brown?

A gentleman and scholar of the old school, Dr. J. L. M. Curry* was a member of the House of Representatives from Alabama in 1861 when his state withdrew. Writing in 1900, he sought to set aright the misrepresentations and falsehoods concerning the Confederacy; and his *Civil History* should be used as a reference text in public schools. He felt it his duty to try to state the legal and moral justifications of the South in secession. Those states, he noted,

> . . . have shared the fate of all conquered peoples; the conqueror writes their history; power in the ascendency not only makes laws, but controls public opinion, a precedent that should make Confederates the more anxious to keep before the public the *facts* of their history, that impartial writers may weigh and properly estimate them in making up the verdict of an unbiased posterity. . . . As they have been the object of persistent misrepresentations, and authentic records have been perverted to their prejudice, descendants are liable to receive and hold opinions hostile and derogatory to their fathers.

On his part there was no wish to reopen old wounds or to revive the arbitrament of war, "slavery," secession, or to inculcate dis-

---

* Jabez Lamar Monroe Curry is one of the little-known American men of letters, a fine scholar, lawyer, educator, clergyman, Congressman, soldier on the staffs of Generals Wheeler and Johnston of the Confederate armies. He was a member of the Confederate Congress and helped to draft the Confederate States Constitution. In 1885 he was Minister to Spain. He was a prolific writer and an agent of the Peabody Educational Fund. Born in Lincoln County, Georgia, June 3, 1825, he died February 12, 1905. Among his works are: *The Southern States of the American Union, Civil History of the Confederate States, Personal Reminiscences, William E. Gladstone, The Peabody Fund, Constitutional Government in Spain,* and *Establishment and Disestablishment in the United States.*

loyalty, but only to present the constitutional side for the South as it indubitably existed in 1860, to vindicate it from accusation and aspersion based on ignorance and injustice. Conclusions had been drawn from false premises and hence injustice done; prejudiced and vicious statements concerning character and motives had been accepted and acted upon as verifiable and undeniable facts.

> In deciding upon the rightness or the wrongness of secession, in passing judgment, it is essential to proper conclusions that condition of affairs in 1860 be understood and accurate notions be had of the nature and character of the Federal Government and of the rights of the States under the Constitutional compact. And right here at the threshold one is confronted by dogmas which are substituted for principles, by preconceived opinions which are claimed to be historical verities, and by sentimentality which closed the avenues to the mind against logic and demonstration. . . . Stubborn historical facts are set aside, and inferences and assumptions are used as postulates for huge governmental theories. These errors are studiously perpetuated, for in prescribed courses of reading in civics and history are books full of the grossest misstatements, teaching sectional opinions and latitudinous theories, while works presenting opposite and sounder views are rigorously excluded.

From a "Union" that the South considered no longer worth preserving, for them, as it was then came "secession"—from "a Union which stank." From secession came the war that took a toll of half a million American fighting men killed, wounded, disabled, with incalculable losses in property, human suffering, and degradation—all to what end? To the end of preserving the American form of constitutional government, one of laws, not of men—a Cause indeed, and not yet lost, but only in abeyance.

Soon after that government was organized in 1789 and took its place among the nations of the world, some amendments proposed by the ratifying states were submitted and were adopted by them. The amendments had no *direct* relation to the immediate objects for which the Union was formed; with few exceptions they were intended to guard against improper "constructions" of the basic charter, abuse of delegated powers, or to protect the government itself in the exercise of its proper functions and to protect the people and the states against federal usurpation. The one that Jefferson called "the cornerstone of the Constitution," the Ninth, prohibits a construction so that the specific rights set forth by the people "shall not be construed to deny or disparage others retained by the people": other rights are *not* to be denied by the enumeration of certain stated rights. The Tenth Amendment is expressed in language that tyranny cannot pervert or dispute. It would seem that language itself could scarcely describe the ultimate authority of the States more explicitly: the general government has no more right to try to enforce its decision against those of the several states that disagree about the extent of their respective powers than the states have to enforce their decisions in a similar situation. This reservation was incorporated into the Constitution from caution—by some then considered excessive caution, because the reservation is of the very essence of the Constitution itself. But time has vindicated the wisdom and sagacity of the fathers in plainly setting forth that the states, instead of *receiving* powers, bestow them.

South Carolina, Virginia, New Hampshire, and Massachusetts were so alarmed at the possibility of the federal government's absorbing unsurrendered powers that at the time they proposed that the amendment state that each state respectively retained every power, jurisdiction, and right that had not been delegated. There was then great distrust of centralization. The proposal was given much consideration, was modified, and was adopted in regular constitutional form as what is now the Ninth Amendment.

What, by 1860, had transpired? What changes wrought? The Union was no longer that Union established under the Constitution that the founding fathers had so hopefully framed.

Dr. Curry was sitting in the House during the events following December 19, 1860, when South Carolina

> . . . by unanimous vote of the convention at Columbia solemnly declared and ordained that "the Ordinance adopted May 23, 1788, whereby the Constitution of the United States was ratified, and all acts of the General Assembly ratifying amendments of said Constitution were repealed, and that the Union subsisting between South Carolina and other States under the name of the United States of America, is hereby dissolved." After the ordinance was engrossed and enrolled with the great seal of the State attached, the president of the convention proclaimed South Carolina an independent Commonwealth.
>
> The vote on the ordinance was telegraphed to the members of Congress in Washington. It was at once made known and in a few minutes every member of the House, of which I was then a member, learned of the great event. . . . Business went on without interruption; some contemptuous expressions and sneers were visible and audible on the Republican side, especially from one representative who later said, "There is an eternal antagonism that must be settled, and we may as well have it settled now as at any other time."
>
> In ordaining separation from the Federal Union, the State acted alone, without waiting for co-operative action, but expressing an earnest desire for, and most cordially inviting, the formation of a Southern Confederacy. Commissioners were appointed to the several Southern States, inviting their co-operation, and deputies were elected to meet those of other States which might secede, for the purpose of forming at an early period a provisional government and to consider and propose a constitution and plan for a permanent government. [*Reminiscences.*]

The flood of wrongs deriving from perversion of the original compact of government had at last broken the floodgates. The intentions of Lincoln (which the experienced political leaders of the new party were patiently and constantly trying to hush up or modify, knowing too well what they faced in Washington) were only too well known in the South. She was to be subjugated and enslaved—or by herself keep herself in freedom and equality. Sons of their fathers of '76, what other choice did they have? Best to hope for a peaceful separation.

Florida, Mississippi, Alabama, Georgia, Texas and Louisiana followed South Carolina. Georgia affirmed that the question of slavery "moved not her people half as much as the fact that their rights as a community were insulted." There were thousands and tens of thousands of her people who did not own slaves; a large proportion of the people owned none. The address concludes: "To avoid these evils we withdraw the powers that our fathers delegated to the Government of the United States, and henceforth seek new safeguards for our liberty, security and happiness."

Dr. Curry, great Southern scholar, wrote:

> In seceding from the Union to which, in the language of Washington and Jefferson, each had acceded as a sovereign, the States by a very simple and orderly process repealed the ordinances by which the Constitution was ratified and agreed to, and by which each State became a party to the compact. Thus the State declared herself no longer bound by that compact and dissolved her alliance with the other parties to it. South Carolina, Georgia and other States sustained the same relation to the Federal Government and the States remaining in the Union that Rhode Island and North Carolina did before they ratified the Constitution and became members of the Union. . . . Not infrequently one hears in speeches, or reads in pretentious treatises, full of vulnerable logic and superficial history, that secession was not a justifiable remedy because the Constitution grants no such right to a State [!].
>
> What is politic or expedient may be entirely different from what is legally right. The right of a mode of redress is one thing; its wisdom or expediency, quite another. One has the vaguest idea of the nature and character of our Federal Government, of its vital and fundamental principles, who searches the Constitution for the rights of the States, or limits those rights to what may be found among delegated powers. Seces-

> sion, or the right to resume delegated powers, or withdraw from the Federal republic, did not come from the Constitution, but from State sovereignty. Such fallacies spring from an entire misapprehension of our Federal Government and of its origin. Historical facts which no one of intelligence or candor can deny, show that the Government of the United States was Federal in its origin and in the common bond. From the Declaration of Independence sprung thirteen separate and distinct republics, and these set up a great Federal republic whose constituents were thirteen distinct, sovereign States.

John C. Calhoun (*Works,* pages 147–48) set forth the character of the new nation succinctly, and it so remains, today, in the organic instrument, no matter in the least all attempts to change it unlawfully and unconstitutionally, as by the three Civil War amendments—which somehow still remain, the Fourteenth especially, an ever increasing stumbling block.

There have always been those who would convert a federal, constitutional, representative republic into a consolidated government of the aggregate population. To them the United States Supreme Court is the ultimate arbiter in the decisions of political as well as judicial questions. Because of its great wisdom and impartiality, supposedly it would be a tribunal on which all might rely. The power of judicial relief from unconstitutional action is a peculiar and beneficial provision of the American system, and it must not be underestimated or not given due appreciation. We know that Europeans can hardly conceive that a court should exercise the prerogative of declaring null and void laws that have Legislative and Executive approval. Probably no other court in the world has surpassed in integrity and ability the United States Supreme Court—in which only two acts of Congress had been found unconstitutional between ratification of the Twelfth and the Thirteenth Amendments and to which the South for over sixty years had furnished Chief Justices.

We should not, however, lose sight of the fact that there is a tendency in all officers to enlarge their own powers, and there is nothing in the judicial station to exempt a judge from that infirmity, or from political bias. We know that the Supreme Court has at times been dominated as much by party spirit as other departments of government have. Attempts have been made to enlarge it, to provide for decisions politically desired at the time. Interpretations of the Constitution by justices may be sought not infrequently in their party affiliations and the history of their times. Except for nominal Senate confirmation, all federal-court and Supreme Court justices come to their benches without being passed upon by the voters of the several states. Decisions may thus often be "colored"; this suggests how much judicial opinion can depend on the men who happen to occupy the bench when a fateful case is heard.

Thus the Court can assume or usurp jurisdiction not allowed by the Constitution, and there is no power in the federal government, either Congress or the Executive, to gainsay it. There seems to be left only the sovereignty of the states to interpose. A single department might deny to others powers they really possess, or confer powers never conceded. A system of laws has been built up by the "legislation" of the courts, leading later to all sorts and forms of pernicious activity. Questions raised by sections of the Fourteenth Amendment the courts must be able to dispose of properly. Fifty states, or three-fourths of them by legislature or convention or two-thirds of their congressional quotas, should act on those troublesome amendments, as forty-eight removed the Eighteenth twenty-five years ago. A century has passed since the Supreme Court, observing the oaths of high office while considering the Dred Scott case and looking within the Constitution, found the answer. But that answer was openly defied by many of the states of the North—those least affected by the decision—and they thereby broke the terms of the Union contract, or compact of association, because they were numerically strong enough to do so. Except for a four-year war, they still are getting away with it, but without proper changes in the organic instrument of law according to its prescribed methods.

Speaking of the compact, Calhoun thought

> . . . that in that character [of thirteen sovereign states] they formed the old Confederation, and when it was proposed to supersede the Articles of Confederation by the present Constitution, they met in conventions as States, acted and voted as States, and the Constitution, when formed, was submitted for ratification to the people of the several States. It was ratified by them as States, each State for itself; each by its ratification binding its own citizens; the parts thus separately binding themselves, and not the whole the parts; and it is declared in the preamble of the Constitution to be ordained by the people of the United States, and the Article of Ratification, when ratified, to be binding between the States so ratifying. The conclusion is inevitable that the Constitution is the work of the people of the States, considered as separate and independent political communities; that they are its authors—their power created it, their voice clothed it with authority; that the government formed is in reality their agent; and that the Union, of which the Constitution is the bond, is a Union of States and not of individuals.

Herein lay the great error of the Lincolns and the Websters, of Story and Marshall to an extent: in attempted deforming of the organic charter of the nation from what it actually was to something that would divert great unconstitutional powers unto *them,* making men, not laws, the foundation. This the South disputed, and Calhoun pointed out the closing words following Article VII of the final draft: "Done in Convention by the Unanimous consent of the States Present"—followed by the names of the deputies from the states.

The almost universal discontent in the states of the southern section of the Union Calhoun had noted, and he sought for its cause. Beginning about 1835 organized movements initiated in the North began harrowing the southern regions with anti-slavery propaganda. Presses were established; lecturers went throughout the North to excite the people; incendiary literature was scattered over the whole of the South through the mails and by furtive night runners and agitators. A situation arose that was dangerous and threatening in the extreme to the lives and property of the planters, and they became thoroughly aroused, held meetings, adopted resolutions calling upon the North to put a stop to that evil and promising to take measures for their own protection if the vicious practices were not suppressed. But it went on. The fanatical leaders who had begun it all would today probably be considered mentally unbalanced and held for observation in mental hospitals. But at that hour they were affiliating themselves with political groups that were to give them a powerful voice in making decisions in the North.

The North had acquired a decided ascendancy in every department of the government and, through it, control of all powers of the system. A single section, governed by the will of the numerical majority, had control of the federal government and all its powers. Calhoun reasoned that, had this situation developed slowly over a period of time without the interference of the government, the South would have had no reason to complain; but that was not the case. It was caused by the legislation of the government, a government that had been appointed as the common agent of all and charged with the protection of the interests and security of all. On *that* the Union had been founded.

There had been a series of acts by which the South had been excluded from the common territory belonging to all the states as members of the federal Union. Ironically, most of the territories had been added to the Union by southern efforts and under southern leaders. Virginia alone had ceded a princely empire from which were carved the present states of Ohio, Indiana, Illinois, Michigan, Wisconsin, and half of Minnesota; and two other states, Kentucky and West Virginia, were once her territory. The great Louisiana Purchase from Napoleon had been the doing of Jefferson, a Virginian; the additions after the Mexican War had come under President Polk of North Carolina and Tennessee; others, like Texas, Florida and Oregon, had been secured by southern diplomacy. But the South, outnumbered in Congress, had slowly lost the position of equality that she had earlier held when the sections were equal. When the territory allotted to the North was vastly extended and that to the South restricted, immigration into other territories still further increased northern numerical superiority in both houses of Congress.

There was also adopted a system of revenue and disbursement by which an undue proportion of the tax burden was imposed on the South and an undue proportion of the proceeds appropriated by the North. This was followed by a system of political measures by which the original character of the government was radically changed so that entire control passed into the hands of the northern section.

As the election of Mr. Lincoln in November, 1860, was followed by the secession of seven States, and later by four others, to form a Union or Confederacy of their own, it is perhaps not out of place here to review some of the odd circumstances of the election. It is nowhere better portrayed than by one of the participants, one who was himself nominated for the place, Mr. Jefferson Davis. He says, "The people of the United States now had four rival tickets presented to them by as many contending parties, whose respective positions and principles on the great and absorbing question at issue may be briefly recapitulated as follows:

"1. . . The Constitutional Union Party, as it was now termed, led by Bell and Everett, which ignored the territorial controversy altogether, and contented itself with a simple declaration of adherence to the Constitution, the Union, and the enforcement of the laws.

"2. . . The Party of 'popular sovereignty,' headed by Douglas and Johnson, who affirmed the right of the people of the territories, in their territorial condition, to determine their own organic institutions independent of the control of Congress; denying the power or duty of Congress to protect the persons or property of individuals or minorities in such territories against the action of majorities.

"3. . . The States Rights Party, supporting Breckinridge and Lane, who held that the territories were open to citizens of all the States, with their property, without any inequality or discrimination, and that it was the duty of the general government to protect both persons and property from aggression in the territories subject to its control. At the same time they admitted and asserted that the right of the people of a territory on emerging from their territorial condition to that of a State to determine what should then be their domestic institutions as well as all other questions of personal or proprietary rights without interference by Congress and subject only to the limitations and restrictions prescribed by the Constitution of the United States.

"4. . . The so-called Republicans, presenting the names of Lincoln and Hamlin, who held, in the language of one of their leaders (Greeley), that slavery can exist only by virtue of municipal law, and that there was no law for it in the territories and no power to enact one, and that 'Congress was bound to prohibit it in or exclude it from any and every Federal territory.' In other words, they asserted the right and duty of Congress to exclude the citizens of half the States of the Union from the territory belonging to all in common, unless on condition of the sacrifice or abandonment of their property recognized by the Constitution—indeed, of the only species of their property distinctly and specifically recognized as such by that instrument.

"On the vital question underlying the whole controversy—that is, whether the federal government should be a government of the whole for the benefit of all its equal members, or a sectional government for the benefit of a part, the first three of the parties above described were in substantial accord as against the fourth. If they could or would have acted unitedly, they could certainly have carried the election and averted the catastrophe which followed. Nor were efforts wanting to effect such a union. Bell, the Whig candidate, was a highly respected and experienced statesman, who had filled many important offices, both State and federal. He was not ambitious to the extent of coveting the presidency, and he was profoundly impressed by the danger which threatened the country. Breckinridge had not anticipated, and, it may safely be said, did not eagerly desire the nomination.

He was young enough to wait, and patriotic enough to be willing to do so if the weal of the country required it. Thus much I may confidently assert of both of those gentlemen, for each of them authorized me to say that he was willing to withdraw, if an arrangement could be effected by which the divided forces of the friends of the Constitution could be concentrated upon someone more generally acceptable than either of the three who had been presented to the country. When I made this announcement to Douglas—with whom my relations had always been such as to authorize the assurance that he could not consider it as made in an unfriendly spirit—he replied that the scheme proposed was impracticable, because his friends, mainly Northern Democrats, if he were withdrawn, would join in the support of Lincoln, rather than any one of those who should supplant him; that he was in the hands of his friends, and was sure that they would not accept the proposition.

"It needed but little knowledge of the status of the parties in the several States to foresee a probable defeat if the conservatives were to continue divided into three parts, and the aggressives were to be held in solid column. But angry passions, which are always bad counselors, had been aroused, and hopes were still cherished, which proved to be illusory. The result was the election, by a minority, of a President whose avowed principles were necessarily fatal to the harmony of the Union." (The electoral votes we have already shown; Mr. Davis here further analyzed the results.)

"Of 303 electoral votes, Lincoln received 180, but of the popular suffrage of 4,676,853 votes, which the electors represented, he obtained only 1,866,352—something over a third of the votes. This discrepancy was owing to the system of voting by 'general ticket'—that is, casting the State votes as a unit, whether unanimous or nearly equally divided. Thus in New York, the total popular vote was 675,156, of which 362,646 were cast for the so-called Republican (Lincoln) electors, and 312,510 against them. New York was entitled to 35 electoral votes. Divided on the basis of the popular vote, nineteen of these would have been cast for Lincoln and sixteen against him. But under the 'general ticket' system, the entire 35 votes were cast for the Republican candidates, thus giving them not only the full strength of the majority in their favor, but that of the great minority against them superadded. So of other Northern States, in which the small majorities on one side operated with the weight of entire unanimity, while the virtual unanimity in the Southern States counted nothing more than a mere majority would have done."

(We see readily that Mr. Lincoln was not the Presidential choice of the great majority of the American voters in 1860, nor, as we shall see, in 1864 either. The country had fallen into the clutches of what could be termed nothing but political embezzlers and demagogues of the most sordid character, moral debasement, and corruption.)

"The manifestations which followed this result in the Southern States did not proceed, as has been unjustly charged, from chagrin at their defeat in the election, or from any personal hostility to the President-elect, but from the fact that they recognized in him the representative of a party professing principles destructive to 'their peace, their prosperity, and their domestic tranquillity.' The long-suppressed fire burst into frequent flame, but it was still controlled by that love of the Union which the South had illustrated in every battlefield from Boston to New Orleans. Still it was hoped against hope that some adjustments might be made to avert the calamities of a practical application of the theory of an irrepressible conflict.

"Few if any, then doubted the right of a State to withdraw its grants to the federal government, or in other words to secede from the Union; in the South, however, this was generally regarded as the remedy of last resort, to be applied only when ruin or dishonor was the alternative." (Davis, Chapter 7)

There may be some history texts in our American public schools which set forth these undeniably important facts to American pupils and students, but if so, I have not been able to locate them. Why any concealment? What need?

The most positive exposé of the falsity and chicanery underlying the Abolitionist and anti-slavery agitation movements in the North may be found in the first several chapters of Davis's *Rise and Fall.* It seems incomprehensible that the whole of Chapter 1 of this work should not be incorporated, *in toto,* in every school text professing to be intended for use in the teaching of American history to our children. The accuracy and honesty of this presentation concerning slavery is beyond argument or refutation. Non-presentation leads to false concepts of mid-19th-century America, placing a premium erroneously on the new governmental form, falsifying our genuine history, permitting continual perversion and distortion of the American form of government which the Fourteenth Amendment brought to this nation, lawlessly, unconstitutionally, wrongfully.

As an example of historical equivocation and error, I have before me a late work, the *Encyclopedia of American History.* In volume 1, page 227, there is given, under the heading "Presidential Election," the following, "Had the Lincoln opposition combined on a fusion ticket (attempted unsuccessfully in several States), it would have changed the result only in New Jersey, California and Oregon, for a total of eleven electoral votes. Lincoln would still have had 169, a clear majority." Compare this with the figures of Mr. Davis, concerning 'general ticket' voting. New York alone would have lessened Lincoln's electoral vote by sixteen votes; with some other States counted by popular vote, Lincoln could *not* have won.

By whatever forced count or adroit political maneuver, it is still seen that Mr. Lincoln received 1,866,352 out of a total vote of 4,676,853; his opponents had 2,810,501. As said, Lincoln received a bit more than one-third, his opponents a bit less than two-thirds, which indicates, surely, that the majority of Americans did not want Mr. Lincoln for President in 1860. He received not a single electoral vote from the South. Opposition against his acts and the conduct of the war throughout his administration was so virulent in the North that only a lawless seizure of total and dictatorial powers, an overthrow and ignoring of the Constitution by him permitted that war to be carried on. From every available source of information, the election of 1864 was won by Lincoln through similar questionable methods, such as marching Union troops to the polls and voting them by regiments. Even so, in 1864, Lincoln's majority was only approximately 400,000 votes out of a total of four million cast. His assassination then put Andrew Johnson into office, whose successor was General Grant. Grant got in the White House through the Negro vote in the South obtained by carpetbagging controls there, under the lawless Reconstruction acts, and the rule of martial law. These truths need pointing out to our school children so that they may know some of the real facts of American history, and the past experience of their fathers, and especially it is needed in the South, where the treatment of truth and facts by Northern texts have sometimes been fantastically distorted.

As Mr. Davis pointed out, "No rash or revolutionary action was taken by the Southern States, but the measures adopted were considerate and executed advisedly and deliberately. The presidential election occurred (as far as the popular vote, which determined the result, was concerned) in November, 1860. Most of the State legislatures convened soon afterwards in regular session. In some cases special sessions were convened for the purpose of calling state conventions—the recognized representatives of the sovereign will of the people—to be elected expressly for the purpose of taking such action as should be considered needful and proper under the existing circumstances.

"These conventions, as it was always held and understood, possessed all the power of the people assembled in mass. Therefore, it was conceded that they, and they only, could take action for the withdrawal of a State from the Union. The consent of the respective States to the formation of the Union had been given through such conventions, and it was only by the same authority that it could properly be revoked. The time required for this deliberated and formal process precludes the idea of hasty or passionate action, and none who admit the primary power of the people to govern themselves can consistently deny its validity and binding obligation upon every citizen of the several States. Not only was there ample time for calm consideration among the people of the South, but for due reflection by the general government and the people of the Northern States.

"President Buchanan was in the last year of his administration. His freedom from sectional asperity, his long life in the public service, and his peace-loving and conciliatory character, were all guarantees against his precipitating a conflict between the federal government and any of the States; the feeble power he possessed in the closing months of his term to mold the policy of the future was, however, painfully evident. Like all who had intelligently and impartially studied the history of the formation of the Constitution, he held that the federal government had no rightful power to coerce a State. Like the sages and patriots who had preceded him in the high office that he filled, he believed (and so stated in a message on December 3, 1860) that 'our Union rests upon public opinion, and can never be cemented by the blood of its citizens shed in civil war. If it cannot live in the affections of the people, it must one day perish. Congress may possess many means of preserving it by conciliation, but the sword was not placed in their hand to preserve it by force.' He kept his oath of office; the radicals in the Congress had forgotten theirs."

Samuel Adams, speaking of "Our Rights," said, "Among our natural rights given us is the right to have liberty, to hold property, together with the right to defend these rights in the best manner we can." But Abraham Lincoln, speaking on "Our Faith," said, "Let us have faith that right makes might and in that faith let us, to the end, dare to do our duty as we understand it." His understanding seemed to be that to rob the people of the South of their liberties through subjugation and of their properties by a species of dictatorial common theft, was a kind of American faith. Even eminent domain called for payment. And let us remember that he never represented all, but only a minor portion of the American electorate and ended his career at the hands of an assassin. Probably the last distinct words he ever heard were those of Virginia's motto, *Sic semper tyrannis*—Ever thus to tyrants.

He had permitted himself to be swayed and moved by the most callously vicious and remorseless elements of his party, backers of the John Browns and Abolitionists and the Thad Stevenses, the Charles Sumners, the Ben Wades and their ilk. When Andrew Johnson, his successor, opposed them, standing up manfully for those sacred constitutional principles he had sworn to uphold, these men infamously attempted his impeachment, bringing what was doubtless the most disgraceful, dishonorable page to American politics. The presidential oath was put in the Constitution for the specific purpose of forestalling dictators.

CHAPTER 4

Southern Slavery and New England Abolitionism

NEGRO "SLAVERY" in the southern regions was in no way the responsibility of northerners. Each state took care of its own domestic matters, and unless northerners came South for a visit, as Mrs. Stowe did, or settled there for business or commercial pursuits as some did, "slavery" was only an abstraction that did not affect them. Yet they came, in the amazing campaign that the Abolitionists still carried on, to be hostile in varying degrees toward southerners. It was a "sin," and the Abolitionists were under sacred obligation to destroy it. It was a "crime," an offense against humanity. They were bound to use all possible efforts to be rid of it. It was "a blot and a stain" upon what they called the character of the nation, and they felt themselves bound accordingly to give it no support or tolerance. Whether they were right, wrong, or in part both, the burden was still left upon the South, not the Abolitionists, to care for a large body of ignorant, improvident beings who could not work even to support themselves in that day except under the system of old-time southern "slavery." It had long been asked, "Kill slavery . . . what to do with the corpse?" It was dying out all over the civilized world; left alone in the South, it would have died a certain if lingering death. Many prominent southern leaders were in favor of doing away with it and colonizing the Negroes outside the States. One effort was to send them to Liberia; another to the now free West Indian Greater Antilles, to Haiti or San Domingo, to Central America or Panama.

It was doubtless the venomous, insulting, long-continued campaign of hate carried on against them that contributed to the resistance of the exasperated owners. Long they had pleaded, "Let us alone. Do nothing to us, and say what you please about slavery." They knew that it embodied a social relation that could not be destroyed without subjecting both whites and blacks to calamity and the region to poverty, desolation, and wretchedness.

We hear Lincoln say that the war was due "somehow" to slavery. Could he not, with his position and all that power, put his finger on something less vague than the abstraction of a "somehow"? It was a cover-up, an excuse. General Grant made the same explanation, and others followed the specious tale. We say that slavery was *not* "somehow" the cause of the war; it was an incident of it. In one of his brief appearances on the floor of Congress in 1847 the Hon. Abraham Lincoln, representative from Illinois and a Whig, stated bluntly that any people anywhere, being inclined and having the power, "have the right to rise up and shake off the existing government and form a new one which suits them better"; it was a most sacred right, one he hoped and believed would liberate the world. The English historian Goldwyn Smith in a laughing comment said that the South could not have asked for any clearer support than those very words of their later Nemesis, one of the Erinyes.

We would not teach sedition or condone human slavery; rather, we would reveal some facts long belittled in or concealed from our history. When the South seceded, she merely acted, quietly and orderly, by Ordinances of Secession on what was fully believed to be (and what we aver was and still is) her undoubted constitutional rights, and was only following threats and examples that had been suggested by northern states in 1803, 1814, 1845, and 1857. And when the South today blandly ignores a Supreme Court decree, she only follows—with far more justification—acts of ten northern states that refused to accept that Court's 1857 Dred Scott decision. Present-day southern laws have been on the books a long time, and there are ample precedents for nearly a century comparable to those acts of 1830–60 in many northern states which Daniel Webster himself called "treasonable" when he warned his section against their lawlessness and defiance of plain provisions of the Constitution. One state, Rhode Island, repealed hers, convinced of their inconsistency and illegality under the organic law of the land and the voice of the Supreme Court; most others, however, did not, but stood upon their "states' rights," no matter what the Court might decide. One prominent publicist proclaimed that there is "a higher law"! Why then, today, should a South waver an iota before a Supreme Court decree on far less genuinely constitutional grounds than that of Roger Taney's Court a century ago?

Charles Warren (Vol. I, page 388) thought that "states' rights" are based not so much on dogmatic political theories or beliefs as on the particular economic, political, or social legislation that a Supreme Court decision happens to sustain or overthrow. No section, he said, had found difficulty in adopting or opposing the theory when its interests lay that way. Perhaps he is right; nevertheless, the Constitution *must* be looked to in all constitutional questions. Where Justice Taney looked into it, Mr. Justice Earl Warren went outside, to upset precedents of more than fifty-eight years pronounced by some of the most eminent jurists who have ever sat on the high court, which had declared that it has no power to amend the Constitution. The same year of the Warren school-integration decision his Court held that "nothing new can be put into the Constitution except by the amendatory process"—language certainly plain enough to all.

Thomas Jefferson thought it dangerous to consider the Supreme Court as the ultimate arbiter of *all* constitutional questions: "The Constitution had erected no such single tribunal. . . . First, to check these unwarranted invasions of States' rights by the federal judiciary . . . the government was divided into three branches in order that each should watch over the others and oppose their usurpations." Lincoln's words were, "A Supreme Court ruling is not the law of the land. . . . It is the law of the case before it." In *Marbury* v. *Madison,* Justice Marshall noted that it was the province and the duty of the Judicial branch to say what the law is, and he went on: "The Constitution is the superior paramount law, unchangeable by ordinary means, or else it is on a level with ordinary legislative acts and like other acts is alterable when the legislature shall please to alter it"—a situation that would render a constitution an absurdity, ephemeral and legally ambulatory or changeable. A fifth justice, in a 5–4 decision, to remake, or unmake, a Constitution covering the whole nation? Hardly.

Of the strange decision in the 1954 school cases, the governor of Virginia, a man of scholarly legal attainments, experienced in the law and well versed in the history of his country, remarked that

> . . . the confusion, tortuous, irrational opinions and usurpation of power by the federal judiciary, has come about under the guise of interpreting the Fourteenth Amendment. . . . What is there to justify it? Nothing, absolutely nothing . . . Those who want to stretch the Constitution, those who want to "liberalize" it, those who want it to grow with the times, have seized upon Section 1 of that Amendment as an excuse for philandering with the rights of the States, in the cloak of safeguarding the rights of the individual. . . . The last section of that Amendment provides that "the Congress shall have the power to enforce by appropriate legislation the provisions of this Article" . . . and the Congress has never enacted any legislation that would implement to the extent of giving the federal government control over schools maintained and operated by the States and the localities. . . . We of the South, where members of the two races have lived in harmony for more than 300 years, are concerned with what the Supreme Court threatens to do to these good relations, as well as what it is doing to our Constitution and the rights of States.

Emphatically, the Court should not upset or overrule precedents long recognized, accepted as the reasoning of some of the most eminent jurists who have adorned the American bench, and thereby create dismay, disorder and near chaos in a large section of the country in a matter that, pre-eminently, is the affair and business only of the States of the Union themselves. It is not by any stretch even of legal imaginations a matter for remote control by non-lawmakers decreeing from afar and intruding into the strict duties of governors and their legislatures, whom the sovereign peoples of the sovereign units have lawfully elected to govern them under the republican forms of the country.

What is the best argument today against the general principles of home rule, or states' rights, on which the country was founded with a decentralized, not consolidated, government? Recently in a Virginia city I called upon an old friend, dean of one of the South's most respected law schools, and in the course of conversation happened to ask that question. His reply was rather general: It was a large question. Yes, he said, these are no longer "horse and buggy" days; the world, men, industry, science, are growing. Uniform laws might be best, on the whole, though some would probably be best left in the hands of the states, some in the hands of the federal government, with gradations in between. To my query about the present-day world-wide experiments by the British Commonwealth of Nations to extend home rule so as to permit London to become more or less free of the forms of remote control, imperialism style, he raised his eyebrows, smiled, but did not reply. I did not press him.

In August, 1862, a group of free Negroes assembled at the White House at the invitation of President Lincoln to hear an address he delivered. He long had expressed a wish "to see all men free and equal everywhere." In a discussion of proposed resettlement outside the United States, Lincoln said bluntly to them:

> You and we are of different races; between us exists a broader difference than between any other two races. Whether it is right or wrong I need not discuss, but the physical difference is a great disadvantage to us both, as I think. You suffer greatly by living among us; we suffer on each side, ours from your presence. . . . It affords a reason we should separate . . . but even when you cease to be slaves, you are yet far removed

> from being placed on an equality with the white race; the aspiration of men is to enjoy equality with the rest when free, but on this broad land not a single man of yours is made equal to one of ours.

It is not known how the audience reacted or responded, or what their own views were, at this meeting which preceded by a month another White House meeting at which the President astonished his Cabinet first with a "funny" story, then with the outline of the Emancipation proposal to become effective the following January 1. But the return to Africa (possibly the best solution) seemingly died aborning, much as had Lincoln's talk about "compensation" to slaveowners. His duplicity reveals him as no friend of the South, regardless of the piety, platitudes, great-heartedness, etc., and all the protestations of the astonishingly large Lincoln cult. A few historians, painstakingly reviewing the vast stores of data, have felt obliged to appraise his real feelings toward southerners as of concealed and resentful malignancy; he had received not a single electoral vote there.

Probably the best account of the inception of the Emancipation Proclamation can be found in the diary of Secretary of the Treasury Salmon P. Chase for the year 1862.

> Sept. 22, Monday. To Department about nine. State Department messenger came, with notice to Heads of Departments to meet at 12.—Received sundry callers.—Went to White House.
>
> All the members of the Cabinet were in attendance. There was some general talk; and the President mentioned that Artemus Ward had sent him his book. Proposed to read a chapter which he thought very funny. Read it, and seemed to enjoy it very much—the Heads also (except Stanton) of course. The Chapter was "Highhanded Outrage at Utica."
>
> The President then took a graver tone and said:—
>
> "Gentlemen: I have, as you are aware, thought a great deal about the relation of this war to Slavery; and you all remember that, several weeks ago, I read to you an Order I had prepared on this subject, which, on account of objections made by some of you, was not issued. Ever since then, my mind has been

much occupied with this subject, and I have thought all along that the time for acting on it might very probably come. I think the time has come now. I wish it were a better time. I wish that we were in a better condition. The action of the army against the rebels has not been quite what I should have best liked. But they have been driven out of Maryland, and Pennsylvania is no longer in danger of invasion. When the rebel army was at Frederick, I determined, as soon as it should be driven out of Maryland, to issue a Proclamation of Emancipation such as I thought most likely to be useful. I said nothing to any one; but I made the promise to myself, and (hesitating a little)—to my Maker. The rebel army is now driven out, and I am going to fulfil that promise. I have got you together to hear what I have written down. I do not wish your advice about the main matter—for that I have determined for myself. This I say without intending any thing but respect for any one of you. But I already know the views of each on this question. They have been heretofore expressed, and I have considered them as thoroughly and carefully as I can. What I have written is that which my reflections have determined me to say. If there is anything in the expressions I use, or in any other minor matter, which anyone of you thinks had best be changed, I shall be glad to receive the suggestions. One other observation I will make. I know very well that many others might, in this matter, as in others, do better than I can; and if I were satisfied that the public confidence was more fully possessed by any one of them than by me, and knew of any Constitutional way in which he could be put in my place, he should have it. I would gladly yield it to him. But though I believe that I have not so much of the confidence of the people as I had some time since, I do not know that, all things considered, any other person has more; and, however this may be, there is no way in which I can have any other man put where I am. I am here. I must do the best I can, and bear the responsibility of taking the course which I feel I ought to take."

The President then proceeded to read his Emancipation Proclamation, making remarks on the several parts as he went on, and showing that he had fully considered the whole subject, in all the lights under which it had been presented to him.

Note in the above that there had been some "objections" from members of the Cabinet and that Lincoln had had their views, but that he "did not wish their advice about the main matter, for that I have determined for myself." The story he read from Artemus Ward's book of humor consisted of about a page, with a relation of how, while Ward was showing his wax figures at Utica, New York, the one of Judas Iscariot at the Last Supper was grabbed by an outraged Utican, and that Ward himself was punched around the room with a demand to know why he had brought that "pussylanermous cuss here." Said Ward, "Yu egrejus Ass that 'air is a wax-figure of the false prophet or Apostle." But the irate Utican (who it seems was later indicted for arson in the third degree) was unsatisfied. "That's all very well for you to say, but I'm tellin', old man, that Judas Iscariot can't show hisself in Utica with impunity by a darn site."

The Cabinet found it difficult to see just what was so funny about all that, even though Lincoln was greatly amused by it. Their laughter was mild and polite. What the connection was between that story and the next act of the President was over all their heads. (Stanton did not even smile.) Perhaps to Lincoln's mind he was demonstrating subtly to his advisers that he, too, was pummeling a wax figure of a Proclamation that freed no slaves, put no black men as soldiers in the field to replace whites, or provided any solution as to what to do with the hordes of near savages he would loose upon a white civilization. The talk about "colonizing them in Central America, the greater Antilles or Africa," had begun in talk and it ended so—in talk.

The Abolitionists, with Lincoln's aid, perverted the war from its originally declared purpose of "preserving the Union" into a crusade for freeing the slaves and confiscating Southern property, but it did not have the support of the Northern people. On January 1, 1863, as we said, the Proclamation was made, declaring that all slaves in areas still in rebellion were "then, thenceforward, and forever, free." The Congress already had gone as far in partisan legislation on the subject, and the Proclamation applied only to areas over which the United States government exercised no control. Specifically exempted were those areas under the bayonets of the federal military occupation forces.

We must take exception to the words "in rebellion." The Confederate States were not "in rebellion." That term would assume that the Northern States, or Lincoln, held a sovereign power over them. What power, under the United States Constitution did the North ever hold over the South? The South was almost half the Union and, like the North, had sent senators and representatives to create a "Union."

Resettlement in the Monrovian Republic of American Negro former slaves was sporadic,* none too successful, and not undertaken by them with enthusiasm. The plan had originated about 1816 because of statutes in the slave states which required a number of stringent observations whenever a black was emancipated—e.g., posting bonds, certifications of character, the requirement of leaving the state within a specified period (in Virginia within one year after gaining "freedom"). By 1847 Liberia was an independent republic, with its own Constitution modeled after that of the United States and with its own "slavery." The institution of slavery was the subject of an official investigation under a League of Nations Commission in 1929–31, which uncovered conditions of actual slavery existing by government sanction, and with the frauds, corruptions, cruelties, evils, uncivilized practices often found when former slaves have been separated from the master class of owners (as, for instance, in Haiti, and San Domingo—now the Dominican Republic).

General William T. Sherman, who conducted one of the disgraceful dragonnades of modern history through the Carolinas and Georgia (January–April, 1865) "freeing" every Negro in sight, nevertheless had written to his brother, Senator John Sherman, in July, 1860: "All the Congresses on Earth cannot make the negro anything else than what he is; he must be sub-

---

* *Virginia Historical Society,* Vol. 59, No. 1, pp. 72–88.

ject to the white man, or he must amalgamate or be destroyed. . . . Two such races cannot live in harmony save as master and slave." Six months earlier, in December, 1859, when the Abolitionists were roaring in high fettle, stamping on the floors and pounding on the desks in both houses of Congress, he had said, "I would not if I could abolish or modify slavery."

Having stated opposite views on the matter in previous weeks, Lincoln in a different milieu, looking south with apparent sympathy, could say, "I cannot blame the Southerners for not doing what I should not know how to do myself. . . . Were all earthly powers given me I would not know what to do as to the existing institution." Yet some years later, as if indeed all earthly powers had been given him, he took it upon himself—and wholly outside the Constitution—to declare forever "free" nearly four million uneducated, childlike blacks, not one in thousands of whom had the least notion of what it was all about. They were suddenly propelled into a highly organized white civilization that moved and existed by means of the function of money, hired labor, production, consumption, and where sentiment was incongruous if not grotesque. This was a wrong done by a reformer of juvenile moral stature, accomplished by an outrageous ukase that no Czar of the Russias would have dared to utter.

Frederick Law Olmstead traveled through the South for several years following the 1850 compromises. In *Cotton Kingdom* he writes that he found the Negro field hands

> . . . a very poor and a very bad creature, much worse than I had supposed before I had seen him and grown familiar with his stupidity, indolence, sensuality and duplicity. . . . He seems but an imperfect man, incapable of taking care of himself in a civilized manner, and his presence in large numbers must be considered a dangerous circumstance to civilized people. A civilized people within which a large number of such creatures has been placed by any means not within its own control has claims upon the charity, the aid, if necessary, of all other civilized peoples in its endeavors to relieve itself from the dangers which must be apprehended from their brutish pro-

> pensities, from the incompleteness of their human sympathies—their inhumanity—from their natural love of ease, and the barbaric want of forethought and providence, which would often induce desperate want among them. The people thus burthened would have need to provide systematically for the physical wants of these poor creatures, else that the latter would be liable to prey with great waste upon their substance. Perhaps the very best thing to do would be to collect them into small herds, and attach each herd to a civilized family, the head of which would be responsible for its safe-keeping. Such a superintendent, of course, should contrive if possible to make his herd contribute in some way to the procuring of its necessary sustenance. If besides this, he even turned their feeble abilities to such good account by his superior judgment, that they actually procured a considerable surplus of food and clothing for the benefit of others, should not Christendom applaud and encourage his exertions, even if a certain amount of severity and physical restraint had been found necessary to accomplish this success? [Vol. II, Ch. 18, pages 564–65.]

At the time Olmstead was considered not to have drawn a wholly fair picture of the South, the cotton plantations, and their sustaining capital-labor elements of planters and "slaves."

Jefferson Davis, unlike Abraham Lincoln, was not a "reformer." His own might have been looked upon as a model plantation. The life he inherited from his forefathers, his experiences as soldier and farmer, his education, contacts, acts, common sense—not to mention the often exasperating, even insulting outbursts and petitions ever appearing on the floors of Congress to excite passions or to delay legitimate legislation—long led him to reply evenly and courteously to opponents in that day of envenomed exchanges in the august Senate. He had a reputation for keeping his head, and using it, not infrequently swamping adversaries by ready facts and figures as well as by the charm of his manner and voice. It was early noted that whenever he rose to speak the chamber listened with that attention usually accorded mastery and eloquence. With patience and civility he would endeavor to point out errors. It was unusual for him to make violent or impassioned answers, though there were occasions when vileness and vulgarity or untoward vehemence moved him to protests. In February, 1858, concerning charges of the South's tolerance of "the sin of slavery," he answered: "No population whose density is so great as to trade rapidly on the supply of bread, is willing to keep and maintain an improvident population, to feed them in infancy and care for them in sickness, protect them in age; it would thus be found in history that whenever population has reached that density in temperate zones, serfdom, villenage, slavery, whatever called, had disappeared." New England, the North, might starve, freeze; the southern states were lands of Goshen. He defended them, though he too disliked the "institution" fastened upon his section.

It is an historical fact that Massachusetts men of letters and agitators had been foremost in spreading the insane crusades against "slavery." To many of them the Mexican War was a southern plot to extend slave territory. The heart of New England, Massachusetts, had contributed not only some of the best but some of the worst of the many ideas that influenced our national character and development. One of these was fanaticism and intolerance. Abolitionism had there its strongest hold, and John Brown's murderous raid was financed from there in large part. Its Puritan spirit, commendable in many ways, degenerated into uncompromising, fanatical, dogmatic aspects, and it seems that no effort was made to understand the point of view of other sections (though never have they questioned their own). James Truslow Adams, one of the state's foremost scholars and writers, bitingly points this out:

> That this state, and all New England, would take an unyielding attitude on slavery questions, in so far as it appealed to her moral and fanatical inhabitants, was a foregone conclusion, even though they had no solution to offer. . . . The Republican orators played on the racial and economic fears of the Northern laborers and mechanics, asking how they could expect two dollars a day when Southerners spent but ten cents a day on their slaves (which was bunkum). One of the chief economic

disadvantages of slavery was its costliness and waste. . . . The orators took no account of the fifteen hundred to twenty-five hundred dollars that a slave cost to buy, of the possibility of his death, of the need of keeping him in sickness, off-seasons, dull years, of the need of feeding, clothing, physicking him, or of his inefficiency. . . . But the fear served. The Northerner had no love of the Negro, who in many ways was treated worse there than in the South; even that troublemaker, the free Negro, had better chance to rise above the laborer class in, say, Louisiana than in New York or Connecticut. . . . In two respects the North was in the line in which the world then was moving, away from slavery, but towards the exploitation of men and women in highly industrialized communities. . . . The conflict had to be rationalized; . . . it was characteristic of the North and especially of New England as the centre of the process that the whole stress should be laid on a single issue which could be moralized. The average Northern workman cared a great deal more about the Negro as a competitor than he did about him as a being in God's image who was entitled to life, liberty and pursuit of happiness. There was precious little that a Negro could do in the way of pursuing happiness in most Northern communities, as Connecticut could bear witness. [*Epic of America,* Little, Brown & Co.]

Two contrasting and antagonistic types of civilization had developed within the political and geographic unity. They needed reconciling, but how?

CHAPTER 5

The Republican Dictatorship of Lincoln

THE THEME THAT ENSLAVEMENT of the African Negro in wide stretches of the American South was *the* cause of, brought on, a brothers' war seems difficult to eradicate from popular belief even today. Why is this almost complete fallacy so widespread and so difficult to dispel? It must be that school textbooks in history, beginning with the mid-nineteenth century, try to justify a great wrong perpetuated against a great section of the American people, who did not counteract it much. It also is due to the memorials, statues, monuments, biographies, and forced traditions of pretended patriotism or statesmanship, some of which, grotesquely enough, adorn our public squares as others flood the nation's literature with panegyrics—especially those from New England.

In his *Epic of America* James Truslow Adams felt that the southerners were justified in leaving the Union as it was composed in that day. "Many did so, believing that the only way out was to leave the shelter of that Union from which they were being driven by the blind bigotry of a North which, in its industrial development, had grow away from the old 'live and let live' of the Constitution." It threatened now the lives and property of the South,

> . . . denounced its standards of morality, and was seemingly insanely anxious to create a uniformity of thought and life through the whole length and breadth of our great land. . . . The South too had loved the stars and stripes. . . . It had taken more than its full part in the first founding of the nation; the earliest successful settlement had been on its shores, not on those of New England. . . . The man on whom the success of

the Revolution had finally depended had been a Southern slaveowner and had been the first President. In the drafting of the Constitution and the statesmanship of the early republic no names have shown brighter than Jefferson, Madison, Marshall, all Southerners and slaveowners. . . .

There can be no gainsaying it; yet the material victory of force of arms by dictatorship in 1865 relegated the most important facts of American governmental history to near oblivion because a salient point of American jurisprudence, of constitutional law, had to be harassed out of sight and worried into hypothetical nonsense, principally by so-called lawyers and jurists, mostly of the Supreme and federal courts, over that "dead and buried and forgotten" phantom known as "states' rights." They had been ended by Lincoln: so, at least, they would have us believe. But this is *not* America, but *the United* States *of America,* now and forever. And we make a blunt statement of our own: Nothing destroys states' rights while the Constitution stands and all public officers under it faithfully observe their solemnly sworn oaths to support it. *Take notice!*

Abraham Lincoln did not observe that oath, and his administration is best known by its great number and variety of unconstitutional acts. We have already noted an item in his first Inaugural Address. Between inauguration in March, 1861, and the convening of Congress in July the new Republican President had brought a war upon the country and, in addition, through connivance with northern governors presented an army to fight it, to bolster the Congress and his own (as yet) unavowed intentions. All this was done outside the party, thereby obviated certain internal feuds, acrimonious debates, and delays sure to have embroiled even the almost fully partisan Congress. Declaring war is reserved to the Congress, not to the President, who seized that power—an amazing act!

The war itself was prosecuted in the same illegal, high-handed manner. Fiat money was made legal tender; states were brought into line by use of Executive favors and patronage. The

President has vast appointive power, and Lincoln lost no time in using it; generals and paymasters were appointed wholesale. Word was passed to put the quietus on sympathies expressed particularly in such border states as Maryland, Missouri, Kentucky, and Delaware. The Maryland legislature was prevented from assembling in the state Capitol at Annapolis and went westward to Frederick; but even there some of its members were stalked, seized, and rushed into the federal detention pen at Fort McHenry near Baltimore. They appealed to Chief Justice Roger Taney, a Marylander also, who decided that they were being illegally held and ordered their release. No attention was paid to his order when it was delivered to the fort, and from Justice Taney's lips came some token of the terrors then prevailing in many of the sovereign states of the Union. He proposed to reduce his judicial opinion to writing, take it himself to the White House, and demand that the President carry out his constitutional duties. The imprisoned legislators were not released; the President of the United States by his own order suspended the ancient writ of habeas corpus—something that, according to the organic law, only the Congress can do, on specified occasions. Thousands of citizens, men and women, were thrown into prison indiscriminately. The phrase "iron hand of the dictator," strange language to Americans, no doubt, is quite descriptive of what went on in the land under the new Republican regime in 1861.

Imagine yourself sitting in the quiet comfort of home or office, when suddenly you are startled to hear the front or back door being kicked in. Then a file of foreign soldiers in blue uniforms—men not in the country six months and speaking Polish or German or broken English—under a Union provost officer crowd into the room, seize you, carry you off to a stockade or an improvised army prison camp or fort, where you are held without accusation being lodged or made known and unable to communicate with family or friends. Then imagine this happening to many citizens.

In Maryland alone, where Governor Bradford and the legislature in 1861 had been elected by the federal soldiers and kept in office by their bayonets, even the judiciary found itself prevented from making independent decisions without first securing the approval of the Union commander in the area. In a message to the Maryland legislature then at Frederick, Governor Hicks told of the seizure of the state Capitol by General B. F. Butler and New York and Massachusetts militiamen under orders from Lincoln because secession sentiment was nearly unanimous at Annapolis before the regiments arrived.

In the same month, May, on the Eastern Shore Judge Carmichael was dragged off the bench at Easton by United States troopers and confined for six months with no charges lodged against him. He had at a previous court sitting instructed a grand jury to enquire into the manner of recent elections. Next month another judge, J. L. Bostol, was jailed without explanation.

Elihu Riley (*History of Annapolis*) tells of "test oaths," intimidations, civic frauds, and how 250 Union soldiers quartered at the United States Naval Academy voted there. Nonresidents of the state, "placed on their *voir dire,* these men declared they had entered Maryland thirteen months previous with intent to make Annapolis their residence"; on this the judges of elections received their so-called votes. One Captain Francis Keffer, a provost officer there, made prisoners of a dozen or more prominent citizens, most of them lawyers, one former Governor Pratt, when they refused to take an oath unknown to the Maryland law. They had come to vote in a state election, for which the state law provided governing regulations, and when turned away from the polls they declared their intention to have the election judges indicted before the Anne Arundel Grand Jury for preventing them from exercising their right as citizens to vote. For that they were arrested and sent to Baltimore under the charge of a Major-General Schenck.

Lincoln thus was having citizens jailed without charges being preferred against them, and held for months. He assumed the authority which is strictly Congress's for raising armies and making war against, and attacking and invading, the states that had peacefully seceded. Stupid military officers were given power to arrest citizens, kidnap them, commit them to jails or fortresses without warrant or indictment. He brazenly defied the very First Amendment to the Constitution and permitted his subordinates to raid newspaper offices, arrest editors, and stop publication of what was not favorable in tone. He paid out millions of dollars of Treasury money without authority, and to persons not authorized to receive it. The currency and financial obligations of the new Confederate States he allowed to be counterfeited, openly sold in the city streets, and distributed to soldiers for use in the Confederacy, where his armies were threatening and destroying. The vital American freedom of speech and of press was suppressed.

Mind you, we are not talking about a St. Bartholomew's Eve or a Reign of Terror, but the United States of America in 1861 and succeeding years. What was the necessity, why was it done? The answer is surprising. It was "to preserve the Union and the Constitution," Lincoln said. But that is what the Confederate States were trying to do, and their own organic law, the Confederate Constitution, unanimously ratified March 11, 1861, is incontrovertible proof of that. (The doubter is referred to the reprint of that Constitution in Part 3, Chapter 13.) The simple answer is: The black race was "freed" and enfranchised to keep the Republican Party in power, and these were the start.

We see at this point that the average American, back in the little red or the large and imposing granite or brick schoolhouse, was not told all the tale in history class, by any means. In fact, most of what he was told and allowed to study was the false front of "humanitarianism," flag-waving, and spread-eagling as performed by the experts of their hour of triumph. Let us look at one, none other than the famous poet of *The Vision of Sir Launfal*—now not so highly rated by southerners or even by some of his Massachusetts compatriots (e.g., *Bigelow Papers*). In the *North American Review* of January, 1864, James Russell

Lowell in an essay on Lincoln compared him to Henry IV of France, promulgator of the Edict of Nantes (who, by the way, like his predecessor and like Lincoln, also died at the hand of an assassin). Lowell thought that there had been many "painful crises since the impatient vanity of South Carolina hurried ten prosperous commonwealths into a crime whose assured retribution was to leave them either at the mercy of the nation they had wronged, or of the anarchy they had summoned but could not control, when no thoughtful American opened his morning paper without dreading to find that he no longer had a country to honor and love."

This, nothing but nonsense, is almost humorous. That the "vanity" of one state should hurry ten others into a "crime" indeed? And what was that anarchy? Where was it? Not in the South was there any knowledge of it. Surely there was far more anarchy in the North during most of the war years, in the Draft Riots in New York and elsewhere, and in the manner by which the federal government was to "guarantee" a republican form of government to the states. States like Maryland, Kentucky, Tennessee, Delaware, and Missouri would almost certainly have followed the seceding states out of the Union, on the states'-rights question alone, except that they were held through treachery in an iron military grip that had been imposed in each case in stealth and by trickery. Their citizens, confident in their constitutional rights and guarantees, were awakened to their violation in the most brazen, unprecedented manner ever attempted in the land before or since. The seceded South, now on its own, was singularly quiet, orderly, and determined in unusual and almost unanimous support of their governors, and the conventions were a solid front with their President in determination to achieve their purposes of divorce from the perfidity of their former partners and to go their own way in independence, a new nation.

To Lowell (1864),

> . . . the Republicans have carried the country upon an issue in which ethics were more directly and visibly mingled with politics than usual. . . . Their leaders are trained to a method

> of oratory which relies for its effect rather on the moral sense than the understanding . . . their arguments drawn not so much from experience as from general principles of right and wrong. When the war came their system continued to be applicable and effective, for here again the reason of the people was to be reached and kindled through their sentiments. . . . It was one of those periods of excitement, gathering, contagious, universal, which, while they last, exalt and clarify the minds of men, giving to the mere words *country, human rights, democracy,* a meaning and a force beyond that of sober and logical argument. . . . What is called the great popular heart was awakened, the indefinable something which may be, according to circumstances, the highest reason or the most brutish unreason. . . . Nothing is so pitilessly and unconsciously cruel as sincerity formulated into dogma.

It is always demoralizing to thrust sentiment into matters where it should not intrude, we agree. A President, his fingers unopposed in the public Treasury to persuade purchasable northern executives and hordes of importunate petitioners, needed but the "sentiment" to secure the seat of the dictator.

Widespread arbitrary arrests over the country—particularly in, though not confined by any means to, the border states and contiguous regions—made governors uneasy and filled the people with dejection and nameless terror, "cast them down and made them distrustful not alone of Washington, but even of their own governors and legislatures and state officials." The appearance of United States marshals in the street was a signal for frightened scurrying and hiding, for closing doors abruptly, suspending conversation, even by peaceable and conservative townsmen. They were troubled most of all by the extreme radicals, some of whom occupied gubernatorial mansions, as for instance Governor Yates of Illinois, who had been heard to say of a certain citizen who had remarked that he "would like to see Lincoln in Beauregard's hands" that the citizen "should have been hanged the moment he said it."

Consider an Executive Order authorizing the immediate arrest of "all persons suspected of being guilty of any disloyal practice, resisted the draft, or discouraged enlistments." Or a Secretary of War who provided marshals in the states "to report treasonable practices, detect spies, seize disloyal persons, arrest deserters." An intended result of the habeas corpus suspension was intimidation of voters in the elections that came shortly after the Emancipation proposal. In New York, New Jersey, Delaware, Massachusetts, Michigan, and Kansas, surprisingly enough, results showed the people unquestionably opposed to conscription, Emancipation, the Negro, the war itself, and the encroachment of government upon individual rights. Only stricter repressive measures could save his party, and Lincoln, apprehensive at the words and showing of Governor Seymour in New York, dispatched an aide to Albany with orders "to take Seymour to the mountain and show him the kingdom"—that is, let him know he can be approved as the President's successor. But the governor refused to bite. Meanwhile voting was conducted under the supervision of United States marshals on special pay. Union troopers stood at the booth windows, "raising drawn swords to permit entry of those who carried Union tickets, while Democrats faced delays, test-oaths, arrest, or were deprived of their tickets and compelled to cast Republican ballots."

Was it Noll and the Ironsides all over again? The "great public heart" was indeed awakened—with fear and uncertainty. Sentimentality was interfering with retributive reform. Lowell was of the opinion (in that essay) that it is corrupting to morals "to extend the domain of sentiment over questions where it has no legitimate jurisdiction; and perhaps the severest strain upon Mr. Lincoln was in resisting a tendency of his own supporters which chimed with his own private desires while wholly opposed to his convictions of what would be wise policy."

It required only the first break in the military picture, however, the drawn battle of Antietam, to bring out the great Executive theft of the Emancipation Proclamation—an act as "constitutional" as most of their other acts. In his war to "preserve the Union and the Constitution," it was an act wholly apart that fitted in nowhere except to prove the well-defined fears of the

South when he was announced elected President in November, 1860, and declared the rights and property of the South "to be in no danger from the incoming administration"!

The Union was made by the Constitution, and the South had always abided by the Constitution, revered it, and looked to it for protection; but what about a Constitution violated? The Union violated? Was that their Constitution? Or their Union? Righteous, impartial observance of its terms was all they asked, from the start of differences—no more, no less. When their inalienable rights were violated, were they to be true sons of their fathers? They were the best fighting people in the world (and, history shows, they still are).

It was not only Daniel Webster—who had been among the first to orate on the theme of a "whole" people and to oppose the arguments of southern statesmen of his day—who put it flatly that a contract broken on one side is broken on all sides. Many other northerners agreed on this most ordinary point in law. The North had unquestionably broken the contract; but note Mr. Lincoln, again in his first Inaugural: "One party to a contract may violate, break it, so to speak, but does it not require all to lawfully rescind it?" In legal contemplation the Union was perpetually confirmed; no state on its own mere motion could get out of the Union. But, by the Constitution, why not?

Mr. Lincoln simply intended to be President of *all* the states. No matter that a majority of the voters did not want him; he would be President of a "forced" Union, whether or not that was right morally, legally, constitutionally. A Constitution? His oath of office? All that mattered were his personal predilections, and though the most prominent members of his own party and outstanding editors and citizens over the nation urged caution and moderation, he ignored their advice. Taking all events of early 1861, each in its place from the November 6, 1860, election, we have a sorry spectacle of the ominous hours from that election day to the convening of Congress in July, 1861.

The governor of Virginia had invited fellow governors to a

national "peace conference" at Washington to try earnestly to solve the questions and to keep the country from the suicidal conflict that was beginning to hover like a Brocken specter over the land. Border-state executives responded, as did New York and a few other more moderate states. Minnesota and Michigan refused even to consider the invitation, and radicals in other states declined to co-operate—Dennison of Ohio, Andrew of Massachusetts, Morton of Indiana, and others. The New York legislature, told that the great mass of northern people desired peace, demanded "that no honorable effort to maintain it be left untried." There was much adverse comment in editorials across the country. When the Confederate Constitution was adopted, it was published in full in the New York *Herald,* March 16, 1861, which commented upon it as both a peace offering and an ultimatum and suggested that the Congress be called into session and an attempt made to reconcile the differences pointed out there. (See Conclusion, following Part Three, below.)

Congress was not called. Troop movements continued in and around the capital. Secret mobilizations of an armada went on in northern ports while a Confederate Peace Commission talked to Secretary of State Seward. The commissioners were assured that no hostile action was being contemplated, and they believed that Seward was speaking for the President.

Lincoln seemed to think that it was up to him to say what the Constitution was and who would interpret and enforce it. He had no registered oath to disintegrate the Union, but only to preserve it; yet only three years earlier he had said that the Dred Scott decision of the Supreme Court should be reversed, and "we mean to reverse it." Would he take over the functions of both the Congress and the Supreme Court?

Answering enquiries of Governor Yates of Illinois about recommendations to be made to legislatures and what to do about sending delegates to the proposed Virginia peace conference, Lincoln said that he would rather be hanged by the neck from the Capitol than beg or buy a peaceful inauguration

—hardly the expression of one hoping to avoid war. What so nationally public a figure has to say must always have profound and far-reaching consequences to all. There can be no refutation; he is bound by his answer. Here is what he had to say about slavery and states' rights in his first Inaugural Address:

> I have no purpose directly or indirectly to interfere with the institution of slavery in the States where it exists. I believe I have no lawful right to do so, and I have no inclination to do so. . . . And more than this, they placed in the platform for my acceptance, and as a law to themselves and to me, the clear and emphatic resolution which I now read:
>
> "*Resolved,* That the maintenance inviolate of the rights of the States, and especially the right of each State to order and control its own domestic institutions according to its own judgment exclusively, is essential to that balance of power on which the perfection and endurance of our political fabric depend, and we denounce the lawless invasion by armed force of the soil of any State or territory, no matter under what pretext, as among the gravest of crimes."
>
> I now reiterate these sentiments.

As for the Supreme Court, he criticized the then recent (1857) decision in the Dred Scott case:

> . . . the candid citizen must confess that if the policy of the government upon vital questions affecting the whole people, is to be irrevocably fixed by decisions of the Supreme Court the instant they are made, in ordinary litigation between parties in personal actions, the people will have ceased to be their own rulers, having to that extent practically resigned their government into the hands of that eminent tribunal. Nor is there in this view any assault upon the court or the judges. It is a duty from which they may not shrink to decide cases properly brought before them, and it is no fault of theirs if others seek to turn their decisions to political purposes.

True; and that Court had decided by 7 to 2 a constitutional case that ought to have settled a long-standing dispute. It was decided on strictly constitutional grounds; there was nothing else that the Court could have found unless they went outside their sworn obligations to support the Constitution. They looked into it, found the answer; a country should have abided by it. Did they? The North did not, and Lincoln supported the dissenting states. Speaking at Chicago on July 10, 1858, he had declared, "Someone has to reverse that decision, since it is made, and we mean to reverse it, and we mean to do it peaceably." By "we" he meant, of course, himself, the Abolitionists, and their Republican Party supporters. What should have set a grave, disturbing question at rest had only added fuel to the flames, warward.

Whether merely dismissing the plea of Scott—as many afterwards thought the high court should have done—and omitting entirely from the lengthy opinion the *obiter dicta* would have had any soothing effect is highly improbable. Practically the whole country was looking to the Supreme Court for an answer —which it got, pleasing to the South, infuriating to the North for the most part and especially to the Abolitionists. Suppositions, opinions, theories, were many, in 1857. Boudin, in his *Government by Judiciary,* expressed the opinion that Taney and a majority of his associates felt that the moment was opportune for the Court's taking a hand in the greatly disturbed condition of the country then existing, "to attempt to re-establish, by judicial decision, that 'peace and harmony' which Congress had been unable to establish by legislation." That insults the Court, which had a case before it to determine, not a "declaratory" judgment in jural relations.

John Brown's raid at Harper's Ferry had shocked the North. Even in Massachusetts Governor Banks and many of the state's prominent citizens and politicos unhesitatingly condemned it as the act of a mad fanatic. Not so, however, one John Andrew, soon to become governor there. Like other demagogues of the day, he saw an opportunity and from the housetops endorsed Brown, declared him "a martyr," took up a collection for his defense, and as a lawyer, one would think, was guilty of misprision of a felony when he privately advised a number of citizens of Boston who had contributed money and ammunition and arms to Brown to fly from the state when it seemed that Governor Banks might honor a Virginia demand for their extradition to be tried for treason by Virginia along with John Brown.

In a speech in 1859 at Columbus, Ohio, Lincoln told an audience that the Republican Party "believes that there is great danger that slavery will spread out and be extended until it is ultimately made alike lawful in all the States of the Union; to forestall that is the original and chief purpose of the party." But he knew from debate with Douglas the futility of continuing slavery in northern regions. At Cincinnati, a city tied to the South by numerous strings, an audience was told, concerning slavery, that the Republican Party "would not interfere . . . not withhold an efficient fugitive Law, but would forestall any 'extension' of it, and opposed the slave trade, with desires for a territorial slave code." And so the agitations and political campaigning over slavery went on and on, a lurid fog obscuring the issues that moderates and conservatives held to, to become a mad, feverish war dance ever increasing in volume, fanned out by fanaticism.

On February 4, 1861, a distinguished, able, patriotic group of men met at Montgomery, Alabama, united and grim in their determination to put an end to the equivocal position of the southern states in the Union. At the same time another group of delegates from some twenty-one states had gathered at the Willard Hotel in Washington with the ostensible purpose of trying to devise ways and means of holding the Union together, but the composition of that group was such as almost to ensure defeat of that purpose from the start. Charles Sumner had begged his own governor and legislature "not to cave in"; Charles Adams had recommended for his state and other radicals "to send men who would defeat the peace men." Despite the fanatics and despite the success of radical congressmen-delegates in preventing northern members from yielding on any Republican principle, there did finally emerge a number of proposals. Seven proposed amendments to the Constitution were presented to the Congress, where "they were received without enthusiasm and rejected almost without debate"—the South being unrepresented on the floor because her members had walked out, each upon the withdrawal of his state.

A Michigan senator had written to his governor and state legislature that in his opinion, "without a little bloodletting, the Union would not be worth a rush." He was not alone; the southern Ordinances of Secession had brought forth too much fire. The governor of Massachusetts, now John Andrew, became positively bloodthirsty. Himself at a safe distance from possible battle fronts, he was frantic in war preparations—drilling the militia, inventing murderous "plots" supposedly being planned in Washington, calling upon General Winfield Scott to lay out lines of march for Massachusetts "troops," and even inducing his legislature, so sure was he of large shares of Executive patronage, to offer the federal government $100,000 as an "earnest of willingness to make sacrifices for the Union." His own people became disgusted, but other radicals elsewhere fell in with his proposals and activities. In the West and the North were other acts and threats: the Mississippi "would be snatched from the secessionists"—no aliens to hold that!

President-elect Lincoln at Springfield, wearied by hordes of importunate political suppliants and "advisers," left his home for a swing around the North to sample public opinion and to visit state governors and legislatures. It was an uninspiring trip, almost mountebank in nature, filled with contradictory, insipid, or vague trivia. He was devoted to peace; he would put the firm foot down. Seward prevailed upon him to alter the defiant tone at the end of a speech to the more poetic appeal with which it actually closed when it went forth to the nation as it was delivered as his first Inaugural Address.

It was a day of remarkable men in the Congress of the United States. Among them was crippled, sour, Thaddeus Stevens of Pennsylvania. For a moment we listen to this odd, dour specimen from Vermont, now representing a Quaker-Amish district in Pennsylvania, as he comes to the House floor on February 29, 1850. At attempt to pass the Wilmot Proviso had failed by a vote of 105 to 71. Stevens had always opposed slavery, not that he knew intimately much about it, although he is credited with having lived much of his adult life with a comely Negress, a widow, who attended him in his Lancaster home and presided over his Washington, D.C. housekeeping. Now, he took as his opening point what another member (Clingman) had said in behalf of the slave-owners, feeling that the country had been thus notified "that unless Congress submitted to settle the slavery question according to Southern demands, there would be no legislation, even to the passage of ordinary appropriation bills to sustain the government." "I doubt not that before he ventured upon so high a threat, he had full assurance from a sufficient number of Southern gentlemen to bring it into effect . . .

"Here, then, we have a well-defined and palpable conspiracy to disorganize and dissolve (the government). I doubt if there is another legislative body in the world where such sedition would not be followed by prosecution and punishment . . . but in this glorious country where two-thirds of the people are free, we can say anything within these walls or beyond them with impunity, unless it be to agitate in favor of human liberty—that is aggression! While I announce my hostility to slavery in every form and place, I also avow my determination to stand by all the compromises of the Constitution, some of which I much dislike, and were they now open to consideration they should never receive my assent. But I find them in the Constitution, formed in difficult times, and I would not disturb them. By these compromises Congress has no power over slavery in the States. I greatly regret that it is so, but I know of no one who claims the right or desires to touch it, within the States. But when we come to form new governments for territories acquired long after the formation of the Constitution, and to direct new States whose only claim for admission depends on the will of Congress, we are bound so to discharge that duty as shall best contribute to the prosperity and glory of the nation. Does slavery contribute to either of these? Is it not rather subversive of them? Let us first view it in the light of political economy.

"Slave countries never can have an intelligent and industrious yeomanry . . . the white people who work with their hands are ranked with the other laborers, the slaves. Their minds and conduct generally conform to their conditions; the soil occupied by slavery is much less productive than a similar soil occupied by freemen. Men who are to receive none of the wages of their labor do not care to multiply its fruits; the land being neglected becomes poor and barren. . . . Take Virginia. She has a delightful climate, a soil naturally fertile, is intersected by the noblest rivers; her hills and mountains filled with rich minerals and covered with valuable timber; her harbors are among the best in the world. At the time of the adoption of the Constitution, she was the most populous State—her population being double that of New York. It was the boast of her statesmen that she was *prima inter pares*. What is she now (1850)? The population of New York is more than double—I think the next census will show nearly treble hers. Her land cultivated by unwilling hands is unproductive. Travel through the neighboring states of Ohio and Pennsylvania and you will see that the land produces more than double as much as the same kind of land in Virginia. In the free States new towns are everywhere springing up and thriving . . . in Virginia there is scarcely a new town within her borders. Her fine harbors are without ships except from other ports; and her seacoast towns are without commerce, and falling to decay. Ask yourself the cause, sir, and I will abide the answer."

A dismal, sombre, false portrait!

His picture was deservedly laughed at by the South for its absurdity. The writings of Dew, Harper, Helper, Hammond, E. B. Bryan, Christy, Calhoun, Cooper, Stephens, Davis, Simms, Grayson, Hundley, Dabney, Fitzhugh, Campbell, Pufendorf, Bledsoe and numerous others can be read with interest for their ideas, first-hand, on the slave and planter condition in the South, where it had been grossly misrepresented by fanatical Abolitionists of the Stevens ilk. Simply, then, it (slavery) was a necessity at worst; with many a positive good, long established, difficult to upset, dangerous to overthrow. Alexander Stephens, later Vice President of the Confederacy, wrote, "The slave so-called was *not* in law regarded entirely as a chattel, as had so erroneously been represented. He was by no means subject to the absolute dominion of his master. He had important personal rights secured by law. His service due according to law, it is true, was considered 'property,' and so in all countries is considered the service of all persons who according to the law are bound to another or others for a term however long or short. So is the legal right of parents to the service of their minor children. True liberty was the enjoyment of the peace in society for which one was fit." The perversion of the Constitution had kept out of the South millions of the immigrants whose influx had so largely built up all those "new" towns, and new "prosperity," and created the great, simple majorities of the North which were prostituting the "Welfare clause" to its ends, and to the loss and injury of the South. And here was one of their representatives, Thad Stevens, holding such injuries and distortions to be the South's fault by a reason *only* of "slavery," which his own compatriots of New England had, profitably, fastened upon the region!

Jealousy of the South's great prosperity, her real culture and manners of gracious living, her long hold on the offices of the government and her pre-eminent place in the Congress from early days had much to do with disparaging criticism. The "humanism" theme was open hypocrisy. Climate alone was much of an answer to all the latter could offer. Were Americans willing to turn over their semi-tropical regions to an alien and semi-savage black race, centuries separated from them in culture and background? Hamilton Fish wrote in 1860 of the "madness" of the anti-slavery doctrines, "If it is limited in its range, rascality begins where madness ends; the North was teaching it to be a duty of the 'slave' to kill his master, to kill all who would restrain him of his 'freedom.'" Such gentle doctrines bound up no gulf between North and South, only widened it.

While the historians and the texts do not delineate on it, there were several tries, in Congress, before Thaddeus Stevens was enabled to put through his notorious creation, the Fourteenth Amendment. That the Fourteenth Amendment was an overthrow of the American form of government cannot be successfully refuted. Some of the supposedly astute Constitutional law authorities have both condemned and upheld it; but it is our own opinion the best of these upholdings are but "the veriest dry bones of legal reasoning and a sophistry of juristic abstraction." Withal, and without a shadow of doubt, it converts the original American form of decentralization into a centralized absolutism located at Washington, D.C., with a United States Supreme Court to order, and a President be he disposed (as Jackson was not) to enforce its decisions with the nation's armed forces, even over the protests of the people's elected representatives. It was, as has been stated, forced through Congress by a Joint Resolution, a method that Congress is without the Constiutional power to do; and is usurpous of the Constitutional powers of three-fourths of the several States alone. The Congress is powerless to act until three-fourths of *all* the States have acted on the proposed ratifications. And three-fourths of the States, as we said, *never* ratified the proposal. How, then, can this amendment be a valid part of the United States Constitution? Obviously, it cannot.

Stevens introduced his proposal in the House on December 5, 1866, and right over the head of the Judiciary Committee, where it had been for some time held up. The first proposal was:

> Representatives shall be apportioned among the several States, which may be included in the Union according to the number of their respective legal voters; and for this purpose none shall be considered as legal voters who are neither natural-born or naturalized citizens of the United States of the age of twenty-one years, Congress to provide for ascertaining

> the number of said voters. A true census of legal voters shall be taken at the same time with the regular census.

It will be noted that the above did not confer the voting franchise upon Negroes, the States were not "forced." But some of Stevens' coterie (Blaine was one) made vigorous objections, so the proposal was changed to read as follows:

> Representatives shall be apportioned among the several States which may be included in this Union according to their respective number, counting the whole number of persons in each State, excluding Indians not taxed. Provided that whenever the elective franchise shall be denied or abridged in any State on account of race or color, all persons therein of such race or color *shall be excluded* from the basis of representation. (Italics are the authors.)

One of Lincoln's desires was to confer the privilege of voting upon "the very intelligent among the Negroes" and upon those "who serve our cause as soldiers."

Lincoln's astuteness, his "statesmanship," is nowhere poorer shown than in these proposals, if they are carefully examined. Would the Confederates be willing to confer franchise upon former slaves who had taken up arms against them? It was but another of the confusing contradictions which pervaded his entire four years in office, his obtuseness of comprehension.

An oddity in Stevens' proposals was the absence of "male" as a voter's qualifications. When queried in regard to it, he demanded, "Why crusade against women in the United States Constitution?" He did not think the Constitution "ought to be disfigured with such a provision." Nor, he asserted, would he ever vote "to insert the words 'white' or 'male' in the Constitution. Let it be attended to by the States." By the States! Yes!

The debates on it makes interesting reading from the Congressional *Globe,* and it was very hotly debated up to the closing speech by Mr. Stevens on January 31, 1867, where he pointed out that the proposal would not force any State to give the elective franchise to its Negroes. It was here that Stevens displayed the foresight, political acumen and practicality which Lincoln so obviously lacked.

And his statements stand out above all the uproar and confusion of the times. He held, "The states have the right, and always have had it, to fix the elective franchise within their own States; this measure did not take it from them."

The key to Stevens' strange stand seems to have been that if the ex-slaves were given the vote without a period of preparation for them to be educated up to it, the whites of the South, particularly the leaders among the former slaveholders would merely use them to increase their own representation, without benefit to the freedmen, or, for that matter, to the nation. From among much of the long arguments (his and others of his belief) what he wanted was to have *all* national and State laws equally applicable to every citizen, with no discrimination to be made on account of race, or color, or even sex.

Finally, the proposal was carried in the House by a 120 to 46 vote, and sent to the Senate.

Here it was to be stopped by Charles Sumner of Massachusetts. Like Stevens in the House, Sumner in the Senate was the Negroes' all-out champion. We cannot go into the intricacies of the arguments in the Senate. Despite Sumner's polish, oratory, and complete belief in his own superiority, it is seen that Stevens was more practical, more wily, and more compromising than the prolix and pontifical gentleman from Massachusetts. To him, if disloyal white "rebels" were to be allowed to vote, why should ignorant, loyal black men be denied? He immediately objected to every objection to a Constitutional amendment which conferred the vote upon the Negro of the South. That many of the Northern States prohibited a Negro from voting (Connecticut, for instance, had rejected by a plebiscite Negro voting), appeared to have no weight with him, and he was extravagant in arraignment; he outdid himself in invective; and those guilty of its perpetuation brought to his thought "Pontius Pilate with Judas Iscariot on his back."

His scathing denunciation caused the Senate to reject the

proposal; the two-thirds vote needed could not be obtained. Sumner had spoken. It went back to the House.

Congress seemed not able to agree on any conditions that would keep the Southern States *out* of the Union until what was wanted of them would be complied with. What was that? The House could not decide. A number of proposals were offered, altered, rejected, re-offered in slightly changed form. The Fourteenth Amendment came out of the Congress to be presented to all the States (for acceptance or rejection). Congress offered the hemlock cup to the South, and saw it rejected. The legislatures of Louisiana, Mississippi, Florida said "no" with unanimity; Virginia gave but one vote for it, Georgia two, Arkansas three, Texas five and Alabama ten out of 106 and North Carolina eleven out of 146. In unmistakable, even peremptory, manner, the South rejected the Fourteenth Amendment. Stevens now led in placing the South under military rule through the "Reconstruction."

Though the North was largely opposed to Negro suffrage, it was to be *forced* upon the South. Even before the Fifteenth Amendment, Negroes were voting under carpetbaggers all over the South. It was claimed that the Fourteenth's ratification was legal because three-fourths of the Northern States ratified it. Ratified it for the South, where it was to be immediately and intimately felt in ways no State of the North was to know? *But,* the Constitution requires that three-fourths of all the States must ratify for validity. The "United" part of the U.S.A. now was the North; the South was an appendage merely hanging on and held up with bayonets. This was a Union restored?

What is known as the "Reconstruction" period of American history extended from the war's end in 1865 to the spring of 1877. It is a page of incredible horrors. It may be said to have actually begun under Lincoln, when in 1862, he appointed provisional governors for Louisiana, North Carolina and Tennessee, in each of which States some limited occupations by the Union armies made possible pretense of legal restoration of Union rule under martial law. To Mr. Lincoln the seceded States had never left the Union. If a tenth of the 1860 electorate, agreed to emancipation and took an oath of loyalty, amnesty and return to the Union was offered. Arkansas and Louisiana were considered to have taken such steps in 1864, but the radical Congress refused to seat their representatives. What was called the Wade-Davis Bill of July 4, 1864 was the Congressional plan for reconstruction. The electorate of each Confederate State was to swear to past as well as present loyalty as a condition precedent to re-entry into the Union, which was obviously meant to prevent any voting except by Negroes. The measure was pocket-vetoed by the president, bringing on him the excoriation of the radicals. Horace Greeley, in the New York *Tribune* published their denunciations, and this led to attempts to remove Lincoln's name from the Republican Party's 1864 slate, but the success of the Sherman invasion in Georgia (leading to renewed hope of winning the war) brought the radical efforts to naught, and Lincoln was re-elected in November, 1864 by a majority of 400,000 votes out of 4,000,000 cast. Unlike his successor Johnson, Lincoln would not stand up to the ferocious radicals of the Congress, who were beginning to resent openly the great expansion of Executive powers he had so unconstitutionally taken for four years. When Andrew Johnson came into office, the Congress was to learn he did not favor their grim proposals concerning a program for the South. During recess, he recognized governments set up in Arkansas, Louisiana, Virginia and Tennessee, and granted amnesty to most of the Confederates, making some exceptions of groups (which could ask him for special pardon; these he granted with a free and generous hand). The seven remaining States were organized with provisional governors, with powers to convene conventions (made up of delegates to be elected by loyal citizens, including those he had "pardoned"), to amend the State Constitutions so as to abolish slavery and repudiate the South's war debts. By the year's end, every State except Texas had fulfilled the requirements, and this State actually reported confirmation on April 6, 1866. When Johnson made his first message to Congress on December 6, 1865, he announced that the Union had been re-united and restored, with the ex-Confederates ready to take their seats in the Congress. It seemed as simple as that. But when the Congress convened they had news for Mr. Johnson. They refused to endorse him or accept his policies. He had become anathema to them; a war dance began to unseat him and take his scalp.

The 39th Congress appointed a joint committee of nine representatives and six senators to investigate and guide it on matters of Southern representation and Negro suffrage in the returned States. This committee ruled the Congress and was under the thumb of Thaddeus Stevens of Pennsylvania in the House and Charles Sumner in the Senate. The former declared the ex-Confederate States to be "conquered provinces" and proposed confiscation of the lands and giving them over to freed Negroes, "loyal citizens" he called them. As this individual (whom James Truslow Adams called "perhaps the most despicable, malevolent, and morally deformed character who has ever risen to power in America) came to wield almost dictatorial powers in the House and over the Republican party, the South was given over to the mercy of the wolves. In the senate, Sumner held that the Confederate States had "committed suicide." These interpretations had the result of putting the South completely under Congressional controls. The president was ignored. The night descended, a night of horror.

On the 18th of December, 1865, the Thirteenth Amendment, abolishing slavery, was proclaimed in effect by the Secretary of State. On March 3, 1865, the 39th Congress established the Freedmen's Bureau, over Johnson's veto, to secure by military force the supposed "civil rights" of Negroes. Presumably the whites did not need any.

Johnson balked, on the grounds that Congress had no powers to legislate when eleven States were unrepresented, not to mention the violation of the Fifth Amendment. He was roared down and vilified.

Over his veto, on April 9, 1866, Congress enacted the Civil Rights Act, giving citizenship to the Negro and granting the same civil rights to all persons born in the United States, which was a direct and unconstitutional invasion of States' rights, later to be so held by the Supreme Court in 1883. June 13, 1866 saw the Fourteenth Amendment concocted by the committee of 15 because of the widespread doubts concerning the legality of the Civil Rights Act. The amendment was submitted to the States for ratification three days later. Submitting the amendment to the States, under the United States Constitution, was *all* Congress had the power to do. With this, its powers ceased, but this was a Congress which knew not of the Constitution. When the Southern States rejected the amendment, Congress made its acceptance a condition of restoration of statehood in the Union. Congress, not the States, thus overturned the form of American government, and a political party did so to perpetuate themselves in power, the whole fear among the Republicans being the awful thoughts of any revival of Democratic Party power in the nation; to prevent this, nothing was too lawless, too corrupt, too preposterous.

Was this type of legislative monstrosity, then, to be taken as representative of the American people? We cannot consider that it was. Without doubt, the Republican party, up to the end of Hayes' tenure, was the most devastatingly corrupt organization the country had yet seen; but we do not wish to be here taking sides, for a recent New Deal Democratic Party, forcing into office a weak president for four terms, brought similar disasters and incongruities and wrongs to a country that, from previous experience, should have known better what to expect. Would not a benevolent constitutional monarch do as well? Especially when the Constitution is permitted to be bypassed and an oath to support it allowed to become only a path to the office, to be thrown aside whenever expediency should suggest or hunger for power arise? More Senate control to an extent over presidential appointments, particularly to all judicial benches, and the independent offices, would seem a crying need of this present day. Even the Electoral College could stand an overhauling to try to put it back where the Founding Fathers intended and divorced from party management and control. The States must take back their proper places, resuming their consistent position relative to a federal government if we are to remain the United *States* of America under the world's best hope of a Constitution. Not yet are we just America!

A first effort might be either to remove three questionable wartime amendments, or at least to put the Fourteenth (and the Fifteenth) up to the States again, to ratify or reject, as they see fit, something that was not done when they were placed there by Congress.

By abrogating the three-fifths clause, about twelve additional seats for the South were made in the House, but a reduction in representation in proportion was provided when any State denied suffrage, except for secession or participation in "rebellion."

Now, what did the South actually "rebel" against? The term is quite frequently used, but is wholly mistaken. There must have been a government which held powers over the South if it rebelled, but no such overweening government ever existed. It was the several States which held the ultimate power over their creation, their creature, the federal government.

Rejecting the Fourteenth Amendment, the Southern States (Tennessee excepted, due to peculiarities there) felt that the approaching congressional election would repudiate the whole radical plan of coercion, but it was a vain hope. Times were too close yet to the war. There were race riots in Memphis and in New Orleans and elsewhere, which the Republicans used to persuade reluctant voters. They captured two-thirds of both houses and thus secured effective control over "Reconstruction."

By the First Reconstruction Act, of March 2, 1867, passed over the veto of the president, the South was cut up into five military districts, under martial law. The States were ordered to call new Constitutional conventions. Congress passed supplemental Reconstruction Acts on March 23 and July 19, 1867 and March 11, 1868, which gave army officers powers to discriminate between voters and office-holders. Declaring a majority of votes, no matter, the number, was enough to install a new State Constitution—which was put over mostly by the Negro vote, with no (or few) Confederates participating. The president's hands were tied. Congress had rejected his vetoes. The governments he had set up previously were supplanted when Northern armies numbering over 20,000 men, with Negro militia, were sent into the South to compel acceptances of whatever the radical Congress proposed. Under these new military governments, it is recorded that 703,000 blacks and 627,000 whites were registered as voters in the South. In Alabama, Florida, Louisiana, Mississippi and South Carolina, Negroes, ignorant ex-slaves, outnumbered the whites, while in the other States a coalition of scalawag-carpetbag-Negro groups made up the radical majorities. Late 1867 saw these various elements take control of the former Confederacy to establish new Constitutions for these States guaranteeing universal manhood suffrage, civil rights for the blacks, and disqualifying the ex-Confederate former electorate.

On June 22-25, 1868 by an Omnibus Act, the partisan Congress, under these extraordinary proceedings, considered that seven States were entitled to be re-admitted into a Union which the Supreme Court, in 1869, held that they had never left, and could not leave. (See *Texas vs. White.*) That court had its difficulties.

The Fifteenth Amendment to the United States Constitution proposed February 26, 1869, was declared ratified by twenty-nine of the thirty-seven states, which was false, and was made a part of the Constitution on March 30, 1870. On February 24, 1868, a Resolution was made to impeach President Johnson. He was cleared by a single vote. In November, 1868, General Grant was elected to the White House; his popular vote was 3,163,500; his opponent's was 2,857,500, a majority for him of some 306,000 votes. The Negroes put him in office. The black vote for him was over 705,000. Three Southern States did not take part, six others were under total radical control. Students should find of interest here Supreme Court Cases *ex parte Milligan, Georgia vs. Stanton, Mississippi vs. Johnson, ex parte Garland.*

PART TWO

The Civil War and Reconstruction

CHAPTER 6

Jefferson Davis, Patriot and President

JEFFERSON DAVIS ALSO WROTE a short autobiography. A friend took it down in longhand at Davis's bedside during his last illness, September–November, 1889, at his home Beauvoir on the Gulf near Biloxi, Mississippi. He personally revised and condensed it for publication; it appeared in the January, 1890, issue of the *Belford Magazine*. Excerpts were also selected for inclusion in a new edition of *Appleton's Encyclopaedia* at the publisher's request. Davis wrote:

> I was born June 3rd of 1808, in Christian County, Kentucky, in that part of it which by a subsequent subdivision became Todd County. At this spot since has arisen the village of Fairview, and on the exact spot where I was born was erected the Baptist Church of the place, the site of which I donated in Richmond, Virginia, 1880, at an occasion in the St. Paul's Church, though I am not a Baptist; my father, Samuel Davis, was. He had served in the Revolutionary War, first in what was called the mounted gunmen, and afterwards as a captain of infantry at the siege of Savannah, 1779. During my infancy we removed to Wilkenson County, Mississippi; I, then a baby, was the youngest of ten children. . . .
>
> After passing through the country academy, I entered Transylvania College, Kentucky, and was advanced as far as the senior class when, at the age of 16, I was told I would be appointed by President James Monroe, on recommendation of Mr. John C. Calhoun, to the United States Military Academy at West Point, New York.
>
> I entered in September, 1824, and graduated in 1828, and then in accordance with the custom of cadets, entered into active service, with the rank of lieutenant, U.S. Army, serving as an officer of infantry at Prairie du Chien in Wisconsin and

other points on what then was called the Northwest frontier until 1833. After a successful campaign against the Black Hawk Indians, I resigned from the army, 1835, being anxious to fulfil a long-standing engagement with Miss Sarah Knox Taylor [daughter of General Zachary Taylor and related through her mother to the Lees of Virginia], whom I married, not after a romantic elopement as has been stated incorrectly, but at her aunt's house, near Louisville, Kentucky, after which I became a cotton planter in Warren County, Mississippi. It was a great misfortune early in my married life to lose my dear wife, and for years thereafter I lived in seclusion on the plantation in the swamps of the Mississippi. I took no part in public life until 1843 when I was elected to be one of the presidential electors-at-large of the State, and the next year I was elected to the House of Representatives, December, 1845.

When hostilities with Mexico commenced, my military education permitted me to take a prominent part, and in June, 1846, on organization of a Mississippi regiment of volunteers, I was elected colonel.

He served under General Taylor at Monterey and at Buena Vista, where he was wounded in the right foot and was left crippled for some time afterwards. In his detailed report of the action General Taylor gave high praise to Colonel Davis and his men for their part in the engagement. When the young Lieutenant Davis of the regular army had asked to marry Sarah Taylor, Old Rough-and-Ready had objected; he knew the hardships that women with the army had to undergo, and he did not propose that his daughter should have any part of it. There also seems to have been some animosity toward the young man. It was later, after her death and the Mexican War and before the general became twelfth President of the United States, that he acknowledged to Davis that his daughter was "a better judge of men" than he was—an amazing thing indeed from a tough, experienced soldier like General Taylor.

His victories over enemy armies much superior to his in force made the general a favored candidate for President. Jefferson Davis, a Democrat, did not vote for his father-in-law, who ran on the Whig ticket, after he had nosed out his superior in Mexico, Winfield Scott, and the famous Henry Clay of Kentucky at the Whig convention at Philadelphia in 1848. His administration was short, for he died July 9, 1850, after only a year and a half in office, in the midst of the furor over the "Compromises."

Jefferson Davis's ancestry was Welsh and Scotch-Irish. His great-great-grandfather, Dolan Davis, had emigrated from England to Pennsylvania with two brothers. A grandson of Dolan, Evan Davis, had moved southward through Maryland, Virginia, and the Carolinas to Georgia, where he married a Mrs. Williams who had been Miss Lydia Emory. The widow had two sons, and her third, born of this marriage, was named Samuel, who in turn married a Miss Jane Cook of South Carolina. These were the parents of Jefferson Davis, last of ten children in a family of five boys and five girls, all log-cabin-born.

The boyhoods of Jefferson Davis and Abraham Lincoln, though they had been born not far apart and were both of pioneer stock, were quite different. Jefferson Davis had gone with his parents to Mississippi, where his father was a great planter who owned many slaves and many acres; and he received what was probably the best formal education that his parents could find for him in that day and setting. Lincoln was of a poor family. His illiterate father was an indifferent farmer and without ambition. His mother, of the Hanks family, died when he was ten, and the family moved to Indiana, then later to Illinois.

It was at the home of one of his married sisters, Ann Davis Smith, on her plantation Locust Grove on the Bayou Sara near St. Francisville that Davis's wife was stricken with malaria fever, from which she died only three months after their marriage. Davis was also stricken, but he recovered. To try to assuage the heartbreak and loneliness he plunged into work on some family acres in the Mississippi swamps, where he soon developed a rich cotton plantation that became one of the most productive in the state and was the foundation of his fortune. Later he traveled a bit and visited various cities—Havana, New York, Richmond, New Orleans, Annapolis, Baltimore, Washington.

During the Mexican War he knew Franklin Pierce, a general under Scott at Vera Cruz, and they became close friends. But he took little part in politics, as he said, until elected a representative from Mississippi in 1845, after he had married Varina Howell of Natchez. In 1847 he was appointed senator to replace General Jesse Spaight, who had died, and he was elected senator in 1851 and became chairman of the Senate Military Affairs Committee, an important post to which he made distinct contributions of great and lasting value to the army. His West Point education stood him in good stead. He left the Senate in 1852 to run for governor, but was narrowly defeated by Whig opposition. His illness returned during the campaign, and he was too ill to tour the state to combat a false propaganda campaign conducted by his opponent.

Now his friend Franklin Pierce, who had become President, came forward and offered him the Cabinet post of Secretary of War. Davis's diligence in filling that office provides one of the outstanding records of that Executive department. It is said that President Pierce leaned on Davis, who without doubt was the most influential member of the Cabinet—the only Cabinet, by the way, that remained unchanged throughout the four years of an administration in United States history. When Pierce left the White House, Davis was again elected to the Senate, where after the death of Calhoun he filled the vacancy left by the great South Carolina statesman as "the voice of the South."

It had been his view, no doubt, that had influenced President Pierce to sign the Kansas-Nebraska bill. It has been said (doubtless with considerable exaggeration) that he was the real President of the United States, though Pierce had the name. Those were times of extravagant statements about public figures, and such a remark must be taken with caution. But there is no doubt that Davis had grown tremendously in political stature. As Secretary of War he had enlarged and modernized the United States

Army, had introduced new weapons and a new manual, made surveys of the West, beautified the national capital, increased coastal and frontier defenses, and experimented with camels on the Utah and southwestern deserts as possibly useful for army transportation. He reorganized the Signal Corps, helped provide a retired list for commissioned officers, and without fear of political or other favor appointed subordinates on merit, regardless of party. He retained that trait throughout his life, and it no doubt contributed to bringing the charge against him that he was no politician at all. But in a day when "politician" meant little more than "a shady character, a fixer, a demagogue," etc., the allegation can hardly have been considered insulting.

With due respect for such great men as Washington, Adams, Jefferson, Jackson, and others, it is however not irrelevant to point to a fact seldom dwelt upon by writers of American annals—that Jefferson Davis, in addition to his talent for great and valuable service in the public interest not only in the South but to the whole nation as a statesman and scholar, was a polished and cultured gentleman, of a distinguished and commanding presence at once obvious and moving, the like of which is rare in those early times of crudity and balderdash. Descriptions by his contemporaries are all but unanimous. If we are to believe the professions of those who knew him best, there was about him always an elevation of character and a dignity impressive and compelling, indicative of uncommon intrinsic mental and moral excellence. In the Senate after Calhoun's departure it was with this kind of aura, almost like that of biblical prophets, that he moved among his colleagues and, by his oratorical talent and unusual voice and flair for debate, held an almost hypnotic sway over audiences, whether supporters or opponents.

His was a spirit founded upon sure faith. As in the Old World the king was *parens patriae,* father of his country, to Jefferson Davis in the New World it was the states. As senator he indeed looked upon himself as part of the government of his country, but, in the light of the last sentence of Article V of the Constitution, also something like an ambassador from his state.

To him the Constitution was the Bible and *vox Dei* of the best of governments, and faithful observance of it would assure perpetuity to the best of countries, a Union of equal states. The tragedy was that there had not been impartial observance but repeated movements by the North away from it, so that at last the injured states found themselves faced either with surrendering inalienable rights or with parting company with their usurping associates. There was no dissatisfaction with the old Constitution, only with its administration; and the avowed and manifest purpose of the seceding states was, as the framing of the Confederate version of the Constitution attested, to restore the integrity of the Constitution and to secure for the future its faithful observance.

The South's action, affirmed and reiterated, was deliberate, publicly announced, long known to be in the realm of possibility; the North had even threatened that it would act if the others did not of their own volition quit the Union. It was no surprise, then, that the cotton states exercised a right well known and long claimed by them—in fact, by most of the original states—and nowhere denied in the charter but retained at its ratification and adoption. This can be seen even today in the Constitutions and acts of a number of states (Massachusetts, Rhode Island, Pennsylvania, Maryland, Virginia). The seceding states neither desired nor expected resistance to their action. The power to coerce states had been explicitly rejected in the 1787 convention, at which Hamilton asserted that to coerce the states was one of the maddest projects ever devised; no provision had then been made by any of the states to meet resistance to their withdrawal from the partnership, as the *Madison Papers* show (pp. 732–61, 822, 914).

There was no appeal to the arbitrament of arms in the South, no guns, no establishments to manufacture or repair them; not a soldier, a sailor, a ship had been provided for offensive or defensive war. The desire, on the contrary, was to live in peace and in friendship with their recent partners of the Union, and every necessary step was taken to secure the desired result. One of the first acts of Jefferson Davis was to send peace commissioners to meet with the new federal administration. When it published the new Confederate Constitution in full, the New York *Herald* commented editorially upon it and pointedly suggested that Mr. Lincoln should immediately call Congress to consider the points of difference and endeavor peacefully to adjust them, looking to the return of the departed states. In this feeling the greater part of northern people concurred. But, as Mr. Adams in the *Life* of his father, C. F. Adams, strangely says, "it was lucky for the country Mr. Lincoln was more interested in the distribution of offices than in the gravity of the crisis." President Davis and the South realized that Lincoln, of all the administration, was bent on war.

The South differed from the North; Davis knew that the principles, policy, necessity of the South held her to rigid conservatism. Purest freedom and the strongest restraint, though seemingly paradoxical, existed there in complete harmony. Denial to the federal government of a right to resort to and to use undelegated powers, and insistence on adherence to the imposed limitations, made for natural reaction in favor of states' rights and home rule and the individual liberty of the citizen. It was this home rule, and slaveholding, and personal freedom that created a strong sentiment of individualism, of self-control, of local government, of opposition to interference—often fierce opposition—to governmental meddling in local affairs or individual and property rights. It made for manly, chivalrous independence, the sanctity of the family, voluntarism in action, freedom of conscience. As Dr. Curry wrote in *The Southern States* (Chapter XII):

> Under the old system there had been less yielding to popular clamor, more consistency in political action, firmer support of public men, less variation from year to year in elections and more concern for principle than for mere expediency. The Northern States revised their Constitutions, or made new ones, much oftener than did the Southern States. No hardier republicanism, said Gladstone, was generated in New England than

> in the Slave States which produced so many of the great statesmen of America. A justice of the Supreme Court said the basis of the enigma of the so-called slave power lay in the cool, vigorous judgment and unerring sense applicable to the affairs and intercourse of men, which the Southern life mode engendered and fostered. The South was a barrier against libidinous democracy. . . .
>
> In the Revolutionary War, and the nascent, formative period of the Federal Republic, there were no mutinies, no Shay rebellions, no Arnolds, as since there were, up to the reconstruction period and later, no strikes nor labor complications. The great change [of secession] wrought by the States in resuming their sovereignty, was attended by no anarchy, no rebellion, no suspension of authority, no social disorders, no lawless disturbances. Sovereignty was not, for one moment, in suspension. Conservatism marked every proceeding and public act. The object was to do what was necessary and no more and to do that with the utmost temperance and prudence.

This was the background of Jefferson Davis and his associates at the beginning of the 1860's. Many of them found themselves saddled with an "institution" they neither wished to perpetuate nor knew how to get rid of. And the more violent and insensate and aggressive the "anti-slavery" sentiment became, the more apprehensive their region grew, in determined opposition.

The war years at Richmond, the unending burdens and anxieties, we shall pass over. The official archives and the state papers of Jefferson Davis, his Cabinet, and the Confederate Congress tell the inspiring story. Beyond our scope here also are most of the reports of generals and their subordinates, the tortuous vicissitudes of campaigns and battles, of defeats and victories, hopes for peace and efforts to obtain foreign intervention to break the blockade and assist the Confederacy against her enemies, even as the Colonies had been so bolstered by French armies, navies, monies, officers, and envoys of Louis XVI. Foreign aid had all but come by the end of 1862, as France and England contemplated intervening to offer mediation, only to have hopes dashed by delay and inaction as the South lost ground before superior forces.

Jefferson Davis, with his family, was captured in the Georgia pines May 10, 1865, while en route to the trans-Mississippi, where he had hoped forces were still intact to continue the struggle Johnston and Beauregard had given up to Sherman at Durham, North Carolina, on the promise of honorable terms of surrender (which were repudiated by the northern government *after* arms had been laid down). The struggle in the East necessarily ended. The odds now were ten to one; the North was being armed with Spencer-magazine repeating rifles, against the Confederates' muzzle-loaders, to turn the war into mass murder. During four years of war the northern armies had been replenished with large-scale inductions of more than 720,000 immigrant males from Europe, who were promised bounties and pensions that the South afterwards largely had to pay. (See the Union Department of War records.) The armies of the South at peak strength never exceeded 700,000 men. Imported "Hessians" were thus used by Lincoln to crush Americans of the South whose fathers had served in the armies of Washington, Jackson, Taylor, to make the nation, to found its renown!

Taken to Fort Monroe, Virginia, Jefferson Davis was confined in a casemate cell. The two years of imprisonment there, with the indignities and petty, spiteful persecutions, including a short period in iron fetters, are told best in Mrs. Davis's *Memorial* and by the surgeon of the fort, Dr. John J. Craven, in a curious little volume, *The Prison Life of Jefferson Davis*. Both should be read for firsthand accounts not obtainable elsewhere.

Charged with detestable crimes that, it was only too well known, he could not be guilty of, Davis was unable to obtain a hearing, and finally was released. A bail bond of $100,000 had been posted for him, oddly enough, by some of the men who had been his bitterest enemies—Horace Greeley, Gerrit Smith, Vanderbilt, and others among the twenty men who pledged $5,000 each in federal court. There was an "inglorious sequel to these threats to make treason odious," Mrs. Davis wrote. Such a charge requires a closer look; it is no small matter to declare a man a traitor. Davis himself thought that

> . . . by reiteration of such inappropriate terms as "rebellion," and "treason," and the asseveration that the South was levying war against the United States, those ignorant of the nature of the Union, and of the reserved powers of the States, have been led to believe that the Confederate States were in the condition of revolted provinces, and that the United States were forced to resort to arms for the preservation of their existence. . . . The Union was formed for specific enumerated purposes, and the States had never surrendered their sovereignty. . . . It was a palpable absurdity to apply to them, or to their citizens when obeying their mandates, the terms "rebellion" and "treason"; and, further, the Confederacy, so far from making war or seeking to destroy the United States, as soon as they had an official organ, strove earnestly by peaceful recognition, to equitably adjust all questions growing out of the separation from their late associates.

It was Lincoln who "made war." Still another perversion, Davis thought,

> . . . was the attempted arraignment of the men who participated in forming the Confederacy, and bore arms in its defense, as "instigators of a controversy leading to disunion." Of course, it was a palpable absurdity, and but part of the unholy vengeance, which did not cease at the grave.

Article III, Section 3, of the United States Constitution defines "Treason"—the only crime the Constitution does define. It is limited to two offenses:

> Treason against the United States, shall consist only in levying War against them, or in adhering to their Enemies, giving them Aid and Comfort. No Person shall be convicted of Treason unless on the Testimony of two Witnesses to the same overt Act, or on Confession in open Court.

> The Congress shall have Power to declare the Punishment of Treason; but no Attainder of Treason shall work Corruption of Blood, or Forfeiture, except during the Life of the Person attainted.

In the light of the events of 1860–65 that have been mentioned here, and considering the attempt to ascribe to the Confederate President crimes against the internal sovereignty of the state—that is, treason—a question arises, one that stumped even the authorities, even the United States Supreme Court, where now Mr. Justice Chase was successor to Roger B. Taney. What war did Jefferson Davis levy? After all, who perverted the Constitution? Who instigated the break? Who invaded? Who attacked?

We have presented our own findings. Davis failed to obtain a hearing, although the wicked charges against him were never erased but were allowed to lie against him unpurged for "every orator-patriot or penny-a-liner in the North to hurl at his head the epithet 'Traitor,'" as Mrs. Davis wrote. And

> . . . he had asked only a fair trial on the merits; [had been held on trumped-up accusations in] close confinement, with circumstances of unnecessary torture for a year and a half and constrained to remain in Fort Monroe for two years, to the injury of his health, and the total destruction of his interests, not to dwell upon the separation from his family and home; he was denied trial while his captors vaunted their "clemency" in not executing their victim. . . . These accusations were either true or false; he asked neither indulgence nor pardon, but urged a speedy trial, constantly expressing an ardent desire to meet it.

One of his first acts after his capture in Georgia had been to deny the charges and to demand trial. That he could not obtain, but the accusations of complicity, etc., were never withdrawn. He had been borne, unwillingly enough, to the position of Chief Executive of eight million people of the South who knew their rights and thought it incumbent upon them to maintain them. He had been one of the last to yield to the dread necessity of strife, and was among the last to leave Washington, where before the Senate January 21, 1861, he had made a remarkably candid valedictory address presenting his own views and his state's stand —a statement of great bearing on the stress of the times, but nowhere, so far as I know, given in the "history" textbooks.

Many have been the defenses offered for him. We shall note only two here, Dr. Bledsoe's and Severn T. Wallis's. Wallis wrote shortly after Davis was released from prison. Both are apparently censored from the textbooks of history, regardless of their worth. Wallis wrote at first hand from his own experience, having been, as a suspected member of the Maryland legislature in 1861, himself a prisoner for fourteen months because of his sympathies for the South. (Bledsoe wrote *Is Davis a Traitor?*)

Obviously the exercise of a right cannot involve a crime. According to the southern theory of the Union, which is constitutionally unassailable, their state ordinances dissolved the relationship and responsibility of the citizen to the general government. Only an overturn of the Constitution itself could entrench other views—with the results of further wrongs, *ex post facto*'s, attainders, proscriptions, confiscations, seizures, forfeitures, imprisonments, denial of almost every basic individual right the Constitution had been created to safeguard. Might, for the hour, made Right, through "Acts," coercive amendments, armed force.

On May 8, 1867, President Andrew Johnson signed an order to release Jefferson Davis to a United States marshal at Fort Monroe and to conduct him to Richmond, Virginia. There he was to be tried later (December 3, 1867) in the federal court before Justices Salmon P. Chase and Joseph Holt, with legal arguments to begin on a motion to quash the indictment. Mr. and Mrs. Davis left the fort by river steamer. George Davis, a member of the Confederate Cabinet, tells that he chanced to be there and had promised Mrs. Davis that as soon as he had any intimation of what the court was going to do he would come to her and report.

I sat in the court when Chief Justice Chase announced that the prisoner was released; I never knew how I got out of that courtroom, or through the vast crowds that lined the streets.... In a little while I saw thousands and thousands of Richmond people, and scarcely passage was there even for the carriage in which Mr. Davis rode at a funeral gait, and as he rode every head was bared, not a sound heard, except now and then a long sigh. . . . I have said he was a prince. . . . He was far better than that; he was a high-souled, true-hearted Christian gentleman, and if our poor humanity has any higher form than that, I do not know what it is.

Many people had the idea that the President was a cold, severe, austere, unfeeling man. . . . There never was a more untrue opinion; for sixteen months I was head of the Law Department and every sentence of a military court that went to Mr. Davis was referred to me for examination and report. . . . I do not think I am a very cruel man, but I declare to you it was the most difficult thing in the world to keep Mr. Davis up to the measure of justice. He wanted to pardon everybody, and if ever a wife or a mother or a sister, got into his presence, it took but a little while for their tears to wash out the record. He was at the head of one of the grandest armies the world has ever seen, at a time when laws were silent in the midst of arms, and I give you my word, I never saw him attended by a guard or even by an orderly; his domestic servants and his office messengers were all that he needed, and all that he would have....

After two years of the most brutal imprisonment the world ever saw outside of Siberia, unrelieved by the slightest touch of kindness or generosity, he was brought to that trial at Richmond....

He never thought it wise to scoff at mysteries; where he could not understand he rested unquestioningly upon a faith that was as the faith of a little child. . . . That never wavered, made him look fearlessly through life, through death, to life again.

When, many years later, Colonel Charles Marshall, of Lee's staff, stood weeping at the open grave of Jefferson Davis, he felt that he should give voice to his undying respect and veneration for the President. To Marshall it seemed that the imprisonment of the President, with the threat of an ignominious death, the false charges made, the calumnies heaped high, vile falsehoods, had turned upon him the full force of northern prejudice and passion. On the other hand, Davis's suffering, persecution, and above all his high and unshaken courage turned toward him the ardent sympathy and love of generous fellow citizens of the South. It was appropriate at that moment to consider Davis's title to the place he holds in the hearts and minds of his people, and to enquire whether the judgment pronounced against him by almost all the people of the North was warranted, Marshall said.

Fitzhugh Lee, governor of Virginia, and ex-general in the Confederate Army, wrote Mrs. Davis in 1889 to try to induce her to select Richmond as the final resting place of her husband, who had been buried at New Orleans. In an address delivered at the Richmond Academy of Music, December 21, 1889, he spoke of the "shadow which had fallen over all our plains and valleys in the news of the death which had come from the 'Crescent City.' " How appropriate was Virginia's lamentation as she wept for Jefferson Davis . . . in those days of '61, when she had exclaimed, " 'Whither thou goest I will go, and where thou lodgest I will lodge; thy people shall be my people, and thy God shall be my God' . . . if Kentucky produced this hero we do not forget that Kentucky was the daughter of Virginia, and if Mississippi his adopted state, that she is Virginia's sister chained to her by the loving links of a mighty past, bound by holy memories of a present, united in heart and in a future."

CHAPTER 7

The War

FROM THE BEGINNING of those unhappy days of blood and civil strife it had been the custom of northern speakers and writers to represent the people of the South as having been "led astray" by their political leaders. It was an easy cover-all to think of them as having undertaken to destroy the old Union and to try to create an independent government for themselves under some sort of compulsion, and to speak of Davis as their leader. But nothing could be further from the truth. If ever there was a spontaneous movement of any people, that of the people of the Confederacy became one when the Proclamation of Lincoln on April 17, 1861, presented the real issue to their astonished view.

> That proclamation, and the hostile measures which quickly followed it, forced the most reluctant to admit to themselves what they had long refused to believe—that the real issue between the people of the South and those into whose hands the control of the federal power had fallen involved the continued existence of Constitutional government for the States of the South, indeed for all the States, and the maintenance of rights older than the Constitution and more sacred than either the Union or the Constitution. . . .

Such was the emergency and so vital the interests at stake that they greatly mistake the character of the southern people who suppose that they needed to be led or driven to meet the storm of menacing battle as it rolled down upon them. It is safe to say that up to the middle of April, 1862, the greater part of preparations for war had been made by the states, or by the spontaneous action of the people themselves.

Consider the spirit of southern women. "Far from truth was it that Mr. Davis was in any sense author or leader of the secession movement; he was selected by his people as best fitted in a time of imminent public danger." The heroism of the women of the South and their devotion to the cause and support of President Davis and his administration are beyond description; this alone exposes the false northern and Lincoln claims. R. S. Henry thought that, to most of them, "the war brought not so much an opportunity as an obligation for heroism in the home, less to be noted but more difficult to achieve." The devotion of women to the cause of southern independence, he wrote, was one of the chief sustaining forces, an incredible piety and fervor; they were face to face with the grim task of living, day by day, in a wrecked and torn country, their men away in the armies, the children to feed and clothe. Thomas Nelson Page tells of his mother riding a mule about the countryside of war-wrecked Virginia, often all day, trying to get the necessities of life. And there was little to feed and clothe with as the money, such as it was, decreased in value to the vanishing point, with taxes (after the summer of 1863 collected in kind) continually going up.

Thus the women, often left alone on far-off, lonely farms or big plantations, had none of the sustaining powers of comradeship and stimulation of example which helped lighten the life of the soldier. Yet, says Henry, "with all this they clung to their dream of a nation independent, outfaced the facts of despair, and through long months and weary years of absence and separation, of privations and dangers, maintained their 'front' to the enemy," to whom they were deadlier than their men, according to some Union reports.

No less remarkable than their spirit in the Confederacy was the attitude of the slaves.

> In the wide stretches of the South, especially in the Mississippi Valley and the central South, there were years when there was, in practical effect, no law at all. It was debatable [?] land, swept over by armies, back and forth, wherein the writ of neither government truly ran. . . . The restraint of the presence of white men was gone; there were no more "paterolls" on the highways at night; there was every reason in a time

> of excitement and disturbances, with the heady talk of "freedom" in the air, for the slaves to desert their masters, and, even as had been preached to them by the John Brown sort, to rise in revolt and destruction.

While many of the younger ones did leave, and some enlisted in the Union armies, there was nowhere in the South even the beginning of servile insurrection that might have been expected to occur with the Proclamation. This is the highest tribute to the southern Negro and the southern white man, and to the relations between them, and controverts much wartime propaganda.

In the *Life and Reminiscences of Jefferson Davis* (Baltimore, E. H. Woodward Company, about 1890) are a number of memorials by distinguished men of his times. In the introduction John W. Daniel writes:

> The proud and self-poised spirit of Mr. Davis and his declination to ask pardon angered some. General Lee had applied for pardon and been refused it. Had Jefferson Davis applied it would have only subjected him to humiliation. In not doing so he stood for a principle. The Federal Constitution forbade Congress to enact an *ex post facto* law [see Amendment XIV, Sections 3–4]; that is a law fixing punishment after the offence. Never tried for treason, he was yet punished by the *ipse dixit* of partisan legislation. The Government and the Constitution were revolutionized in order to reach him. A great, fundamental doctrine of civil liberty was overturned. All this will be fully appreciated in time, and many who have derided Jefferson Davis will applaud the integrity, the courage and the unselfish devotion with which he adhered to his convictions. . . .

The assassination of Lincoln had brought a frenzy on the North, where many were lead to believe that it had been prompted by Confederate connivance. A reward of $100,000 was offered for Davis's capture as an accessory to the assassination—a charge so absurd that even those who proclaimed it did not believe it. It was not pressed; like the treason charge, it was made and allowed to lay against him, to fizzle out after the years in the Monroe prison.

As for the charge of "mistreatment and cruelty to prisoners of war," the revelation of the actual facts about Andersonville and other camps are almost incredible but are not told in the "histories." They are, however, available and are damning evidence and indictment. With 60,000 more Union prisoners of war in the South than there were southerners in the North, more than 4,000 more Confederates than northerners died in prisons. "A cyclone of rhetoric could not shake that mountain of fact," wrote Daniel, and he listed a total of seven distinct occasions when the Confederate President attempted to alleviate the suffering of the war prisoners in his hands. The South had little medicine, which had been made contraband by the North, and only a meager amount that could slip through the blockade now and then was available even for the Confederate army. Those seven attempts were either refused or ignored; any argument to convict President Davis of cruelty more fully convicts President Lincoln. Knowing well the great lack of men in the South for replacements in her armies, toward the end the North refused to exchange prisoners. Lee took some 6,000 Union soldiers at Gettysburg, of whom some 3,000 were paroled on the spot; he could not possibly handle all of them. Exchange had been a custom early by necessity; but when there came to be more Confederates taken than there were corresponding Union losses, exchange was denied. General Grant assumed responsibility for this, as is shown by his testimony before the Committee on the Conduct of the War as well as by his letter to General Butler at City Point, Virginia, August 18, 1864. He wrote:

> On the subject of exchange, however, I differ from General Hitchcock. It is hard on our men in Southern prisons not to exchange them, but is humanity to those left in the ranks to fight our battles. Every soldier released on parole, or otherwise, becomes an active soldier against us at once, either directly or indirectly. If we commence a system of exchange which liberates all prisoners taken, we shall have to fight on until the whole South is exterminated. If we hold those caught, they amount to no more than dead men. At this particular time to

> release all Rebel prisoners North would ensure Sherman's defeat and would compromise our safety here.

What more assurance can one need of what the entire South thought about Lincoln's invasion and spoliation of their homes and firesides than this, written in deadly earnestness, by the Union commander even then on the verge of victory?

General Bradley T. Johnson, a Confederate officer of Frederick, Maryland had raised at his own expense a company for the South and served faithfully in many engagements, including Gettysburg. He wrote:

> Every writer on international war, every authority who has laid down principles and practices, and on which civilized warfare ought and must be carried on, condemns the maltreatment of non-combatants and forbids plunder or appropriation of private property unless necessary for the support of the army, and then to be paid for. Scott, and Zachary Taylor, in Mexico procured provisions by regular details under responsible officers, and paid for them in hard cash. . . .
>
> The government of the United States, bound to range itself on the side of civilization, employed Dr. Francis Lieber, the greatest publicist in America, to prepare a code for the government of the American [Union] army in war; it was published by its authority and was law for General Sherman as well as for the meanest "bummer" who flanked his march and disgraced his flag.

Section 20 of this Code is: "Private property, unless forfeited by crimes, or by offences of the owner against the safety of the army, or the dignity of the United States, and after due conviction of the owner by court-martial, can be seized only by way of military necessity, for the support or the benefit of the army, or of the United States."

Section 24 is: "All wanton violence committed against persons in the invaded country; all destruction of property not commanded by authorized officers; all robbery; all pillage or sacking, even after taking a place by main force; all rape, wounding, maiming, or killing of such inhabitants, are prohibited under penalty of death, or such other severe punishment as may seem adequate for the gravity of the offence."

Did Sherman abide? He did not. His sentiment was to "leave the inhabitants only eyes to weep with." In September, 1863, he cleared his army of all ineffectives—sick, wounded, disabled, everybody who could not march was sent North by railroad. By the end of November he was ready to march to the sea from desolate Atlanta, Georgia.

His troops were seasoned and toughened by battle, bivouac, and march. He had pursued Johnston for seventy days, always advancing, never giving ground. His numbers were superior, with high morale and under the best discipline. With him were 65 guns in four-gun batteries, 2,500 six-mule wagons, and 2,500 two-horse ambulances, wagons with 2,500 pounds each. The roads were good; wood, water, provision plentiful; and the weather superb. In the wagons were ten days' rations and fodder.

At the beginning Lieber's Code was enforced; straggling and plundering were strictly forbidden; stragglers in enemy territory might meet with sudden death. And there was no excuse for plunder or for pillage. The army marched toward Savannah on the coast by four roads, keeping in touch at all times so as to be able to concentrate quickly at any point where it might be necessary to. Making fifteen miles a day would bring them to the coast in twenty days. So they started, in orderly and military manner, decent, civilized. But at the end of two days it became evident that there were no white people in the country except women and children and old people; the byroads, paths, and fields were as safe as Central Park at that time was in New York. Then began the saturnalia of the "bummers," says Bradley Johnson.

> The Federal armies contained regiments from many Northern states; in the ranks were men whose ancestors had died at Bunker Hill or fallen at Buena Vista; they were sons of God-fearing, country-loving mothers and fathers, and were as high-minded, chivalrous, generous soldiers as ever carried a musket

> or drew a sabre. But by their sides, in no inconsiderable proportion, were mercenaries who had enlisted solely for selfish considerations; they knew no flag, no country, felt no pulsation of patriotism, no throb of honest enthusiasm. The commercial spirit, which understood that it would pay better to give $1,000 for a substitute, when a man was making $1,000 a day by contract for bogus boots or shoddy coats, or useless hats, than to risk life or limb for the Union, had filled that army with the scum of the world; the proletariat of the old world, the jails and penitentiaries of the new were brought up by commercial Northern dealers who sold them at a profit. . . . There was the Bunker Hill Mutual Assurance Society, the Perfect Substitute Association, to invest in substitutes. The thirty days' march to Savannah was packed with as much human suffering as ever was experienced in the same period in all the history of all time from the "bummers," the outpouring of the jails of the North, the dregs of the mob of the Continental [European] cities. The spirit of the chief inspires the followers. When Sherman reached the sea he received from H. W. Halleck, Major-General, Chief of Staff, a letter, "Should you capture Charleston, I hope that by some *accident* the place may be destroyed, and if a little salt should be sown upon its site, it may prevent the growth of future crops of nullification and secession."

This from a Union general. Can one believe that an American soldier, in high command, would order "salt" on an American city, salt tears, in such an intimation to commit murder, arson, robbery, and pretend it by "accident"? Sherman did; Lincoln approved. Sherman answered on December 24, 1864, that he would "bear in mind the hint . . . do not think salt will be necessary." He caused the burning and desolation of Charleston and Columbia, but blamed Columbia upon Wade Hampton.

> A solid wall of smoke by day forty miles wide, and from horizon to zenith, gave notice to the women and children of the fate that was moving on them. At early dawn the black veil showed the march of the "Bummers." All day long they

watched it coming from the Northwest like the stormcloud of destruction. All night it lit up by forked tongues of flame lighting the lurid blackness; the next morning it reached them. Terror borne on the air, fleet as the furies, spread out ahead, and murder, arson, rapine, enveloped them. . . . The negroes were no safer than the whites. A special object of search was for jewels, watches, women's trinkets. The old galley-slave, fresh from Toulon and the French hulks, with the brand on his shoulder and the limp of the shackles on his leg, found a wide field for the exercise of those talents which had brought him to grief in his own country, now to wear the Union blue of a "Bummer." And between the thieves and their accomplices, officers often, there was organized a rude system of division, according to the law of Prize. In May [1865] a Union Brigadier told that General Kilpatrick had a bushel of watches, trinkets, ear-rings, finger-rings.

That army moved through South Carolina from its SW corner to its NE boundary, diagonally across the State, covering a front of 60 miles with its parallel columns, and the bummers on its flanks, leaving not a house with a brick chimney, not a barn, or a mill, nor a gin-house, nor any building—hardly a fence—nor a beast nor a fowl, not a graveyard where the fresh graves were not dug up. And the Army of Northern Virginia supplied many a fresh grave that winter to South Carolina. Not a woman, black or white, gentle or simple, who was not insulted. . . .

It has been said that all our Christianity and civilization had removed us only three generations from barbarism. This march proved that the philosopher who first made that observation was utterly mistaken, for experience has proved that 60 days is enough to make savages of men with Christian mothers, reared under the influence of the Bible, and with the light of civilization in their lives. No tongue will ever tell, no pen can record the horrors of that march. Ten generations of women will transmit, in whispers to their daughters, traditions of unspeakable things. These things may not be written. Eyes will weep for them, and memories will transmit them for many a generation. Posterity will decide and history will record

> upon whom the responsibility for all this crime shall rest, just as certainly as that the Great Judge on the last day will render judgment for it.

So said General Bradley T. Johnson, CSA, who was there and saw it before his eyes. In the winter of 1865-66, the people of South Carolina appointed a committee, in Columbia, to take depositions, collect and perpetuate testimony about the sack of the cities of that State. It presents a demonic picture and is part of the State archives . . .

Unbelievable, incredible were acts of some of Mr. Lincoln's generals, as is shown by a letter written October 11, 1864, from General Halleck to General Auger in North Virginia.

> Your plan of putting prominent (Southern) citizens in trains is *approved,* and you will try to carry it into effect. They should be so confined as to render escape impossible, and be exposed to the fire of the enemy.

In an invaded land, its prominent citizens were to be made human shields, to protect the invader's trains from the Confederate attackers. This was the section, too, where "a crow crossing over would have to carry his own provisions." Lieber's code was silent about "hostages" or the like, a matter of war usage of medieval days, but used in modern times only by outlaws and criminals, not honorable soldiers.

Yes, Sherman was leaving the inhabitants "only eyes to weep with"; he forgot the memories left behind. General Bradley Johnson, whom we have been quoting, thought that Sherman's *Memoirs* should never have seen the light of day. He made merry over the humors of his bummers, and wrote that President Lincoln, in their last interview, at City Point, Virginia, April, 1865, was highly diverted and greatly interested in the bummers' doings. Few wars in which American soldiers have been involved have been as barbarously conducted as some incidents of the civil conflict were, and few American administrations can be compared with that of "Honest Abe" Lincoln in his conquest and subjugation of the South by the methods he employed and the individuals used.

A member of the Maryland House of Delegates, Severn T. Wallis, a Baltimore lawyer writing in 1868, recounted how he had been seized by a squad of Wisconsin Germans under a Union provost marshal, hustled to Fort McHenry, held a year on suspicion of being a Confederate sympathizer. No habeas corpus, not even Chief Justice Taney's, could release him, though no specific charges were made against him. In an article and in letters to friends he told of the "little book" written by Dr. John J. Craven at Fort Monroe on Jefferson Davis's imprisonment.

> The children were yet clinging around our knees who were born before "State Prisoners" were imagined as a possibility upon our soil, and the generation who preceded them—scarcely half-grown even now—were taught the stories of the Doge's palace, the Tower and the Bastille, of Olmutz and St. Helena and Ham, as a warning against the wickedness of kings and lords, and a lesson of thankfulness to the good God who had made a Republic their birthplace. . . .
>
> There was one thing more than any other, and perhaps than all others put together, in which the Cabinet of Mr. Lincoln displayed especial and remarkable sagacity. Indeed, in summing up their career as an administration, we might perhaps be justified in saying that it was at the foundation of their success, whole success, and stood them throughout in stead of those high qualities of statesmanship, which such a crisis as the Confederate War would have developed in any nation less devoid of really great men than the Northern section of the United States. . . . We refer to that perfect comprehension of the passions, prejudices, susceptibilities, vices, virtues, knowledge and ignorance of the people upon whom they had to practice. They knew every quiver of the popular pulse and what it signified. They could weigh out to a grain the small quantity of truth to which the public appetite was equal, and they perfectly understood and measured the preternatural extent to which the popular digestion could assimilate falsehood. They were masters of every artifice that could mystify

and mislead, and of every trick that could excite hope, confidence or rage. They knew every commonplace and claptrap that would affect popular imagination or temper, as familiarly and as accurately as a stage manager is acquainted with the oldest of his theatrical properties. Understanding their part thus well, they played to it with wonderful tact and effect. They filled their armies, established their financial system [fiat money], controlled the press and silenced opposition by the same universal system of ingenious and bold imposture. . . .

I have before me an editorial article of Mr. Raymond, of the New York *Times,* in which he testifies that on the night after the battle of Bull Run, he prepared an accurate and candid statement of the Federal disaster, and left it at the office of the telegraph to be transmitted to the journal he conducted, but that the censor of the War Department, to his [later] surprise and without his knowledge, caused his report to be suppressed, and forwarded in its place the well-known telegram in which the triumph of the federal arms, at all points, was announced in startling capitals to the delighted North. The equally notorious dispatch of Mr. Stanton to Governor Curtin [of Pennsylvania], after the battle of Fredericksburg, is but one of a thousand evidences that the Carnot—as Mr. Seward called him—of the Lincoln Cabinet, was as notable an adept as his predecessor, in that ancient art, which was practiced with less impunity in the days of Ananias and Sapphira. . . .

It was not to be expected that the War Department of the United States, thus long taught by success the value of judicious falsehood, should content itself with seeking merely to bring into contempt the head of the fallen Confederate Government. The war in itself so violently antagonistic to the whole spirit and principles of the Constitution of the United States could not, of course, be conducted without unconstitutional means and appliances. Among the most iniquitous of the contrivances resorted to, was the anomalous, inquisitorial tribunal called the Bureau of Military Justice. A few years ago no man would have dared to suggest such an engine of persecution to the most unscrupulous of political organizations in this country. If established it would have collapsed in a week under the scorn and indignation of a people yet uneducated by philanthropy in violence and usurpation. Nevertheless, at the close of the war, it exercised almost unlimited power for evil. It was the center of all the schemes of hidden wickedness and mischief which consumed so many millions of secret service money and raised up and debauched such an army of spies and informers throughout the land. It had grown to monopolize the getting up of persecutions, the organizations of military commissions, the fabrication of evidence and the subornation of witnesses. Guided by the constitutional doctrines of Solicitor Whiting, the legal and military ethics of Dr. Lieber, and the systematized and ingenious malignity of Judge Advocate Holt, it could only have been surpassed had Jeffreys, Vidocq, and Haynau been revived to sit in judgment together. Had its plans not been thwarted by the interposition of President Johnson, when the Supreme Court, under the most disreputable political influence, postponed for a whole year the promulgation of its opinion upon the Military Commissions, it would have opened a general campaign of judicial murder, besides which the Bloody Assizes of King James's chief justice would have lost their hitherto pre-eminent infamy. . . .

Under the inspiration of this Bureau, with the sympathetic assistance of Mr. Secretary Stanton, the well-known proclamation was issued, in which Mr. Davis was charged with having been accessory to the assassination of President Lincoln. It was a painful feature of the abominable outrage that the confidence of President Johnson should have been abused by his official advisors to the extent of inducing him, in the first moments of his accession, to put his name to such a paper. To consider even for a moment here, whether the parties by whom the calumny was made to take official shape had any ground for suspecting it to be true, which the bitterest honorable enemy of Mr. Davis would not have scorned to examine, would be an insult to our readers, not less than an indignity to the gallant gentleman against whose life and honor the poisoned shaft was aimed.

It is safe to say that not one of the conspirators at the War Department, ever harbored, even for an instant, a sincere belief in the truth of this charge, either before or after it was made. If it had been honestly started under the passionate influences of the troubled hour in which it saw the light, it would have been manfully disavowed when the excitement was over, and especially after the disgraceful and utter failure of the attempt to maintain it, with other injurious accusations before the military inquisitions which decreed the murder of Mrs. Surratt and Captain Wirz. But it had done its work in filling the minds of the ignorant with prejudice, and stimulating the hatred and fanaticism of Party; and to have admitted its falsehood would have been to create a just reaction in favor of the victim [Davis]. It was therefore allowed to stand without qualification, until the confidential correspondence between Mr. Holt and his agent Conover disclosed not merely the perjury which had been suborned, but the deliberate and disgusting circumstances of the purchase. . . . In the impartial times to come it will be hard to understand how a nation which not only permitted but encouraged its government to declare medicines and surgical implements and instruments contraband of war as well as the fruits of the earth and the implements of tillage, should afterwards have clamored for the blood of captive enemies because they did not feed their prisoners out of their own starvation and heal them in the succorless hospitals. And when a final and accurate development should have been made of the facts connected with the exchange of prisoners between the belligerents, and it shall have been demonstrated, as even now it is perfectly understood, that all the nameless horrors which are recorded of the prison-houses on both sides, were the result of a deliberate and inexorable policy of non-exchange, founded upon an equally deliberate calculation of their ability to furnish a greater mass of humanity than the Confederacy could afford, for starvation and the shambles, men will wonder how it was that a people, passing for civilized and Christians, should have consigned Jefferson Davis to a cell while they tolerated Edwin M. Stanton as a Cabinet minister. [From the letters and writings of Severn T. Wallis (Baltimore, 1871, 1891).]

We have avoided most of the military aspects and battle scenes here, but thoughts occasionally arise. . . . Suppose General

Lee had been able to clear himself from the overwhelming hordes surrounding him then at Petersburg and Richmond. One can imagine what could have happened to Sherman and his "bummers," by that time well into North Carolina and pressing Johnston's and Beauregard's meager and dwindling forces. His ending there—despite the demonstration of his being an able campaigner by keeping carefully in touch with the sea coast and the Union fleet as he advanced—might have made the reappearance of Napoleon in the West after the retreat from Moscow seem a Sunday-school picnic in comparison. So inconceivable is the gap separating men fighting for home and human rights and those serving false gods and propaganda images, or for pensions, benefits, and bounties of the mercenary and despoiler.

CHAPTER 8

Lincoln and Davis: Contrasting Presidents

ONE MIGHT THINK THAT, for a man as much maligned, hated, and insulted over the years as Jefferson Davis was, tributes and praises would be rare; but that is not so. There are warm reminiscences and eulogies almost without number. The only condemnatory work of much pretense at all is by Edward A. Pollard, author of *The Lost Cause,* who wrote a life of Davis as President that purports to report "behind the scenes at Richmond" and a so-called "secret history" of the Confederacy, with hints and insinuations of "veiled mysteries and inner scenes of the weak and anomalous government that wrecked the fortunes of the Southern Confederacy." Many have thought it a book of calculated malice. It should be read perhaps in connection with another work, one by Frank H. Alfriend, former editor of the *Southern Literary Messenger.* Both were written too soon after the war, published about 1867–68—the first condemnatory, Alfriend eulogistic. There are numerous others, by Dodd, Strode, Knight, Eckenrode, Rowland; a *Biography* by his wife, Varina H. Davis; by General Schaff; praises by Franklin Pierce, Zachary Taylor, General Dick Taylor, Albert Johnston, George Jones, Caleb Cushing, the Hon. Judah Benjamin; and the memorials seem numberless. Some writers, carried away by the shadow of the Lincoln apotheosis, seem inclined to pass over Davis, or else to give him meager praise, even for the part he played as Secretary of War or as senator and successor to the mantle of Calhoun.

It was Senator John W. Daniel of Virginia who, in an immortal oration January 24, 1890, at Richmond, said that he thought Jefferson Davis was more misrepresented, more misunderstood, by many than any other character who had figured in the Civil War.

> That denunciation should be directed upon him by his enemies during the war was natural, for he was the head and front of the Confederacy and a blow at him of any kind was a blow at the cause he represented. . . . The war over, a change of feeling instantly began between the combatants. . . . Between actual fighters of the war bitterness rapidly declined. Towards Davis, however, the North very slowly relented. . . . He seemed to stand apart . . . was regarded as responsible for the war and, as its incarnation, the assassination of Lincoln directed upon him a retaliatory spirit.

Moreover, "he was proud and unbending, and had declined to apply for a pardon." A pardon? For defending the Constitution of the United States of America and its Declaration of Independence?

There are many complications and variations in the age-long drama that goes on between the made man and the born man, between learning and originality, between established knowledge and settled usage on one side and creative will and imagination on the other. Not always is one conservative and unimaginative; sometimes it is a struggle against narrowness and obstruction, sometimes the upholding of the standards of civilization against the savage, the egotistical, the reactionary. Those who "were there" knew, and therefore are the best authority.

We have a curious compound of likenesses and differences in those two men who had come to the front in a nation's most crucial hour—an hour seemingly inevitable, yet capable of compromise, of reconciliation, of renewal of old and traditional brotherly ties cemented in years gone by in battle and bivouac to secure the common good and welfare of each—if Cain and Abel could only be restrained an instant so as to be reasoned with, cooled down, cautioned. The hour had been long foreseen, long dreaded; men had earnestly sought to avoid it. This can best be seen in the great document that John C. Calhoun had asked Mr. Mason of Virginia to read to the Senate for him on March 4, 1850. It is an honest, candid, statesmanlike presentation of a matter of vital national importance; but in what common school history textbook can we find it today, to share space with the justifications and platitudes after 1865?

From the death of Calhoun (1850) to the dawn of 1861, Jefferson Davis fought the battle of the South valiantly and forcefully in the halls of Congress as the acknowledged leader of southern sentiment. He was industrious, a hard worker, up early and to bed late, sticking to tasks he had set himself until they were completed to his satisfaction. Early associates mention that his desks, both in his office and at home, seldom were cluttered with papers, and the room or chambers set aside for his work were just that—for work, not for repose or comfort. In stern, almost jejune simplicity, they doubtless corresponded somewhat to the character of their occupant. He had come to Washington to perform a duty to his constituents, his state, and the nation; to that he clung unswervingly, an advocate of political truths and traditional justice, with views based upon the rights guaranteed to each state by the Constitution, which he knew intimately and, as it would seem, far more completely than many of his colleagues did. In this he was a ready and often fierce antagonist whom few cared to face. It is a fact that no one ever dared to insult him to his face; always it must be done in the corner, behind his back, maybe with iron prison bars between. He was a southern type of his day, a kind of American seldom found among us today—to the loss not only of the nation but of the world.

Jefferson Davis, who had declined to take any steps to have his political disabilities removed, died December 6, 1889, at New Orleans at the age of eighty-one years six months. Senator John W. Daniel, speaking before the General Assembly of Virginia in Richmond January 24, 1890, said:

> When news came that he was no more there was no Southern home that did not pass under the shadow of affliction. . . . The governors of the commonwealths bore his body to the

tomb and multitudes gathered from afar to bow in reverence. Thus it was that throughout the South, the scarred soldiers, the widows and wives, the kindred of those who had died in the battle which he delivered, met to give utterance to their respect and sorrow. Thus the General Assembly of Virginia convened to pay their tribute. Completer testimony to human worth was never given . . . and thus a South will build a monument to record their verdict that he was true to his people, his conscience, and his God, and no stone that covered the dead will be worthier of the Roman legend

CLARUS ET VIR FORTISSIMUS.

Sternly he stood for principle, he was no courtier, no flatterer, no word-magician, no demagogue unless that word shakes from itself the contaminations of its abuse and returns to its pristine meaning—"a leader of the people." Like King David's was his command, ". . . there shall no deceitful man dwell in my house." Those who knew his faith knew where to find him, and wherever found he proclaimed that faith as the standard-bearer unfurls his colors. He always was ready to follow his principles to their logical conclusions, to become at any sacrifice their champion, to face defeat in their defense, and to die if need be rather than disguise or recant them. . . . Personal virtue and public services are so different in essence and effect that nations often glorify those whose private characters are detestable, and condemn others who possess the most admirable traits. The notorious vices of Marlborough stood not in the way of titles, honors, and estates which England heaped on the hero of Blenheim, and the nobleness of Robert Emmet did not shield the champion of Irish independence from the scaffold.

But the men of history cannot be thus dismissed from the bar of public judgment with verdicts wrung from the passions of an hour. There is a court of appeals in the calmer life, and the clearer intelligence of nations, and whenever the inherent rights or the moral ideas underlying the movements of society are brought to question, the personal qualities, the honor, the comprehension, the constancy of its leading spirits must contribute largely to the final judgment. In this forum personal and public character are blended, for in great conjunctures it is largely through their representative men that we must interpret the genius of peoples. It was fortunate for the South, for America, for humanity, that at the head of the South in war was a true type of its honor, character and history—a man whose clear rectitude preserved every complication from impeachment of bad faith; a patriot whose love of law and liberty were paramount to all expediencies, a commander whose moderation and firmness could restrain and whose intellectual powers and attainments made him the peer of any statesman who has championed the rights of commonwealths in debate, or stood at the helm when the ship of State encountered the tempest of civil commotion.

Had a man less sober-minded and less strong than he been in his place the Confederacy would not only have gone down to material ruin—it would have been buried in disgrace. Excesses sure to bring retribution, would have blotted its career, and weakness would have stripped its fate of dignity. . . . Had surrender come before its necessity was manifest to all mankind, reproach, derision and contempt, feud, faction and recrimination, would have brought an aftermath of disorder and terror; and had it been based on such terms as those which the critics have suggested, a glorious revolution would have been snuffed out like a farthing candle in a miserable barter about the ransom of slaves. . . . It was well for all it was fought out to the finish without compromise tendered or entertained. The fact that it was fought out gave finality to its results and well nigh extinguished the embers with its flames. No drop of blood between Petersburg and Appomattox —not one in the last charge—was shed in vain. Peace with honor must pay its price, even if that price be life itself, and it is because the South paid that price with no miser's hand that her surviving soldiers carried home with them the consciousness of duty faithfully performed. . . .

[Jefferson Davis was indeed] a great man of a great epoch . . . a son of the South who became the head of a Confederacy more populous and more extensive than that for which Jefferson wrote the Declaration of Independence, and commander-in-chief of armies many times greater than those of

> Washington. . . . He swayed Senates, led soldiers of the Union —and he stood accused of treason in a court of justice. He saw victory sweep illustrious battlefields; and he became a captive. He ruled millions and he was put in chains. He created a nation, he followed its bier, he wrote its epitaph, and he died a disfranchised citizen. . . . He conquered himself, and forgave his enemies, but he bent to none but God.

He had passed on. The beautiful monument at North Davis and Monument avenues in Richmond is the silent, eternal memorial of the South to his memory and that of the millions who stood with him. Senator G. G. Vest of Missouri felt sure that the time would come

> . . . when all would see in the Southern leader that one great quality, which in all climes and ages has commanded the admiration of mankind—constant, unyielding, uncompromising adherence to what he believed a just cause. To Southern people there would be no change in love and reverence for one who never faltered in his love for them, and through all the ages, until constancy, courage and honest purpose become valueless among men, the flowers will be heaped by loving hands upon his grave.

The Rev. Moses Hoge, D.D., who had known President Davis well in Richmond and had often ridden with him along the lines of the wartime fortifications on horseback, believed him to be

> . . . the man required for the times, a statesman with the ability to lead public opinion in ways that are right, instead of waiting to ascertain the popular drift, no matter how base, that he may servilely follow it. Unlike the popularity hunter who never asks what is just, but what is politic, and then trims his sails so as to catch every breeze of public favor, the upright Statesman, with deep conviction that nothing that is morally wrong can be politically right, steers directly for the port of duty along a line in which no deflection can be traced and holds his course in the very teeth of the gale. While the demagogue attempts nothing, no matter how noble, which might

endanger his popularity, the patriot-statesman, when assailed by obliquy, is not greatly troubled thereby, but calmly awaits for the verdict of time, the great vindicator. . . . When the path of duty becomes the path of danger he is not intimidated but remains firm as the rock in mid-ocean, against which the invading waves beat only to be shivered into spray. While the tricky demagogue spends all his energies in directing the tactics of the Party, the broad-minded statesman aspires to build up a noble commonwealth and rises above all that is selfish and mean, because the ends he aims at are those of country, God and truth. Men of great gifts often fail in public life because they lack the moral basis on which character alone can stand. After all, *integrity* is one of the strongest of living forces; and what the people seek when their rights are imperilled is not so much the men of brilliant talents as for leaders whose chief characteristics are untarnished honor, incorruptible honesty, and the courage to do right at any hazard. . . . Even such men sometimes fail to secure the triumph of the cause, but their very failures are nobler than the successes of the unprincipled intriguer.

Admiration was more due to him "who pursues the course he thinks to be right than to one who succeeds by methods which reason and conscience condemn." Defeat was the discipline which trained the heroic soul to its noblest development. And when the conviction came that he had struggled in vain, and must yield to the inevitable, then he might without shame lay down his armor in the assurance that others will rise up and put it on, and in God's good time vindicate the principles which must ultimately triumph." Another of the lessons to be learned from the life of Mr. Davis, he felt, was "the emptiness and vanity of earthly glory, if it be the only prize for which the soul has contended. As like a flower; in the morning it groweth up and nourisheth; in the evening it is cut down and withereth. Surely man at his best is altogether vanity. Wealth, honor, power, military renown, popularity, the constituent elements of what men call glory; how evanescent they are, how unsatisfactory while they continue! What is earthly glory? It is the favor of the fickle multitude, the transient homage of the hour, the applause of the populace, dying away with the breath that fills the air with its empty clamor. What is earthly glory? Listen, All flesh is as grass and grass withereth, and the flower thereof falleth away; the wind passeth over it and it is gone. There is nothing great but God, nothing solemn but death, nothing momentous but judgment."

How could a country, great even in its predatory day of crass politicians and robber-baron adventurers in high places, afford the loss by discrediting a man of Jefferson Davis's stature, an American of Olympian mold? But he had been a "rebel," a "traitor," because he had refused to stand by and see the Declaration of Independence and the Constitution of the United States of America ignored, perverted, trampled underfoot. He was a "barbarian" because he was the owner of the labor of a number of African Negroes working his plantations in a day and place in which no other method of employment was possible in using the poor creatures. The descendants of the men who had brought the slaves' forebears from Africa were now calling down the curses of Heaven upon plantation owners in the prosperous semi-tropical regions of the country because they usefully employed them. The laborer had nothing to offer for sale but his strong arms and back, and his proprietor was building and increasing the basic prosperity of the country out of what, but for those labor conditions, might have remained as it was found, a wilderness, barren, wasted, rotted, given over to Indians, wanderers, wild beasts of the woods and mountains. The alternative was the civilized, beneficial, humane setup, the capital-labor arrangements inherited from a long past and using beings whose very names had been taken from those of the southern families who owned them—but who now were "moral lepers" because of the institution that, though constitutional and lawful, was condemned by those who had never been in the South.

Jefferson Davis's was an elevated and progressive intellect, perhaps domineering by nature but governmental by conviction. He knew, as M. Guizot had, the eternal problem that Providence has imposed on society, the "solution of which it reserves to itself, of that conflict between two opposites, *Right* and *Duty,* and *Power* and *Liberty.* In the presence of these two hostile elements few men can remain either entirely calm, entirely impartial, but [each] reacts by attraction or repulsion according to his individuality." Of this it has been said, "Some are especially inclined to liberty, others more disposed to power; some would play the minister, others the tribune; these have the instinct of authority, those the sentiment of independence."

Davis was above all a man of power and government, and at the same time the most independent of men—submissive to the yoke of self-imposed principle but bearing his head erect in all questions concerning persons, a leader of great worth, estimating himself at that worth, more convinced than enthusiastic, much more proud of the approbation of his conscience than of the homage of the crowds, gifted to a large degree with that strength of will and perseverance that makes the great statesman a mortal foe to all that resembles disorder. What man, other than Jefferson Davis, had the South to call upon in that hour? What could be the outcome of defeat upon her but the most appalling and indescribable disorder? If Lincoln did not see it, most certainly Davis did.

The machinations of the Federal Bureau of Military Justice, 1864 and later, are a grim witches' brew of perjured, trumped-up, rigged, schemed impositions in the name of "justice" that sicken one to read what there is available on it, and little is now to be had; the whole plastered over by a sort of "top secret" label, and much of it later destroyed before Stanton left the War Department office to die four days before he was to take the Supreme Court seat President Grant had conferred upon him. In such a maze of lies, forswearing, bribery and frame-ups, it is next to impossible to obtain any certain extent of the truth reliable enough to found a mystery tale upon; nevertheless we shall endeavor to spread out the web as best it can be and give access to what seems to be some of the underhanded efforts to make the imprisoned and helpless Mr. Jefferson Davis the scapegoat for the whole of the Confederacy's "sins." There was released from Fortress Monroe some time in 1865 a Confederate war prisoner, a correspondent (one-time editor of a Richmond wartime news sheet who had contrived his pardon after capture on a blockade runner trying to escape to Europe), who went, on his release, to work on what he termed a "life" of Mr. Davis, with a "secret history of the Confederacy." To do this work, so that Davis, to the public reading the story, would be condemned beyond hope of pardon, or a civil trial, may, or may not have been the *sub rosa* agreement for the release of this prisoner. At any rate, he did set to work and he produced such a book, and it did attempt to sink the Confederate President in much of its exposition. It was in one volume; at the time never put up for public sale; was paid for by some secret source and fund, from individuals veiled or unknown, and it first appeared in 1867, before Mr. Davis had come to trial at Richmond. When the *nole prosequi* was entered at Richmond, December, 1868, on the "treason" indictment, with the prosecution on that charge dropped and dismissed, the writer of this weird "biography," continuing his comments, surprisingly had this to say:

> After nearly four years of hesitation, after a most injurious exhibition of doubtfulness and weakness, the North managed to rid itself of the awkward prisoner whom the blind rage or the stupidity of Mr. Stanton imposed upon it.
>
> The *nole prosequi* had been foreseen, or it had been strongly imagined; yet it was the occasion of much rejoicing in the South, and of not a little embarrassment and relief on the part of the North. The newspapers of the South teemed with congratulations of Mr. Davis; but they have been generally stopped there in the apprehension of the event and have been singularly deficient in their commentaries on it. Indeed, it is very surprising that the vast importance of this event, as affecting the morale of the past war, and as involving the whole political history of the country, should have escaped the apprehension of the press of the South; and especially, too, when it is apparently so much concerned to discover whatever there is of hope and encouragement for this section, and affects

so much the tone of optimism in public affairs. The most important triumph that the South could have possibly achieved since the war, the most significant event that has happened since its close, the most interesting revelation that has lately been given the world from behind the scenes of our political history, has been overlooked by the dull and barren press. The mere congratulations affecting the person of Mr. Davis, with which the newspapers have generally stopped short in their commentaries on the abandonment of his prosecution are utterly inconsiderable, compared with the true significance of this event, and the extent of the triumph of the whole South on it. There can be no doubt that the North would have been glad to exact of Mr. Davis the furthest penalties of the law if it could have made out a case for the prosecution; that it was immensely anxious to convict him. There were thousands in the North who even clamored for his blood, and many who would have been glad to doom him to the cell of a felon. This, to be sure, was a mistake; for, as we suggested, it is the kind and degree of punishment that determines whether the victim shall be an example or a martyr, and that the true economy of punishments is their moderation. Thousands who desired his conviction in another and indispensible sense—that of "making treason odious," that of obtaining a moral vindication of the North in the past war and securing the future in its interest.

The extent of the anxiety of the North to procure such a vindication—all indeed that was wanting to crown the great victory of its arms and to complete its satisfaction—has never been fully confessed. It has scrupled at nothing. Its whole government in the South is based on the idea of justifying the war; and its system of test oaths in that section was probably designed as well as for other reasons to obtain a factitious declaration of public opinion there, in favor of the legitimacy of its past contest of arms. . . .

The full sense then of the abandonment of the indictment of Mr. Davis for treason is the confession of the North, that it despaired of obtaining such a justification of the war on its side as would have been implied in his conviction; and, in even proportion to this confession, the claim of the South that the balance of justification was on its side, that it held the vantage ground on whatever questions of law the war involved. Here is a vast admission, and it is as unequivocal as it is important. The trial of Jefferson Davis was the trial of the North. It was to determine whether a man could be punished as a traitor for acting on an opinion which had divided three generations of Americans, and even the founders of the federal Constitution; whether the party and sectional dogma on which the North waged war, could be affirmed on the legal decision of a constitutional question. Such a trial the North has declined. It has shrunk from the august arbitration on which it once proposed to enter in sight of the world to "make treason odious"; it has feared to risk the question whether it had really any superiority over the South in any respect but that of the number of its arms; it has decided not to attempt, even at its own judicial bar, the justification of its cause, the determination whether this was the invocation of a violated Constitution, or the temptation of sectional hate and ambition; and it leaves the South whatever implications may arise from the facts of its rival having withdrawn his challenge and abandoned the contest. The release of Mr. Davis has become one of the most important events of his life—not so much with reference to his own fortunes, as in its application to the whole political history of the country. It is interesting in three aspects. It suggests a vindication of the cause of the Southern Confederacy—such a vindication as is to be desired next to success; it supplies some reflections upon the permanence and vitality of the old schools of American politics; and it has the surprising and most remarkable effect of exhibiting a tendency of the American mind to the conservatism of the past, in the midst of the public passions of the day—of disclosing an undercurrent in the mad career to consolidation that is apparently but not really and entirely sweeping everything before it. Perhaps the South may think herself too ready to despair of her record in the war and of restoration to something of her ancient rights, since she has seen the chief of her so-called "rebellion," a defiant and feared litigant in a federal court of justice, and walking forth released, even from accusation. Such the unexpected loftiness and interest of his exit from the stage of American politics.

Thus Pollard ends a rather remarkable tale of a "life." Strode thought he wrote in calculated malice. It is a writing of which but too little is known today; it is read by too few, studied by still fewer; in fact, I do not know whether the work can now be obtained. My own copy happens to be one which my grandfather obtained about 1869 in Baltimore, Maryland. On the front page of it is written in longhand the words "Life of the Traitor Jeff Davis," Middletown, Conn., July, 1869. The frontispiece illustration of Mr. Davis, "engraved by one J. C. Buttre of New York from a photograph taken from life," has written over it, in the same longhand, the words "The Traitor." Who did this, and when, is not known to me. I was given the book long after my grandfather's death at the Confederate Soldiers Home, Pikesville, Maryland, and, consequently, had no opportunity to ask him. The book contains the original preface of the author; and was, "entered according to an Act of Congress, in the year 1869, by J. R. Jones, in the clerk's office of the District Court of the United States, in and for the Eastern District of Pennsylvania." It is one of my heirlooms. To it, and to Alfriend's more eulogistic work, I am indebted for some of the thoughts expressed in this treatise. Alfriend's work was published in 1867, a year previous to Pollard's; both writers wholly supported the Confederacy, but took opposite views of Mr. Davis. These two volumes, with the two volumes of Davis's *Rise and Fall of the Confederacy* and Mrs. Davis's two-volume biography of her husband are indispensible to informed views of the hour; all four works must be read.

Woodrow Wilson said that he had studied many of the biographies of Lincoln and "had sought out with greatest interest the many intimate stories told of him, narratives of near-by friends, the sketches at close quarters in which those who had the privilege of being associated with him had tried to depict the man himself in his habit as he lived; but he had nowhere got the impression in any narrative that the writer had in fact penetrated to the heart of his mystery, or that any man could penetrate to the heart of it. His was a brooding spirit that had no real familiars, never spoke out in complete self-revelation or revealing itself completely to anyone: a lonely spirit comprehending men without communing with them, as if, in spite of all its genial efforts at comradeship, it dwelt apart. It saw visions of duty where no one looked on, a holy and terrible isolation for the conscience of every man who sought to read the destiny in affairs for others as for himself, for the nation as for individuals. His was a privacy that no man could intrude upon, a lonely search of the spirit for the right which no man could assist, keeping company with invisible things, born into no intimacy but that of its own silently assembling and deploying thoughts." . . . Such in one view was the man who came to the presidential office in 1861.

According to some of the superstitions of Negroes and poor whites of the South, on the contrary, Lincoln had sold his soul to the devil in return for the office of the American Presidency, and that sable gentleman had come to collect the debt on the night of April 14, 1865, at a theater in the capital.

There can be little doubt that absurdities, pretenses, incongruous ideas of his ideals and principles, and downright falsehoods about Lincoln have overwhelmingly increased over the years. He was poor, poverty-stricken, abused, "underprivileged," in the sense that that word has been tormented in recent years. The facts are that he began life in lowly, negligent frontier circumstances, and he died a wealthy man for his day—had not taken too long or waited till too late to reach that stage. As a youth in Illinois he failed as a storekeeper, made no advances as surveyor or letter-carrier, but prospered as a lawyer, no matter the paucity of his early formal education or competent legal training, in rude and violent surroundings like those described in *The Hoosier Schoolmaster*. He received fees of $1,000 often, and once a railroad paid him a $5,000 fee. He was not poor but considerably rich, as he came to be known, with bank accounts, stocks, shares, notes, bonds, lands, tenements, often with money to lend, for which he charged 10 per cent interest—the standard rate of that time.

We sometimes wonder why his countrymen have so long permitted themselves to be hoodwinked by the legends. Perhaps it is time we try to be done with some of the Honest Abe fairy tales of the weeping poets and sob sisters, all those who would make silk purses out of sows' ears. Maybe, after all, in this case a little learning *was* a dangerous thing.

It would seem, from a good source, that his first impressions of Negro slavery came from sights he saw and incidents he encountered as a youth during two flatboat trips down the Mississippi River to New Orleans. There he met some of the seamy side of slavery, no doubt. If he had made similar trips through New England he would have had opportunity to see some of the seamy side of some white "wage slavery" just as bad, and perhaps less excusable, though more prevalent and more fully ignored than the black "slavery" that he is said to have remarked at the impressionable age of nineteen far from home.

He was President by accident, because of political insurrection in the Democratic Party. Considered unfit for the office by prominent party members, he was described variously as a huckster in politics, a baboon, an ignoramus, a mountebank, "the geriller Linkon." Far from being well known favorably, in the late 1850's he was reported as a shifty, cunning stump speaker from the backwoods of the West, a tall, somber, lanky, joke-cracking "railsplitter"—a clever rabble-rouser, but President? . . . Impossible!

Lincoln's place in letters is curious. With men as with nations, their literature and culture are to be known not by the worst but by the best. His writings, after study, cannot be considered the blown-up masterpieces of literature that so many "authorities" on the "martyr" would inveigh upon us. The office of President requires exemplary exposition in all documents emanating from it; there are secretaries, editors, writers, amanuenses, ghosters galore, and there were in Lincoln's day. Whatever he prepared underwent editing and correction. His Cabinet advised, when he permitted; others revamped, rewrote. It was the third rewriting of the Gettysburg Address that finally appeared.

There was little polish or culture about Lincoln. As one of Davis's biographers wrote, "The elite world of Europe early commented on the marked contrast of the latter's [Davis's] polish and eloquence with the conceits and uncouthness of his opponent, whose tangled grammar and literary peculiarities had come to their eyes." Lincoln had always at least three private secretaries at hand; the southerner had none, assigned none, did his own editing and composing, with scholarly results that shine through his writings. In addition to William O. Stoddard, Lincoln's secretaries were John Hay, also American-born, and John George Nicolay, German-born. The Hay-Nicolay biography is *the* life, from which all others derive and thereby help to perpetuate myths, traditions, and some nonsense about Honest Abe. Employing three with such experience and competence to do the spadework hardly entitles another to a place in literature.

None of the three secretaries was a second-rate craftsman. Nicolay also wrote *The Outbreak of the Rebellion* (1881). His daughter Helen, born in Paris, where he became United States consul and Hay legation secretary in 1865, was the author of a number of lives of Presidents and seems to have been steeped in her father's Lincoln-worship. Nicolay also later became a United States Supreme Court marshal. Stoddard wrote a number of boys' stories, *The Boy Lincoln, Lives of the Presidents, The White House in War-Time, Lincoln at Work,* and others.

John Hay came to Lincoln's notice at his admission to the Illinois bar in 1861, and was appointed secretary. He spent a short time in the field so as to get the brevet of a colonel. After the death of Lincoln he and Nicolay got together in Paris to write the *Life*. Hay had a considerable diplomatic career, at Madrid, Vienna, London, and was Assistant Secretary of State in the Hayes administration and later Secretary of State (1898–1905). He was also an editor of *The New York Times.*

We mention these accomplishments of the 1861–65 White House secretariat to suggest the method of apotheosis that made a Constitution-defying President a legend, while his scholarly constitutionalist counterpart, after the defeat of his Cause, has been left in obscurity without laurels or place. How differently might Jefferson Davis have fared with similar "authorities," even in defeat. *Vae victis!*

Many believe that the Emancipator's known *belles-lettres* cannot be considered the marvels that misguided zealots imagine them to be. They are replete with contradictions, exceptions, nonsense, illogical reasoning, and deceit. His debates, letters, addresses, replies, etc., are confusing and confounding to an astonishing extent. Did the man believe he addressed a nation of yokels? Take the remarks at the Gettysburg dedication, with its prattle about the "new birth of freedom," which in reality he had been trying to strangle for more than three years. At the very minute that he was intoning "government of the people, by the people, for the people," Union troopers were with his knowledge patrolling the booths of Delaware polls not a hundred miles away, deciding who might and who might not vote. In this novel conception of a people's government, his hand, as Jefferson Davis said,

> . . . had been laid upon the ballot-box, with the declaration that it was not safe to trust the people to vote except under the inspection of its authority. . . . A government had come upon the land which, whenever it pleased, could set aside all the rights of men, whenever it willed, destroy them. . . . Unalienable rights had become unknown to the war-begotten theory of the Constitution. . . . The day had come in which mankind beheld this government founding its highest claims to greatness and glory upon deeds done in utter violation of those rights which belonged to its own citizens in every State North and South. . . . The Bill of Rights, the limitations of powers, the written Constitution, had lost their sacred authority, and not a man or a State dared, single-handed, gainsay the will of the agency which, feeling power, had forgotten right.

Of what Lincoln wrote or declared there seems no "best" to be selected. The old world of culture in Europe did not early fail to note "the cranks and tangled English" of the Republican President and to make unfavorable comparisons with the polished and finished products of the leader of the Confederacy, whose state papers are considered models of composition and rhetoric. They must be read to be appreciated.

What are we to make of the specious inaugural statements, of most of the debates with Douglas, in which Lincoln founded a political reputation of a kind? Of the "house divided," taken with the Greeley reply of "freeing none, or all, or some"? Of the jealousy and trammeling of McClellan? Of innumerable letters written to the northern governors for backing for his moving regiments to home districts during the 1864 elections, when the Republican Party despaired of being returned to office by the war-weary and dissenting North and West? Of the Emancipation Proclamation, its exceptions, its withholding content and grisly intention?

His writings cannot be held of impressive content or ablaze with truth and sincerity. The Gettysburg Address, for example, cannot possibly be taken seriously. "Four score and seven years ago" our fathers did *not* bring forth on this continent a new nation: they had brought forth thirteen new nations, each distinct in itself, each independent and sovereign, each with different constitutions or charters, laws, customs and statutes, each of different origins and ideals, each wholly independent. To be sure of this one should read the peace treaty made with His Majesty George III of England. In the "house divided," the replies to Greeley, the first and second Inaugural Addresses, the Douglas debates, and others, it may seem at times that they are set in a simple glow of lucid and persuasive prose and seeming odd magic phrases of beauty—that of a dead lunar world; apparent purity, patriotism, and an odd charm (or chill) of manner like the thrill of *Clair de lune*. But they are in turn deceptive, meaningless, contradictory of other declarations just as beautifully toned and high-sounding, replete with errors of logic and reasoning.

The speeches and assertions of many public appearances are so contradictory and deceptive that no one could imagine where he stood, or what he really stood for. It was one thing one day at one place, something else next day at another place. It was demagoguery at its worst, with no trace of statesmanship discoverable, and it pervaded his whole public career. It is difficult to believe that all of it is to be laid to the homely ignorance of a well-meaning soul; such a person would have no business in high office and, what is more, could never get there, even by accident. What else could it be if not the crassest politics, in which the hearer is told what he wants to hear, and the deliverer sometimes comes to the office and salary and emoluments that he covets?

Victory in the war, the asserted preservation of the Union, and Lincoln's assassination rather easily if astonishingly "sanctified" the dictator, the first in American history, whose birthday is still celebrated in the North and West (though not in the South, where the monuments are all dedicated "To our Confederate dead"). The real monument to the Great Emancipator is the maiming of the United States Constitution, though done after his death, and the imposition upon the nation of a Negro race problem that progressively grows.

The opportunity to ride into office on others' coattails in a specific issue much contested before American voters (who until 1890 cast their ballots openly, in public) came again in American politics with the Douglas debates, August–October, 1858. Lincoln came to the fore now, although it was difficult to determine his actual stand from the avowals and denials in his public remarks. The prominent revolutionary German immigrant Carl Schurz gives this picture of him on a train to Quincy, Illinois, after a speech at Galesburg. A companion had pointed to a tall, solemn-looking man who had just come into the train surrounded by an excited crowd, and said, "Why, there's Lincoln himself."

> I looked and there he stood, taller indeed by several inches than those around him; a tanned face, with strong features, deep furrows, and melancholy eyes; on his head he wore a stove-pipe hat, his neck emerged long and sinewy from a white collar turned down over a thin black tie. His lean body was

> clad in a rusty black frock-coat with sleeves that should have been longer, and black trousers permitted a very full view of his large feet. On his left arm he carried a gray woolen shawl which evidently served him for an overcoat in chilly weather; his left hand held a cotton umbrella, and also a black bag that bore the marks of long and hard use. . . . A large number of friends were awaiting him when we arrived at Quincy, and next morning the country people began to stream into town for the great meeting, some singly, some on horseback, on foot, and some in small parties of men and women and even children in farm-wagons. [Beveridge, *Lincoln,* Vol. II.]

Although he was defeated in the election and Douglas was returned to office, Lincoln had started on the road to the White House. Some of his reputed sayings, now preserved for posterity as immortal gems of incalculable philosophical worth, originated in those debates—as, for instance, that inanity about fooling all of the people some of the time, some of the people all of the time, but "you cannot fool all of the people all of the time." Yokel vaccination that "took." In the same weeks the foremost prospective leader of the new Republican Party, William Seward of New York, pronounced radically on the sectional controversy as an "irrepressible conflict between opposing and enduring forces."

CHAPTER 9

Lincoln and the Postwar "Reconstruction"

DECLINING IN 1861 the earnest pleas and sensible advice of adherents, refusing to accept the southern peace offerings, and later going over bodily to the Abolitionist camp with the Proclamation, Abraham Lincoln cast the die and paved the way for the unspeakable enormities of the "Reconstruction," the most mysterious, skirted-around, frantically covered-up chapter of American history. Light is needed to disperse the shadows in the corner. (See such books as Bowers, *Tragic Era,* Pike, *Prostrate State,* and Trowbridge, *The Desolate South.*) Imagine the House leader saying, of measures to "restore" the states, that he would not so far stultify himself as to say that they were constitutional! Lincoln had lit the train of fuses that led to these explosions.

He had assistance not only from northern and western natives but also from a large body of foreign-born immigrants, by far the greater number of whom knew nothing of the South, slavery, or the sectional problems but who, finding that opposition to them promised political possibilities, espoused Abolitionism—none with more glow and enthusiasm than the German revolutionary refugee Carl Schurz of Wisconsin. As a student at Bonn, Schurz had meddled in some obscure local political broil and had had to flee. He was an educated man, of higher type than the usual stolid peasant arrivals, and he at once saw the opportunity of advancement in the new land by supporting Lincoln and denouncing "slavery" on lecture tours. He received, by his own admission, $1,800 from national and state committees to stir up sectional hatred. His reward from Lincoln was appointment as minister to Spain in 1861. On his return to the United States, offering to raise some troops of Germans, he became a colonel. He was frankly a place-hunter, and quipped that it was "a hunt in which the hunters shoot each other." Of the plum of diplomatic appointment the Milwaukee *News* of April 12, 1861, said, ". . . an audacity that couldn't be repulsed, impudence had triumphed over all obstacles. . . . This foreign adventurer and mercenary soldier, this impudent mendicant, who entered the Presidential mansion a homeless vagrant, went forth clothed with the high dignity of a first-class ambassador of State."

After his return from Spain in 1862, as a brigadier general he took part in some of the Union's worst defeats—the second Bull Run and Chancellorsville—and was at Gettysburg. At Johnson's request he even made a three-month tour of the postwar South in 1865 on a survey.

Schurz had been one of the organizers of the Republican Party in Wisconsin. With no knowledge of the sectional problem, he still had urged the Emancipation on Lincoln, who, wanting to build up more decided public opinion for his plan, commissioned Schurz to go privately about the country to stir up sentiment and conscience against slavery. A speech, the draft of which Lincoln saw and approved, was delivered at the Cooper Institute in New York City on March 6, 1862, and was given much acclaim.

It is interesting to note the large number, types, characters of these foreign-born opportunists who fattened on the South's woes. No history book that I know of gives more information on them than the pension list of the Fourteenth Amendment, Section 4. Much of the fantastic horrors of what went on in the South from 1865 to 1878 can be laid to the account of these (as the Confederates called them) "human vampires" from both native and foreign aeries. No wonder historians gallop by with heads averted, like Ichabod at the bridge. There is need for reorientation, because very little of the blunt truths and bare facts of the inflicted wrongs of that nightmare hour are found in the textbooks approved today for classroom study of American history. To portray the period convincingly is difficult without attaching a mass of recorded statistics from the public archives of the tortured regions. We cannot attempt it here, except now and then to cite an accepted authority, an eye-witness, or an interested party's *ex parte* views or to refer the reader to some published source.

The "Reconstruction" to return the seceded states to a Union which, the Supreme Court decided (*Texas* v. *White,* 7 Wall. 700; 19 L.Ed. 227; 1869), they had never been out of was a program of vengeance and destruction, not of construction, as General Richard Taylor of the Confederate Army, son of Old Rough-and-Ready General Taylor and brother-in-law of Jefferson Davis, noted in his book. Others North and South concurred. The South was to be made a veritable graveyard of white people governed by Negroes under the protection of United States armies stationed where it appeared they might be needed and commanded by Lincoln-appointed patronage generals whose whim or direction took the place of constitutional and established civil law.

The once-great sovereign states of South Carolina, Georgia, and Florida were to be set apart—even then it was considered desirable to separate the races—as the new homelands of the freed Negroes. The conquered lands were to be divided into farm tracts of set size to be given *gratis* one to each freedman—once set at "forty acres and a mule." What was left over, if anything, was to be sold, and any funds realized to be used to indemnify men "loyal" North and South, and to curtail the national debt. One whom the South called "that Diabolus Tad Stevens" publicly proposed this, and asked what loyal man could object to it. The whites were to be robbed, disfranchised, left to disappear or to be amalgamated, mongrelized, or exterminated, as one said, "under the African hoof."

To achieve such acts of hate and revenge, three amendments were forced upon the organic law, and there remain today. Constitutions, laws, are meant for the betterment, not the destruction and degradation, of people. If the Prohibition Amendment could be removed—which was comparatively harmless compared to those monstrosities—why should the Thirteenth, Fourteenth, and

Fifteenth be permitted to remain, in opposition to the Ninth and Tenth and to Article V? This attempt to force alteration of the form of American government, the result of a villainous war, should be removed, certainly the Fourteenth, at least. A recent lack of *restraint* on it, by the Supreme Court, has aroused the whole country to indignation. (Note the restraints of 1873-1929.)

Worse than the war, if anything could be worse than civil war, were the misnamed "Reconstruction Acts," supposedly intended to "bring back into the Union" all the seceded states now overcome by *force majeur*. But it was a Union "preserved" from disintegration by bald dictatorship and armed might, not by constitutional law and the rights of men, and by imposition on the national charter of the three extraordinary amendments. As mentioned earlier, there can be "amendments" proposed that are so far out of step with American character and government as to be impossible of serious consideration, so *outré* and strange as to raise at once the question of the power of any Congress to propose them or of any state to attempt to ratify them. These three postwar coercive alterations can be placed in no other category. They exist today as anomalies on the organic law of the land, against the form and origin of the founding fathers' efforts to provide against remote control by a centralized government, and are destructive of local responsibility and home rule by transforming the decentralization of government to a consolidated, absolute form.

Under them, in the guise of assisting the freed Negro to citizenship and attempted equality—which would occur only in the South, with the North largely unaffected—frauds and corruption grew to astonishing excess. Carpet-bagging and Union League activities raised all the debts of the former Confederate States to huge amounts. The very name officially given to the Freedmen's Bureau—i.e., the Bureau of Refugees, Freed Men, and Abandoned Lands—offers a key to a sad story. The bureau could take over abandoned or confiscated lands in the South and sell or grant them for three years in designated acreage units to Negroes under protection of the Union army, while sales for "taxes" grew and innumerable families were robbed of ancient inheritances. Powers previously exercised by the United States Treasury and War Departments to seize and sell the lands of the Confederate States, along with private lands left desolate by withdrawal of the former slave laboring gangs, provided money proceeds that were used to keep and to "educate" the ex-slaves—in reality often to keep them voting wards of the new Republican Party.

Proceeds from such sales were used to found in Washington, D.C., in 1867 the all-Negro Howard University, named for General O. O. Howard of Maine, first president of the University and former director of the Freedmen's Bureau. The bureau was abolished by Congress in 1872 because of financial and political scandals that had become a national disgrace. Yet Congress even today appropriates for the university approximately $1,000 a year per Howard student in what can only be class legislation for a single group. By what right has a Negro student to such a grant that a white should not also have it?

New situations born of the Emancipation and the Fourteenth Amendment brought indescribable economic and social conditions. The locusts were upon Goshen. The new freedmen would not work; the plantations stood idle and overgrown with weeds and the jungle was closing in, because the owners had been killed in the war, had fled the country, or returned as hopeless refugees to their own land. Droves of blacks wandered aimlessly about the countryside, stealing and pilfering in all directions. The occupying Union army itself took steps to reinstate a semblance of industry and order; and the state legislatures, many of them composed of large numbers of untutored Negroes, met to enact laws and regulations to meet the crisis.

These "black codes" were no more different for curbing vagrancy than similar ones long in use in Massachusetts, Indiana, and Wisconsin. Yet when attempt was made to return the blacks to work—all that was left for them if anarchy was to be replaced by responsible government—newspapers like the Chicago *Tribune* thundered that "Northern men will convert Mississippi into a frog-pond before such laws will be permitted to disgrace a foot of the soil." So unaffected, so ignorant of the chaos, so afar off were the editors licking the boots of sadists in the Congress. Not one of them had faced a Confederate musket or cannon in battle, or even "suttled" for a Union regiment at the rear. The Parkers, the Wendell Phillipses, the Pastors Brooks, Beecher, and others, joined in such shameful choruses.

Judge Lamar summed up the "Reconstruction" policy of Sumner and Tad Stevens:

> It was the offspring of misconception and distrust of the Southern people. . . . Its theory was that the Federal success in arms was only a partial one . . . that the sentiments, passions, and aims of the Southern people were still, and would continue to be, rebellious to the authority, and hostile to the nation's policy; that the termination of the war having put an end to military control, it became necessary to substitute another organization which, though not purely military, yet would be no less effectual in its functions of repression and force. . . . Its unmistakable purpose was the reversal of every natural social and political relation, on which I will say not only the civilization of the South but of the World and the whole Union rested. . . .

Races so distinguishable can meet side by side, "but are far more immiscible than Jew and Gentile, Greek and Moslem." It required the combination of all the strength, prestige, character, patriotism, patience, intelligence, spirit of the South, sustained by constitutional conservatism in the North, to prevent the country from becoming a second San Domingo. Better work was never done for the Negroes than defeating the policy and purpose of "Reconstruction"—the most outrageous Executive, Judicial, Legislative knavery and fanaticism ever visited on a civilized people in modern times.

The Union was "saved"—and this was to be its outstanding accomplishment? One is tempted to compare that Union with the unions under investigation by Congress today, many of them so rotten with corruption, crime, violence, and accumulated evils that they are not worth saving, or preserving. Can one say for the South that at that time a Union so rotten, decayed, evil, was worth the saving? Saved it was, by force of armed might and notorious legislation, Acts, and amendments. One needs only to read that remarkable and insolent Fourteenth Amendment and the Acts of the so-called "Reconstruction" that followed it to see a worthy section of America, even to the sea, "giving up its dead" in the night that descended on it in 1866.

How much better, and nobler, for an American President and an aroused Congress to recommend the removal of those festering additions to the United States Constitution, and let the Supreme Court take it from there. Although they *appear* not to, who from their station would know better the utter flouting of the true form of American constitutional government than the justices? We cannot believe that they lack the old-time traditional American sterner stuff which their distinguished predecessors Marshall, Miller, Taney, Hughes, Taft, never failed to display when the urgent occasion arose.

In a copy of the Constitution, read the amendments through the Fifteenth. Note amid the five sections of the Fourteenth how citizens are to be forced upon the states, although in Section 2 it expressly admits that the states alone, absolutely, have the say as to who shall be citizens in them. Yet this Section 2 attempts to control the states in their choice. Note what it does *without repeal* of Article I, Section 2, of the Constitution. Then examine Section 3 of the amendment, look up Webster's definitions of "*ex post facto* laws" and "bills of attainder," and note that the Constitution forbids both being passed by either the state or the federal governments. What Confederate was ever hanged for high treason? Not even the Number One man was even tried for the crime; federal authorities of that day dared not so bring him to trial, though the shameful, unproved, patently false charge so lays against him to this very day. Section 4 of the amendment is but a concoction of more wrongs, thefts, and illegalities. Under Section 5, for the most part, the courts threw out as invalid and unconstitutional most of the small amount of legislation attempted therein, and that, early.

There is no basis in our constitutional federal republic for saying that anything is constitutional or admissible simply because the Executive, the Legislative, or the Judiciary, or the moral convictions of the citizens approve, or even if the country will benefit by it.

The Constitution is federative in the power that framed it, in the power that adapted and ratified it, in the power that sustains and keeps it alive, in the power by which alone it can be altered or amended; and the government is federative in the structure of all its departments. In no sense is the federal government a democracy, nor do the people rule en masse. The doctrine of restraints dominates the whole system of checks and balances and was purposely meant to do so. It was this that made our system unique. It is up to us to keep it that way. Make no mistake, the South, at least, intends to try!

The South from the beginning had been a minority section and, although a delectable country, had been more or less shunned by immigrants because of the climate and the blacks. The whites who remained, owners of the region and heirs of their forefathers, must perforce get on as best they could. Being a widespreading rural empire with agriculture its chief occupation and pursuit, and individualistic as planters and farmers always are by the very nature of their lives, it adhered to what is known as the Jeffersonian, or "states' rights," school of politics. Those doctrines contain the only principles truly conservative of the American Constitution; apart from them, checks and limitations are of little avail, and a central government so disposed could increase its powers indefinitely.

The states of the South, in fact almost all of the original states at one time or another,

> . . . held to the fact that they had entered the Union *quoad hoc*: to the extent of the powers delegated in the Constitution. So far as related to the powers reserved, undelegated, Well, they were *out* of the Union. To them it was plain enough that the government of the United States had no *inherent* powers whatever, none by virtue of the fact it was a government, all its powers being derivative, named in the bond, specifically granted, delegated, and what was not named or implied, was reserved to the States or to the people.

One of the texts that Jefferson Davis, Lee, Jackson, Grant, Sherman and others studied at West Point was Rawle's *On the Constitution,* which taught that any state has the right to secede if it sees fit to do so. This is wholly supported in the Declaration of Independence and is nowhere denied in the United States Constitution to this very day.

There can be little to question about the education, training, aptitude, experience, displayed talent, character, of Jefferson Davis in comparison with that of Abraham Lincoln. The war came because they were in "reversed positions." Lincoln wanted to be President; he wanted the power, and he early showed his Cabinet that he, not any of them, would make the decisions. There would be nothing of the kind of a Jeff Davis in a Franklin Pierce Cabinet to run or influence him or the new administration. He would do that, and he proceeded to do it. Advice to move slowly, cautiously, was disregarded. The Confederate peace commissioners were lulled, while the assembling of an armed military and naval expedition continued in New York and other northern ports, to descend upon Charleston, South Carolina, to force a war in 1861.

Jefferson Davis, while still in the United States Senate, had hoped against hope that Lincoln would hold the anti-slavery men in check. He wanted to see no war, and counseled patience and tolerance. President Buchanan had publicly declared that he had not the constitutional power or thc will to make war. There was nothing in the Constitution to permit states to secede, but there was nothing there to prevent them. True, the Constitution did not give the States the right to secede but found them in possession of that right. Davis looked to taking a command in the field, if war came, as he had in the Mexican War. When word of the withdrawal of his state arrived, he made a sorrowful valedictory speech to the Senate and, shortly after, left for his home. There he immediately found himself commissioned a major general to organize the state military forces. Then came a telegram notifying him that he had been elected President of the newly formed nation. Mrs. Davis wrote that, as he stood before her reading it, "he looked so grieved that I feared some evil had befallen our family. . . . After a few minutes' painful silence he told me, as a man might speak of a sentence of death. . . . As he neither desired nor expected the position he was more deeply depressed than before." But he was no quibbler or balker; resolutely he faced what had come unasked. He assembled the plantation Negroes, informed them of the message and of his decision to go, and made them an affectionate farewell, to which they responded with expressions of devotion. Next day he left for Montgomery.

He could have refused that unprecedented American office, declined the honor, warded off the terrible responsibility of inconceivable burden that he only too well appreciated was being put upon him. He would be facing a superior military power headed by an untried politician who had not "found" himself (but who would seize and hold more power than any Englishman had since Oliver Cromwell). That he accepted the appalling honor demonstrated the kind of man he was.

Jefferson Davis, coming to high office, was a man who had found himself or, in the words of Woodrow Wilson, had "come to himself." Lincoln, it would appear, had not yet "arrived," though he came to the office of President at the age of fifty-two, the sixteenth President of the United States but almost a political unknown—in reality a "dark horse." He as titular head of the Republican Party had become President because of a split in the Democratic Party, whereby of a total popular vote of 4,680,869 he received 1,866,329, the three candidates opposing him polling a total of 2,814,517, though the electoral vote was divided 180 for Lincoln to 123 for the others. Thus a minority President, Lincoln had no mandate from the American people either to preserve or to break up the Union. The action he undertook was solely his own, on his own initiative and, at the start, against the advice of his Cabinet, of General in Chief Winfield Scott, and of prominent members of his own party, not to mention a large and insistent editorial voice in the North and a very considerable so-called "peace" party there, later to be scoffed at as Copperheads.

There was also Union and non-secession sentiment throughout the South, but it never attained anything like the proportion of the Copperheads in the North, who during four years of war were a formidable thorn and acute threat to the ambitions of Lincoln. We can dismiss them without further discussion by giving here their 1864 party platform, which tells better than volumes could the sentiment of a large portion of the northern population. It was brief and to the point: "The Constitution as it is, the Union as it was, the Negroes where they are."

But for the ruthless iron hand of the dictator strangling all opposition in patent violation of the United States Constitution and his oath to support it, it is more than possible and even likely that the war would early have ground to a halt in the discouragement of Union military defeats alone, with undoubted prospects of restoring old ties, compromising differences, and re-union. Peace and preventing an avoidable war were blocked only by a dictatorial President grasping far beyond Article II, ignoring his oath of office, and trampling underfoot the organic instrument of that Union—and backed soon by corrupt and ruthless men in Congress, by patronage-bought northern governors and a war-prosperous North bent to the dictator's will, and behind all the ferocious, fanatic Abolitionists. It was tragic and deplorable, and of no credit to Christianity, civilization, or political philosophy, to see how long-standing differences of opinion that had run parallel to the whole history of the Union should have to be "settled" by resort to arms instead of to some other arbitrament. Even a truce.

Little indeed was settled of the quarrel itself. The attempted forced changes did not come to full fruition by any means. The destruction of the rights of the sovereign states and the transfer of all power to Washington, D. C. as feared by Thomas Jefferson, was attempted but failed. Even Alexander Hamilton, Jefferson's political opponent, despite his leaning toward a strong central government had said:

> The state governments are essentially necessary to the form and spirit of the general system. With the representative system a very extensive country may be governed by a confederacy

> of the states in which the supreme legislature has only general powers, and the civil and domestic concerns of the people are regulated by the laws of the several states. State governments must form a leading principle. They can never lose their powers till the whole people of America are robbed of their liberties.

Long had that question of centralized versus local self-government thus agitated the country's politics. Was the general government a federal, or a consolidated, one—a constitutional or an absolute one?

To a rather astonishing extent it has been assumed that the Civil War did "settle it," that the Fourteenth Amendment destroyed states' rights. Nothing could be further from the truth than the statement of a *federal* judge that the rights of states had been, or could be destroyed; yet judges even today have been heard to make the same statement, adding ". . . although the states are just beginning to find it out." Such a judge by that statement has demonstrated his unfitness for the bar or the bench because of his naïveté and abysmal ignorance of the Constitution itself, the progress of constitutional law, its origin and precedents, and the history and traditions of the nation.

When the Confederacy's last days came with the dawn of 1865, even before there were any new amendments to the Constitution, it was clear that "states' rights are dead" to the northern states, and to that peculiar war-bought group their governors and the legislatures that met that January. As one proclaimed, "There is and can be under the Constitution only one paramount authority, sovereign authority; the war has been a lesson worth its costs, many a hero dead, many a household draped in mourning, many a broken heart; but who would take it back?—that is precious which was bought with blood," etc.

By that time the formerly important state executives had become mere army recruiting agents for Lincoln's administration, which had been returned to office in November, 1864, principally through the use of troops at the polls. It is probable that at least eight northern states had been carried by the soldier vote, or by military intimidation of private citizens at the polls—though no standard history textbook notes this fact.

Writers were not wanting, then or today, to cheer for the new "nation." Lincoln was its architect; his great victory of nationalism, centralism, over localism and states' rights was "a victory over men of lesser minds." To some it appeared that the new "nation" had in the last analysis emerged from the Civil War not solely as a result of the military defeat of Jeff Davis's armies—starved, blockaded, dropping arms at last but not begging for peace when overwhelmed and surrounded by swarming hordes, with repeating rifles, at Appomattox—but because that political and military victory was equally the result of Lincoln's peasant mind and personality. Had he at last succeeded in driving that great nation, which his own forebears had helped to bring forth painfully by the tears and blood at Lexington and Yorktown and the 1787 convention, back to the very thing from which they had seceded—the consolidated centralism of remote-control, autocratic government, one not of laws but of men? Was that the single achievement of his coming to the White House? For, after all, the quarrel had been over whether the states had inviolable rights or the general government was possessed of all of them, with total and supreme authority.

So there was a second inauguration at Washington March 4, 1865. But there was to be none at Richmond, because the Constitution of the Confederacy made its President's tenure of office six years, and Jefferson Davis still had two years to serve. That spring the future of the Confederate States looked dark indeed, and only the indomitable spirit of their President seemed to be holding them together for the final hour, as it turned out, just ahead.

Having as he thought destroyed the American form of local self-government, Lincoln now was all for peace and conciliation, without which it would not be possible to hold the material victory of the war, no matter the enemy's defeat and desolation. Therefore, after a short inaugural ceremony with a hypocritical plea and pious platitudes, Lincoln the next month went to Richmond, a battered, smoke-smudged heap of debris, a ruin of smoldering buildings that flared up fitfully amid black smoke or collapsed in sullen, quaking clouds of dust. There was no need for his presence or personal authority there, as he stood awhile, gazing at its scattered stones; the visit would seem to have been just an empty, incongruous gesture, like a pontifical wave of the hand deprecatingly, rather like the *Sic Semper Tyrannis* of the seal of Virginia in reverse—the wrong foot on the wrong neck. There was nothing he could learn or accomplish by going to that dead city. The Confederate government had retreated to Danville, then continued farther southward when news of Lee's surrender to Grant was brought by courier.

Joseph E. Johnston's and Hampton's cavalry had just administered a licking to Sherman in North Carolina, where soon Jefferson Davis was to plead earnestly with his two remaining generals near by, Beauregard and Johnston, not to give up the fight. "With arms in hand the South was unconquerable . . . was suffering from a panic; it yet had resources to continue the war; it was for those who still had arms to give an example to reanimate others, and erect declining resolution again for the whole country." That President was setting an example, even as had the great Washington before him, of sublime courage, of fortitude and hope, while the other stood staring, musing, in the strange atmosphere of his trophy, the abandoned Confederate capital, surrounded by ecstatic, masterless, uncomprehending Negroes.

CHAPTER 10

The Real Cause of the Provoked War

IN THE SPECIOUS SECOND INAUGURAL ADDRESS of Abraham Lincoln, which weeping poets have sometimes described as "a lasting memorial to, and a perfect portrait of, Lincoln's great soul," he well knew the utter falseness of his remarks when he said:

> . . . one eighth of the whole population are colored slaves, not distributed generally over the Union but localized in the Southern part of it. These slaves constituted a peculiar and powerful interest. All know that this interest was, somehow, the cause of the war. . . . To strengthen, perpetuate, and extend this interest was the object for which the insurgents would rend the Union, even by war; while the government claims no right to do more than to restrict the territorial enlargement of it.

Where, in the Constitution, do we find the justification or explanation of that "somehow"? This, as we have shown, was a direct, deliberate, unblushing falsehood. The colored slaves were *not* the cause of the war, and under the Constitution of the United States never could have been the cause of it. But the speaker was in need of such amazing untruths to bolster, try to justify, his trampling of that Constitution and his callous disregard of his oath to support it. Moreover, his declaring those colored slaves "free" by the Emancipation Proclamation was a brazen act of theft and misuse of Executive powers on the pretense of the public necessity and in a part of the nation in which he had no constitutional or military authority. The Negroes in the North, a negligible minority, were free. That President was trying to justify his four dictatorial years of lawless seizure of power and attempted overthrow of the American form of government and to lay the groundwork for perpetuating his own new political party in power by creating a new southern black electorate.

He went on: "Neither party expected for the war the magnitude or the duration which it has already attained. Neither anticipated that the cause of the conflict might cease with, or even before, the conflict itself should cease. . . . Each looked for an easier triumph, and a result less fundamental and astounding." That is an incredible statement, but no protests seem to have been voiced publicly.

So the entire Civil War, in which both Union and Confederate armies suffered casualties of between 35 and 40 per cent of the participants—more than half a million men—and a half-billion-dollar war debt, was just to rob a few southern planters of their labor forces, which they had lawfully bought and paid for under their own state and the United States constitutions and had employed to the prosperity of the whole Union—a humane "institution," a workable capital-labor arrangement for hot climates that was mislabeled "slavery"? We are asked to believe this obvious and preposterous falsehood, and to consider its declarer one of the anointed and deified "saints" of American history.

A whole separate category of literature, both scholarly and puerile, has been amassed for his sanctification, and magnificent monuments have been erected far and wide over the land in his commemoration. There is one in the national capital itself that constitutes a daily, gratuitous insult to every man who wore the gray, from Jefferson Davis to the least of his tattered troopers, and to their descendants now living in the desolated regions.

The conqueror writes the history and makes the public opinion of the vanquished, and the South's history, if accepted in future years as now written, will, as Dr. Curry wrote,

> . . . consign her to infamy. . . . If she were guilty of rebellion or treason, if she adopted and clung to barbarism, essential sins, and immoralities, then her people would be clothed, as it were, with the fabled shirt of Nessus, fatal to honor, to energy, to noble development, to true life. . . . So was there any

sanctity or infallibility in acts and opinions relating to the South, that they should escape historical criticism, or be exempt from all the tests of truth and justice?

The so-called "slavery" of the American South was in no way like that of Lincoln's bald presentation—that "any men should dare to ask a just God's assistance in wringing their bread from the sweat of other men's faces." What about the other men's bread: how was that to be secured? Or did they eat bread? Then, "we pray that this mighty scourge of war may speedily pass away. . . . Yet if God wills that it continue until all the wealth piled by the bondman's two hundred and fifty years of unrequited toil shall be sunk, and until every drop of blood drawn by the lash shall be paid by another drawn with the sword, as was said three thousand years ago, so still must it be said, 'The judgments of the Lord are true and righteous altogether.'" An extravagant assumption without base, this picture of two hundred and fifty years of lashing to death $1,500–$2,500 Uncle Toms. The price was the cost risk for the possible lifetime labor or services of a rude black who might die next day—or be rendered useless for some time by those "lashings" that Lincoln vividly imagined. These sound like the ravings of a man whose mind had become unbalanced, rather than the sober thoughts of a President who had deliberately brought on a war "to preserve the Union and the Constitution" and who had distinctly rejected in his first Inaugural all intention of interfering with "slavery" in the states where it existed when he quoted and reiterated the platform resolution of his party to that effect, in 1861.

The second Inaugural Address closed with the speaker solemnly affirming what could indeed have been his own epitaph:

> "The Almighty has his own purposes. . . . Woe unto the world because of offenses! for it must needs be that offenses come; but woe to the man by whom the offense cometh." If we shall suppose that American slavery is one of those offenses which, in the providence of God, must needs come, but which, having continued through His appointed time, He now wills to re-

> move, and that He gives to both North and South this terrible war, as the woe due to those by whom the offense come, shall we discern therein any departure from those divine attributes which the believer in a living God always ascribe to Him?

The hands of the Abolitionists and of the White House secretariat, perhaps also of the Cabinet, are seen here. Jefferson Davis was a churchgoer, a steadfast Christian church member. On the Sunday that news came to him from Lee, of the lines broken at Petersburg, he was seated in the family pew of the St. Paul's Church, in Richmond, where he and his family, and the Lees, worshiped, as Episcopalians. His counterpart, even in the Presidency at Washington, D. C., so far as can be determined, never joined or identified himself with any Christian church or religious denomination. Why is not known.

The "peculiar institution" of the South was seldom called "slavery" there. Many southerners, among them Vice-President Alexander Stephens, felt that there was no such thing as genuine slavery in most of the section. Hordes of naked, bought and kidnaped savages had been brought in continually from the wilds of Africa from early colonial days. Their only use then was to work on plantations raising the staple crops of the region, cotton, indigo, rice, tobacco, sugar, naval stores, etc. Some, it is true, were found educable and capable of being trained as efficient, trusted house servants. Each of the great plantations, where most of the slaves were congregated in field gangs, was a small, self-sufficient, self-contained and self-supporting world in itself, each different from others in subtle ways.

All of the slave states had enacted laws for the slaves' protection, by which their life and limbs were protected from violence inflicted by masters or others. In the United States a slave was a person (albeit counted as three-fifths of a person for purposes of electoral and representative apportionment), and as such was capable of committing evil, crimes, of receiving his freedom, of being the subject of homicide, and very materially of modifying by his own volition the rules applicable to other species of property. His existence as a person being recognized by law, that existence was protected by law; the relations of husband and wife, parent and child, etc., were recognized by statutes concerning public sales and by the courts in all cases in which such relationships were relevant to elucidating the motives of these acts. The slave had, of course, no political rights, the government of that time being the sole judge of who should be its citizens. His civil rights, though necessarily more restricted than the free man's, were based on the same foundation—the law of the land—and he had none but those that are by that law and the law of nature given to him. Slaves legally could not acquire property, their acquisitions belonging to their masters; but in the southern states they frequently were permitted to obtain, and retain, property.

There was a rule of common law that a slave could not be a witness except for or against slaves or free Negroes; only a free man was worthy of taking an oath. The rule of exclusion was enforced in all cases in which the evidence was offered for or against free white persons (whites also often being in bondage), in most states by statute. A slave could sue only for his freedom; for all other wrongs he appeared through his master, for whose benefit recovery would be made. The master must support, defend, his slave, however helpless or impotent; and cruel treatment was a penal offense. "Manumission" was withdrawal of the master's dominion, making the slave "free" only, not a citizen. In most of the slave states "freeing" a Negro slave entailed some duties before it could be effected—a bond posted so that the freedman would not become a public charge, certification of good character, and in some states payment of passage to Africa and subsistence for six months there.

The "institution" from the beginning was bound to be fastened mostly upon the southern regions because the crops raised there, tobacco, rice, indigo, cotton, etc., flourish in the rich soil of hot, alluvial lands where a Caucasian cannot work well under the broiling sun but a black can, at no harm to himself and without departure from age-old conditions in Africa.

In 1783 the Congress, endeavoring to set quotas of the revenue to be required of the several states, had a problem of apportionment. If the tax burden were distributed according to population, it made a great difference whether slaves were to be counted or not. If they were counted, the southern states would have to pay more than their equitable share into the federal Treasury; if they were not counted, the North argued, southern states would be paying less than their share, and therefore inclined to consider slaves as population, while the South considered them chattels. As a compromise, Madison proposed that a slave count as three-fifths of a free man, and the measure was adopted then and also by the 1787 Constitutional Convention when the question of representation arose. The House of Representatives was to represent the American people, not the American states as the Senate did. Was this representation to be apportioned by wealth or by populations, and if by population, were *all* the inhabitants or only those "free" to be counted? As human beings slaves might be population, but at law they were chattels. The fierce and complicated dispute is probably best recounted by John Fiske, in *Critical Period* (pages 242–68). He thought that, in the chattel-population question, "in politics as in algebra it makes all the difference in the world whether you start with a plus or a minus." Madison, who had offered the three-fifths solution before, offered it again as a compromise to save the convention from breaking up, and did save it, although Virginia above all others wanted to rid the new nation of slavery. Under the circumstances, it was the best possible solution, and resulted in South Carolina and other slave states counting slaves as population and permitted Massachusetts and Rhode Island to continue to bring them into the country.

The Census of 1790 records a total of 697,897 slaves in the United States, distributed as shown in the table. This distribution clearly shows that the "institution" became the South's problem, a heritage from the past, brought originally upon them by old England and New England and fastened upon them by climate, culture, and geography rather than upon the colder North, where it had been found unprofitable and had therefore died out.

North		South	
New Hampshire	158	Delaware	8,887
Vermont	17	Maryland	103,036
Massachusetts	*none*	Virginia	293,247
Rhode Island	952	North Carolina	100,572
Connecticut	2,759	South Carolina	107,094
New York	21,324	Georgia	29,264
New Jersey	11,423	Kentucky	11,830
Pennsylvania	3,737	Tennessee	3,417
Total	40,370	*Total*	657,527

All over the world slavery was still looked upon as necessary and was so treated in all political societies, though from the beginning of the nineteenth century it was being decried in most civilizations of the world and was on its way out in the South before 1860. Except for one of the most amazing propaganda campaigns ever carried on in America, it would early have passed into oblivion, and by the volition of the South. The earliest emancipation societies had been formed in the South, and in the 1787 convention it was the Virginia delegation that suffered defeat when they tried to have slavery outlawed by proposed articles that led to the writing of the Constitution itself. Who helped to oppose it then? None other than a considerable number of northern delegates whose constituents were profitably engaged in importing and selling large cargoes of Guinea Negroes to southern planters. (Doubters should refer to the last sentence but one of Article V of the Constitution beginning "Provided . . ." and consider its meaning.)

Jefferson Davis had early said, "We are not fighting for slavery; we are fighting for our independence." With a force that carried sincere conviction he pointed out the aims and beliefs of his region:

> If a just perception of neutral interests shall permit us peaceably to pursue our separate political career my most earnest

> desire will have been fulfilled. . . . Solemnly in the face of mankind we desire to have peace, at any sacrifice save that of honor and independence; we seek no conquest, no aggrandizement, no concessions of any kind from the States with which we were lately confederated; all we ask is to be let alone; that those who never held power over us shall not now attempt our subjugation by arms; this we will, we must, resist to the last extremity.

That, in the southern point of view, was all the war was; what had slavery to do with it? It was the North that made the attacks, invaded, deliberately maneuvered the firing upon Fort Sumter and immediately seized upon the "firing on the flag" to arouse a nation most reluctant to begin a fraternal conflict. The facts about Fort Sumter have for too long been glossed over, mitigated, or deliberately falsified; the situation actually prevailing at the time and the ramifications both North and South must be uncovered to reconstruct the true picture.

A majority in the North did not want to go to war. By the Declaration of Independence itself the cotton states, if they believed themselves wronged and preyed upon, had the right to alter or abolish the form of government that had become destructive, and "to institute a new government, laying its foundation on such principles, and organizing its powers in such form, as to them shall seem most likely to effect their safety and happiness." Long a powerful voice in the councils of New York, Editor Horace Greeley said, "I have no doubt that the free and the slave States ought to be separated. . . . The Union is not worth supporting in connection with the South"; and he had also said, "If the Declaration justified the secession of three million colonists in 1776 we do not see why it would not justify the secession of five million Southerners from the Union of 1861." He had hoped never to live in a republic "whereof one section is pinned to another by bayonets."

A forced Union is a contradiction in terms. But Lincoln would be President of a forced Union, which could only be a contract by duress. When he was asked in 1860, "Why not let the South go?" his little-known answer, long ignored by those in a position to know, is reported by the editor of the *Southern Literary Messenger* to be, "Let the South go? Where then shall we get our revenues?" Which was mentally echoed in the North: "Let the South go? Where then shall we look for the bounties and monopolies that have so enriched us at the expense of those improvident southerners? Where shall we find again such patient victims of spoliation?"

By 1860 that federal Union that Greeley spoke about was fast becoming no longer "federal." From the very beginning of the republic there had been differences of opinion as to the powers of the general government. Washington's administration had seen two of his Cabinet officers express decided opinions; Washington, on the spot as Chief Executive and faced with unforeseen situations, wanted above all else to see the country launched on a safe and solid base. Through the following years valiant, able, patriotic men, famous in American history, even that of the world, strove to compromise threatening issues and to help steer to success their new kind of government, a "world's best hope." From Washington to Buchanan there were no basic changes, few amendments, made in the organic law, but there had been compromises aplenty.

Each President, regardless of background, education, experience, and inheritance, was to meet and know that strange lesson Walt Whitman mentions: ". . . that provision in the essence of things, that from any fruition of success, no matter what, shall come forth something to make a greater struggle necessary." This the Confederate President knew beforehand and had so intimated in an Inaugural Address. Lincoln in 1860 obviously did not; it lay ahead of him. To him, from below and with little public service or political experience compared to Davis's, political success would seem an enviable eminence to strive and pant for, to be reached through great endeavor or great good fortune —a prize beyond compare. Attained, it appeared more and more a barren, lonely shale, a place sore and dread, a mirage achieved, a slippery fingerhold over an awful abyss of threatened ill and failure, destroying reason and careers, panicking men, bringing suicide and oblivion. Many had so known. Only the truly great and noble among Christian characters, the Washingtons, the St. Pauls, could buckle armor and stand to the very end. Such, pre-eminently, had been Jefferson Davis.

For Lincoln, whatever sure knowledge and value had come with his ordeal in the White House was forever extinguished by an historical act on the night of April 14, 1865, at the Ford Theatre in Washington. Davis, on the other hand, lived through to a ripe old age, to state his case in full for a more impartial jury of maturer peers, in maturer years, for a surer, decisive verdict from the pen of history. He gave the closing years of his life to spelling out the South's right and justification in a monumental work that has never been answered. Indeed, though unread today, *The Rise and Fall of the Confederate Government* is unanswerable.

This work should be read and studied today, as a text in law, politics, government, and history classes, because today there are being appointed to positions on federal, even Supreme, court benches men who are *not* learned in that very law of the land, that Constitution, which they solemnly swear to uphold when they take office by presidential appointment. A well-known and respected jurist who long adorned the United States Supreme Court, Oliver Wendell Holmes, in his *Collected Papers* (1920) gave, inadvertently perhaps, what may be and still seems on the whole to be the dogma of the Court: that "the United States would not come to an end if we lost our power to declare an Act of the Congress void; I do believe the Union would be imperilled if we could not make that declaration as to the laws of the several States. . . . For one in my place sees how often a local policy prevails with *those who are not trained to national views.*" (Italics added.)

Memories of the war and its aftermath, handed down through the years, will ever haunt the South. Other than the great work of her ex-President, and a few of the leaders, the region, like Lee, remained mute; its recollections were too painful. Arnold

Toynbee, in *A Study of History,* thought that in two of the States, Virginia and South Carolina, memory of the great social catastrophe persisted starkly over a long period. The "war" there meant the Civil War, even though two fearful world-wide wars have since intervened. They were living under a spell in which time has stood still; two of the most cultured of the States of antebellum day, each had had so far to fall.

CHAPTER 11

Statesmanship and Abraham Lincoln

SHORTLY AFTER WORLD WAR II, I visited my younger son, who was studying for his Ph.D. degree at Princeton University. Walking around the spacious, venerable grounds, I happened to enter the student co-operative store hidden in an unobtrusive ground-floor corner of one of the massive stone buildings, and there picked up from a pile of students' texts "for sale" a booklet entitled *When a Man Comes to Himself* by a former president of the university, Woodrow Wilson. I read it through while standing there and decided to buy it. It was published by Harper and Brothers in 1901, long before the author became President of the United States. As it seems scarce now (I have never seen another copy), I take the liberty of paraphrasing from it at length. When I first read it I was thinking of the two men we have been discussing here and of the strange hour in history that their lives embraced and helped to shape in the mysterious scheme of things.

Wilson thought it a very wholesome and regenerating change which a man undergoes when he comes to himself. It is not only after periods of recklessness or infatuation when he has played the spendthrift or the fool that a man comes to himself. He comes after experience of which he alone may be aware; when he has left off being wholly preoccupied with his own powers and interests and with every petty plan that centers in himself; when he has cleared his eyes to see the world as it is, and his own true place and function in it. It is a process of disillusionment; the scales fallen away, he sees himself soberly and knows under what conditions his powers must act, as well as what his powers are. He had got rid of earlier prepossessions about the world of men and affairs, both those which were too favorable and those too unfavorable—both those of the nursery and those of a young man's reading. He has learned his own paces or, at any rate, is in a fair way to learn them; he has found his footing, and the true nature of the "going" he must look for in the world; over what sorts of roads he must expect to make his running, whither his goal lies, and what cheer he may expect by the way. Though a process of disillusionment, it disheartens no soundly made man, but brings him into a light which guides instead of deceiving him, a light which does not make the way look cold to any man whose eyes are fit for use in the open, but which shines wholesomely rather upon the obvious path like the honest rays of the frank sun, to make traveling safe and cheerful.

There is no fixed time for this; some never come to it at all. No thoughtful man has ever come to the end of his life and had a little space of calm from which to look back upon it who did not know and acknowledge that it was what he had done unselfishly and for others, and nothing else, that satisfied him in retrospect. . . . Men grow by having responsibility laid upon them, the burden of other people's business. Their powers are put out at interest, and they get usury in kind, are like men multiplied; each counted manifold. Men who lived only with an eye upon what is their own are dwarfed beside them, seem fractions while they are integers. The trustworthiness of men seems to grow with the trust. It is for that reason they are in love with power; it allows an expansion, a large run for their minds, an exercise of the spirit so various and refreshing; they have freedom of so wide a tract of the world of affairs. But if they use power only for their own ends, if there be no unselfish service in it, if its object be only one's own personal aggrandizement, their love to see other men tools in their hands, they go out of the world small, beggared, disquieted, no enlargement of soul vouchsafed them, no usury of satisfaction, having added nothing to themselves.

Necessity is no mother to enthusiasm; she carries a whip. Her methods are compulsion, not love, with no thought to be attractive, but content to drive.

Men come to themselves by discovering their limits no less than by discovering their deeper endowments and the mastery that makes them happy. It is the discovery of what they can *not* do and ought not to attempt that transforms reformers into statesmen, and great should be the joy of the world over every reformer who should come to himself. The spectacle is not rare, the method not hidden; the practicality of every reform is determined absolutely and always by "the circumstances of the case," and only those who put themselves into the midst of affairs either by action or by observation can know what those circumstances are, or perceive what they signify.

No statesman dreams of doing whatever he pleases; he well knows that it does not follow that because a point of morals or of policy is obvious to him, it will be obvious to the nation, or even to his own friends. And it is the strength of a democratic polity that there are so many minds to be consulted and brought to agreement, and that nothing can be wisely done for which the thought, and a great deal more than the thought, of the country, its sentiments, and its purposes have not been prepared. Social reform is a matter of co-operation, and if it is to be of a novel kind, requires an infinite deal of converting to bring the efficient majority to believe in it and support it. Without their agreement and support it is impossible.

It is this which the more imaginative and impatient reformers find out when they come to themselves. Ofttimes the most immediate and drastic means of bringing them to themselves has been to elect them to Legislative or Executive office; it will reduce oversanguine persons to their simplest terms. It is not that they find their fellow legislators or officials incapable of high purpose or indifferent to the betterment of the communities which they represent. Only cynics hold that to be the chief reason why we approach the millennium so slowly, and cynics, Wilson thought, are usually very ill-informed persons. Nor is it that under our modern democratic arrangements we so subdivide power and balance parts in government that no man can tell for much, or turn affairs to his will. Wilson thought that one of the most instructive studies that a politician could undertake would be to examine the infinite limitations that had been laid upon the power of the Russian czar, notwithstanding the despotic theory of the Russian Constitution then—limitations of social habit, of official prejudice, of race jealousies, of religious predilections, of administrative machinery even, and the inconvenience of being himself only one man, caught amid a rush of duties and responsibilities which never halted or paused. He could do only what could be done with the Russian people. He could not change them at will, was himself of their own stuff, and immersed in the life which forms them as it formed him; he was simply the head of the Russians.

Wilson thought also that an English or an American statesman was better off. He leads a thinking race, not one of peasants topped by a class of revolutionists and a caste of nobles and officials. He can explain new things to men able to understand, persuade men willing and accustomed to making independent and intelligent choices of their own; and an English statesman has even better opportunity to lead because there executive power and legislative initiative are entrusted to the same grand committee, the ministry in power, who both propose what shall be made law and determine how it shall be enforced when enacted. But they too have found office a veritable cold-water bath for their ardor for change, going from the most radical to the most conservative. . . . For the first time they had seen in its entirety what it was they were attempting, at last at close quarters with the world, realizing the real nature of the complex stuff of life they sought to work in, its intricate, delicate fiber and the subtle, secret interrelationships of the parts. . . . And so they work circumspectly, lest they should mar more than they mend.

> Moral enthusiasm is not, uninstructed and of itself, a suitable guide to practicable and lasting reformation; and if the reform sought be the reformation of others as well as himself he should look to it that he knows the true relation of his will to the wills of those he would change and guide. When he has discovered that relation, he has come to himself and discovered his real use and planning part in the general world

> of men, has come to the full command and satisfying employment of his faculties. Otherwise he is doomed to live for ever in a fool's paradise, and can be said to have come to himself only on the supposition that he is a fool.

(The places of Jefferson Davis and Abraham Lincoln may not be at once perceivable in this thought.)

Wilson ended on a note of Christianity and love, without which men of purest altruism might yet be as sad and unsatisfied as the Roman emperor Marcus Aurelius Antoninus. Men have both an absolute and a relative capacity; absolute in that a man is endowed with such a nature and such parts and faculties; relative in that he is a part of the universal community of men and stands in such relation to the whole. He will come to himself, when and if he does, in that relative capacity. Political society, the life of men in states, is an abiding natural relationship, no mere convenience or mere necessity, not a voluntary mere association or corporation; not deliberate or artificial, devised for a special purpose, but in real truth the eternal and natural expression and embodiment of a life higher than that of the individual—that common life of mutual helpfulness, stimulation, and contest, which gives leave and opportunity to the individual life, makes it possible, full, complete, by the man himself.

We might fit either Lincoln or Davis into any mold that might be satisfactory enough to us, but would be neither rational nor wholly false or historically true. Historians have left room for different decisions. Those earlier and closer—too close—to the event are inclined one way; later ones, in more impartial judgment, another. Some of the later historians have maintained that Lincoln maneuvered the South into the Fort Sumter incident. Is a man with a cocked pistol pointed at his breast to be considered the beginner of the strife when he knocks the pistol from his adversary's hand before it can be fired? We have shown that Lincoln desired and intended to have power, and that Davis did not; one forced, the other was forced. The end of the war indicated no essential eternal right on the part of the victor, but only that the attempt of the Confederacy proved not practicable at that hour—even as the long struggle of the colonists would have been vain except for France.

Find a word or clause in our charter, the Constitution, proclaiming the nation supreme. It is not there. Why? Sovereignty, inherent, and powers unsurrendered by the states from the beginning remain to them in residuum, as the Tenth Amendment simply states. And that amendment has never been overruled, not lawfully set aside or invalidated or repealed, and has been recognized by the Supreme Court *after* the imposition of the three Civil War amendments (see 109 U.S.C., p. 3). John Marshall early had said, "No political dreamer was ever wild enough to think of breaking down the lines which separate the States, and of compounding the American people into one common mass." But some very prominent men in American history have since tried it, and some have almost succeeded. It is our conclusion that Lincoln's was such an attempt, and he had assistance. In the preliminary Emancipation Proclamation he wrote that "the war hereafter as before will be prosecuted for the object of practically restoring the constitutional relations between the United States and each of the states." Was he incapable of perceiving that the observance of his oath of office would of itself, alone, have gone far toward achieving such a relation, and early would even have initiated possible return of the aggrieved and departed states? He held the power to attempt, at least to try, for that.

The results of the war—the persistent misrepresentations, perversion of authentic records, aspersions and accusations based on ignorance, malice, and passion—remind one of the words of Cardinal Newman in his *Apologia,* where, on the subject of the defeat of good and the success of evil, he thought of the world and man and of the many races, ". . . their starts, fortunes, mutual alienations, conflicts, ways, were exactly described in the Apostle's words, 'have no hope and without God in the world,' a vision to dizzy and appal, inflict upon the mind the sense of a profound mystery absolutely beyond human solution." This was no *ignis fatuus* in the South after 1865.

We must stem the tides of vested fatuities like Lowell's (1864)

> . . . the wisdom of the presidential measures is justified by the fact that they have always resulted in more firmly uniting public opinion [?]; particularly admirable in his public utterances is a certain tone of familiar dignity which, while perhaps the most difficult attainment of mere style, is also no doubtful indication of personal character. . . . There is something essentially noble in an elective ruler who can descend to the level of confidential ease without losing respect, something manly in one who can break through the etiquette of conventional rank and trust himself to the reason and intelligence of those who elected him.

Driveling tripe like this disfigures, and inspissates, bubbles, and hardens to a form, in American literature from Lincoln to Franklin D. Roosevelt.

We have made little mention of the war, but there are some unrecorded historical matters concerning the Fort Sumter incident that require the light of day. South Carolina, upon seceding, had demanded the return to her of the forts in the harbor of Charleston. Originally, any such installation that had been turned over to the federal government for purposes of defense, etc., under the arrangements was subject to return to the state-owner in event of non-use or other stated cause. The deeds by which Virginia granted the lands upon which Fort Wool and Fort Monroe stand contain such stipulations, and there are others in similar grants. There was no payment; the properties were deeded *gratis* by the state concerned and, under specified eventualities, under eminent domain reverted to them. Therefore South Carolina was wholly within her legal rights. The Secretary of State promised to return the holdings, but the Lincoln adherents decided otherwise. While the southern peace commissioners in Washington were being assured of no attempt at violence, Lincoln ordered reinforcements—ships, troops, guns, ammunition, supplies—assembled at New York and other northern ports. The commander of the fort, Major Anderson (who at West Point had been a teacher of Beauregard, the southern general at Charleston), had been receiving regular provisions from the locality under an amicable agreement with Governor Pickens, and the fort was far from want or distress.

Nowadays we find a number of writers (Miss Tarbell, John Mors, and Secretary Welles among them) who tell of a letter Lincoln received from the major indicating that he had sufficient provisions to last at least to April 14—when the reinforcing squadron would be ready to relieve him. Lincoln drafted a letter for Secretary of War Cameron to forward word to Anderson that the expedition "will go forward." Three days later Major Anderson answered by protesting that he should have been notified of the expected invasion force; the officer who was to command it had hinted to him that it would not be carried out. He ended his letter with the words "We shall strive to do our duty, though I am frank to say that my heart is not in the war which I see is thus to be commenced." He saw the treachery.

The straggling squadron arrived off Charleston harbor, but a storm prevented their attempting to enter. Meanwhile, the Confederates, faced with the duplicity, received orders to take the island fortification, and they proceeded to do so in no inefficient way. There were no casualties, despite the terrific thirty-four-hour shelling during which the fort was reduced to rubble. Afterward there was one accidental casualty as Anderson saluted the flag he was hauling down, before marching out to the piping of "Yankee Doodle" and cheered by his recent assailants, who lined the shores and expressed appreciation of his gallantry.

Convinced of Seward's double-talk to the Peace Commission and learning of Lincoln's decision to send an armed expedition to relieve the fort before April 15, which Anderson had set as the time he would evacuate, "should I not receive prior to that time controlling instructions from my government, or additional supplies," Beauregard had demanded surrender of the fort. Anderson had refused but assured the Confederate officers as they were leaving that he would "await the first shot." If not battered to pieces, he would be starved out in a few days anyway. When this was reported to Secretary of War Walker, he revoked the attack order of April 12 and directed the Confederate commander not to bombard the garrison if its commander would set the time when he would leave, thus "to avoid the effusion of blood." But the arrival of units of the enemy fleet off the harbor entrance left the southerners no alternative but to reduce the threat in the inner harbor for their own safety.

The Union Secretaries of War and the Navy were aware of Lincoln's plans, and the Secretary of the Navy wrote that it was "important that the Rebels strike the first blow in the conflict." About the failure of the expedition to make entry into the harbor Lincoln displayed no concern, and he even wrote to the commander not to become annoyed, as both "anticipated the cause of the country would be advanced by making the attempt even if it should fail; it is no small consolation now to feel that our anticipation was justified by the result." Now he could tell the nation that the flag had been insulted and call for 75,000 men, a *posse comitatus,* to quench the insurrection. Historians have skipped over the indignant answers of a dozen state governors; they would furnish no troops to coerce or war upon sister states!

Seward had advised evacuating Sumter, but the President determined upon war. When it became certain that he would attempt military conquest of the seceded states, Virginia, Arkansas, Tennessee, and North Carolina immediately joined their sister states to resist such an unconstitutional, dictatorial, usurpatory proposal. Except for prompt and treacherous military seizures in Maryland, Delaware, Missouri, and Kentucky, undoubtedly those states would also have gone over. Several historians, Masters, Tilley, Ramsdell, among others, charge Lincoln with deliberately maneuvering the South into action—even as, in recent years (though not yet told bluntly; see Admiral Kimmel's *Story*) an American President apparently deliberately maneuvered an Asiatic enemy into destroying the United States fleet at Pearl Harbor to get the nation into a war. Such hellish, hidden acts must not be kept covered. The American people are stout and resolute enough to face facts in so dark an hour. We are no more partial to Democrats than to Republicans in power seizures.

Though urged by members of his Cabinet and by numerous prominent Republicans and others in the North who recognized the suicidal possibilities, and though he had made distinct pledges to the contrary in his first Inaugural Address, Lincoln had determined upon coercing the South to remain in a forced Union.

Sumter was in the nature of a friendly trial suit, and neither of the face-to-face combatants wanted war or bloodshed. General Beauregard reported that after firing the first gun at 4:30 A.M. (touched off by a fiery secessionist, the Virginian Edmund Ruffin), no reply was made before 7 A.M. The garrison had gone into the bomb-proof shelters. Now coming out, they fired a few shots in return. Later, when it became evident that the fort was on fire, Beauregard held fire and sent some aides with a fire engine to assist in extinguishing the blaze. Without any authority and in an open boat under fire, Senator Louis Trezevant Wigfall of Texas pulled up to the embrasures of the burning fortress, climbed in one of them, and, going directly to Major Anderson, begged him to give up the fight on the honorable terms that had previously been proposed. The major reluctantly agreed, and the arrangement was immediately ratified ashore. (He had once thought to go over to have dinner with his old colleague, General Beauregard and was already suspected of "sympathies.")

One historian noted that "never was so costly a victory so easily won." But the attempt to represent the South as the aggressor, Jefferson Davis said, was "as unfounded as the complaint made by the wolf against the lamb in the familiar fable."

Then, threatened by the fifty placed guns of the repaired fort in the center of the harbor, and more reinforcements on the way, that very day there loomed on the horizon off the coast the succoring Union fleet units. The commander, Captain Gustavus Fox, had planned, as he wrote, "to propose three tugs convoyed by light-draft men-of-war . . . the first tug to lead in empty, to open their fire." The gale prevented that, and the fort fell. Coastal guns then readied to drive off the fleet. Under the circumstances it is difficult to accept those historians who would have us believe that the Confederate decision to bombard was "incredibly unwise," or that they should have waited, regardless of considerations to the contrary, for the North to fire the first gun, "even if they had to wait a lifetime." No, their action was not only correct but justified by events at the time.

The Confederacy failed to gain its justified independence because it was unable to obtain foreign support like that of the French armies and fleets of Louis XVI that assured the successful secession of thirteen Colonies from Britain. But the contention that states' rights were "dead" hardly survived their assassin's burial. His successor stoutly and manfully maintained them, even to his attempted impeachment; and scarcely seven years later the Supreme Court, no longer blanching before the mob, largely upheld parts of them by judicial decrees in some civil-rights disputes, beginning with the slaughterhouse cases of 1873; *U.S.* v. *Stanley et al.*, 1875; 109 U.S. 3, etc. In 1883–87 the greater part of the Civil Rights Act of 1875 was declared invalid, by a court with "restraint."

Jefferson Davis never forgot that he was a constitutional President; Abraham Lincoln seems never to have remembered that he was one. Davis amid all the turmoil and agonies of the war held steadfast to the observance of the oath of his office. In this, as was sadly said afterwards by some of his friends, "he was more nice than wise in circumstances that should have led him to temporarily opposing to the vigor of the despotism into which the government of the United States had been converted a corresponding vigor purchased at the same cost to the people of the South." But a thief to catch a thief? Not Jefferson Davis. He was a chief who knew with whom and with what he had to deal, the character and spirit of his people. They were not a docile, led, immigrant-infiltrated kind like those predominant in and characteristic of much of the North. That it took four fearful years to overwhelm them, in the equation twenty-eight million versus eight million, is ample proof of that.

In all the belligerent relations of the Confederacy, Jefferson Davis truly represented the spirit of moderation. In a contest in which all depended, especially on the weaker side, upon Executive energy, concentration, decision, and promptness, he stood reluctant to grasp a single power not confided to him by the Constitution. In a study of contrasts this fact stands out sharply. The federal government and Executive, looking only to success, regardless, and contemptuous of the means by which it might be assured, trampled right and left over every constitutional guarantee, over individual liberty and state authority alike. But Davis confined himself within the limits assigned to him, refusing to take to the evils of full Executive usurpations or dictatorship. Later, of the rights lost with the Confederacy he said that while they appeared lost, the principle for which he had contended was bound to reassert itself, though it might be at another time and in another form.

Was the Confederate Cause lost? Only temporarily, against tyranny and armed might; it had not been wrong, only weak—impracticable at the time. If that Cause were lost, what cause was it? Surely not that of the South only, but the cause of constitutional government, of the supremacy of law, of the natural rights of men everywhere—secured when the Executive, Legislative, and Judicial oaths of office are faithfully attended.

Can the Constitution be casually set aside as Lincoln tried because of war? Not at all. The United States Supreme Court in a famous decision (4 Wall. 2) refused to go along with the proposition, saying that "the Constitution is a law for rulers *and* people, equally in war and in peace, and covers all classes of men with the shield of its protection, at all times and under all circumstances." Martial law cannot arise even from threatened invasion; the necessity must be actual and present, the invasion real, such as to close the courts and depose the civil administration effectually. It could never exist where the courts are open and in the proper and unobstructed exercise, then, of their jurisdiction. It is to be noted that under Lincoln the Constitution was observed largely in the breach; but in the South it was insisted upon and widely observed under the President and the Confederate administration.

Before he had risen to fame either scholastically or politically Woodrow Wilson, then a professor at a boys' school at Middletown, Connecticut (Wesleyan University), delivered the commencement address on, "Leadership," at the University of Tennessee in 1890. He said:

> Leadership cannot always wear the harness of compromise; once and again one of those Influences which we call a Cause arises in the midst of a nation. Men of strenuous minds and high ideals come forward with a sort of gentle majesty as champions of a political or moral principle. . . . Attacks they sustain in behalf of the Cause are more cruel than a collision of arms; their souls are pierced by a thousand keen arrows of obloquy; friends desert, despise, them; they stand alone; sometimes made bitter by their isolation. Yet the leader must not yield. And the Cause must not be born out of time; no man thinking thoughts born out of time, can succeed in leading his generation; that is the product of sympathy, not of antagonism, a sympathy which is insight. Not yielding, the forces of public thought hesitate, waver, come over to the side of the Cause. But the leader is not to be conceived a trimmer, weak to yield what clamor claims, but the deeply human man, quick to know and to do the things that the hour and his nation need. . . . [*Works.*]

PART THREE

The Two American Constitutions

CHAPTER 12

Constitutional Revision for the Confederacy

THE CONFEDERATE CONSTITUTION was modeled on and largely copied from the United States Constitution throughout. The only changes were those that experience had suggested for a better practical working or, as Jefferson Davis stated, "for greater perspicuity."

The preamble to both is the same in substance and nearly identical in language. The words "We the People of the United States" in the one are replaced by "We the People of the Confederate States" in the other, and the perversion that was made of the original expression is precluded in the latter by the addition of an explanatory clause "each State acting in its sovereign and independent character," making it clear that the "People" means the people of the States themselves, not the people of the *whole* United States considered as one body. This perversion was never the intent of the makers of the Constitution, and holding such a view was to destroy the independence and identity of the sovereign states of the American Union and to reduce them to mere provinces of a central power, a national government rather than what was the intention of the makers—a federal union.

The intended meaning, at the time of the formulation of the United States Constitution, was so well known, so well understood, that so labored an explanation would have been deemed superfluous then.

The President's term of office was fixed at six years instead of four, and it was provided that he should not be eligible for re-election. This too was in accordance with the original draft of the Constitution of 1787. The President was empowered to remove officers of his Cabinet, or those engaged in the diplomatic service, at his discretion; but in all other cases cause for removal from the office had to be reported to the Senate.

The Confederate Congress was authorized to provide by law for the admission of Cabinet officers to a seat on the floor of either house of Congress, each with the privilege of taking part in discussion of subjects pertaining to his department. (Note this wise and judicious provision, which would tend to obviate delay and misunderstanding. It was never put into effect by the necessary legislation because of the exigencies of war.)

Protective duties in favor of special branches of industry, which had been a fruitful source of trouble and irritation under the United States government—the tariff issues—were altogether prohibited. The South, a rural empire, had little need for any so-called "protection"; rather, it needed to be able to buy in world markets as cheaply as it could, without the burden of special taxes on the economy. Also prohibited were bounties from the Treasury, and extra compensation for services rendered by officers, contractors, or employees of any kind.

A vote of two-thirds of each house was requisite for the appropriation of money from the Treasury, unless asked for by the chief of a department and submitted to the Congress by the President, or for payment of the expenses of Congress or of claims against the Confederacy judicially established and declared. The President was also authorized to approve any one appropriation and disapprove any other in the same bill.

Impeachment of federal officers was entrusted, as formerly, to the discretion of the Confederate House of Representatives, with the additional provision that in the case of any judicial or other officer exercising his functions solely within the limits of a particular state, impeachment might be made by the legislature of that state—the trial in all cases to be heard before the Confederate Senate.

Any two or more states were authorized to enter into compacts with each other for improvement of navigation of rivers flowing between or through them.

A vote of two-thirds of each house—the Senate voting by states—was required for the admission of a new state.

The Confederate Constitution made it obligatory upon the Congress, on the demand of any three states concurring in a proposed amendment or amendments, to summon a convention of all the States to consider and act upon them. Voting, by States, was restricted to the particular propositions thus submitted. If approved by such convention, the amendments were to be subject to final ratification by two-thirds of the states.

Articles IX and X of the Bill of Rights—the Ninth and Tenth Amendments to the United States Constitution—were incorporated verbatim in the Confederate Constitution as the last two paragraphs of Article VI, which begins with the statement "The Government established by this Constitution is the successor of the Provisional Government of the Confederate States of America. . . ." (Note "thereof" added to the end of Confederate Article VI.)

Other changes worthy of special notice related to internal improvements, bankruptcy laws, duties on exports, suits in the federal courts, and the government of the territories.

Regarding slavery and the slave trade, the provisions of the Confederate Constitution furnished an effectual answer to the false, propagandizing assertion so often made that the Confederacy was "founded on slavery," that slavery was its "cornerstone," etc. Property in slaves already existing was recognized and guaranteed, just as it was by the Constitution of the United States. The rights of such property in the common territories were protected against any hostile discrimination as had been attempted in the Union. But the "extension of slavery," in the only practical sense of that phrase, was more distinctly and effectively precluded by the Confederate than by the United States Constitution, as will be seen by a comparison of Article I, Section 9, of each. The United States Constitution is as follows:

> The Migration or Importation of such Persons as any of the States now existing shall think proper to admit, shall not be prohibited by the Congress prior to the Year one thousand

> eight hundred and eight, but a Tax or Duty may be imposed on such Importation, not exceeding ten dollars for each Person.

On the other hand, we find that the Confederate Constitution ordained:

> The importation of negroes of the African race, from any foreign country other than the slave-holding States or Territories of the United States of America, is hereby forbidden; and Congress is required to pass such laws as shall effectually prevent the same.
>
> Congress shall also have power to prohibit the introduction of slaves from any State not a member of, or Territory not belonging to, this Confederacy.

In the case of the United States Constitution, the only prohibition is against any interference by Congress with the slave trade for a term of years, and the trade was further legitimized by the authority to impose a duty upon it. The term of years had long since expired, but there was still no prohibition of the trade by the United States Constitution. It was, after 1808, entirely within the discretion of Congress either to encourage, to tolerate, or to prohibit it.

By the Confederate Constitution, on the contrary, the African slave trade was forbidden positively and unconditionally from the beginning. Neither the Confederate government nor that of any of the Confederate states would permit it, and the Congress was expressly required to enforce the prohibition. The only discretion entrusted to the Congress was whether or not to permit the introduction of slaves from any of the United States or their territories.

In the Inaugural Address that President Abraham Lincoln made in 1861, he stated: "I have no purpose directly or indirectly to interfere with the institution of slavery in the States where it exists. . . . I believe I have no lawful right to do so, and I have no inclination to do so." If there was no purpose on the part of the government of the United States to interfere with the institution of slavery within its already existing limits—a proposition which permitted its propagation within those limits by natural increase—and inasmuch as the Confederate Constitution precluded any other than the same natural increase, we can plainly perceive the absurdity and the disingenuousness of the pretension (by a factitious sympathy obtained in certain quarters of the North) that a war of invasion, destruction, and subjugation of the whole South was conducted on the preposterous grounds of a war in behalf of "freedom" against slavery—any more than it was a war conducted to preserve the Union against attack and aggression by the South. The North was the attacker, the aggressor, the invader throughout. The South defended itself against attack, and tried at first to settle the whole dispute within the Union frame. Finding it not possible to be safe, free, prosperous, *in* the Union, the South determined to *get out* of the Union, and should have been permitted to go, in peace. Instead, finding themselves unable to live without the South, whose rights and guarantees under the Constitution a ruthless northern majority were violating, the North went to war to drag back and subjugate the weaker southern states, and accomplished it after four bloody years.

Then three amendments, the Thirteenth, Fourteenth, and Fifteenth, were imposed upon the Constitution by force of arms after the South had surrendered, had been disarmed, and was helpless longer to make defense and oppose these wrongs. History was falsified; facts were concealed, misrepresented, and falsely distorted to the injury of the whole South. An investment of about $3,000,000,000 by the South in the capital-labor setup (a misnamed "slavery" institution that had been usefully invoked to the entire and national prosperity) was destroyed, and nothing put in its place but three amendments to the United States Constitution which, under the rights guaranteed to each state of a republican form of government, never had the chance of passage until the states affected had been subjugated and were held in irons by an occupying army. Those amendments are there today, by fraud and not by law, and should for that reason be protested by the South on all occasions when raised or invoked.

The two Constitutions are presented side by side for study in the next chapter, to show how the proposed Confederate Constitution measured up as a wise, temperate, and liberal exhibition of true statesmanship. Some very important and desirable improvements had been made by its proposals (as indicated below *in italics*, and by the blank spaces in the columns).

The problem of "slavery," so called, was an incident, not a cause, of the conflict; this must be kept in mind. "Slavery" was wholly constitutional and lawful, and was so recognized prior to the Emancipation Proclamation and the war.

At the beginning of the nineteenth century, slavery was treated as a necessary and invariable concomitant of almost all political societies of the world. It is doubtful that, without it, the southern states could have been developed and made prosperous. When the Constitution was adopted, all the states—with the possible exception of Massachusetts—had it, though it was numerically greater in the South than in northern sections, with a tendency to continuance in the South and cessation in the North. So it early presented itself as a disturbing element. The provisions of the Constitution, which were known to be necessary for its adoption, bound all the states to recognize and to protect that peculiar species of property. As ex-President Jefferson Davis wrote:

> When at a subsequent period there arose in the North an anti-slavery agitation, it was a harmless and scarcely noticed movement until political demagogues seized upon it as a means to acquire power. . .. Had it been left to pseudo-philanthropists and fanatics most zealous where least informed it never could have shaken the foundations of the Union and have incited one section (the North) to carry fire and sword into the other. . . . The agitation was political in its character and developed as early as 1803. To preserve equilibrium and to maintain the equality of the States was the effort on one side; to acquire empire was the manifest purpose on the other. . . .

Why blame them? To end it in the United States was the great problem. It was an institution that had been fastened upon the

South by old England and New England long before the days of 1861–65. It existed throughout the world, prospering in tropical, dying out in temperate, zones.

The blacks were without any history but that of the most degrading bondage imaginable, in which their ancestors had lived for at least five thousand years, as shown by the pictures and inscriptions on the most ancient Egyptian monuments. This was no fault of the southerners, or anybody else, unless it be construed that of the Negroes themselves. Much had been attempted for them, particularly in the South. Maryland in 1663, for instance, had provided life servitude for them only because an early effort at abolition of bondage "had proved the Negro too childlike to be without a master or guardian." Those brought to America by adventurous, enterprising whites who were exploring and colonizing the world while other races were in somnolent savagery, or little better, came from the western coasts of Africa, such Gulf of Guinea regions as Angola and the Slave and Gold Coasts, and belonged to the true Negro type. Their chief characteristics are a dark brown to black color, frizzy, woolly hair, projection of the jaws, unusually long arms, short flat nose, wide nostrils, thick everted lips, full black eye, thick skull, small cranial capacity, early closure of the cranial sutures, ability to endure tropical suns.

European slavery disappeared after the fourth century A.D. and little was heard of it by the end of the tenth century. Serfdom took its place, binding man to the soil. When that was sold, he went with it, an integral part of the old feudal system which came to an end in England by a peasant revolt 1381. In parts of enlightened, cultured France it did not end before 1789; in Prussia it lasted until about 1811, and in Russia until 1861. This was white slavery, and it shows how very slowly the world moved onward toward "freedom's light." Not overnight came emancipation.

When Europeans came more or less in continued close contact with the African Negro, in the fifteenth century, slavery was revived. In the Central African regions slavery had always been known; tribal chiefs sold own tribesmen and had engaged in slavery from times beyond record. The oldest Egyptian monuments recorded Negro slavery at least five thousand years previous; it was the only workable method known and used by such enterprising peoples as then led the world. It was unquestioned, an accepted part of life.

When the Europeans first came into contact with the blacks of the Guinea regions and noted the lives and conditions, slavery was revived. There were hot lands, colonies, fertile, promising and productive, where a white or Caucasian could not work under a boiling sun but a black could, at no harm to himself and not departing from his ancient condition. There was promise of wealth and progress in a plantation system in the fabulous West Indies of Spain, England, France, and many other parts of the New World in the Northern and Southern Hemispheres, growing cotton, tobacco, sugar, rice, coffee, and the like.

The Negroes, particularly those of the Central African regions, were people of another color and race, so different that they seemed to be scarcely human. Early Portuguese navigators carried them to Europe and to the New World colonies, where the native Indian had often been nearly exterminated by such use. The Negro stood up far better, enduring the toil and conditions; soon a booming slave-trade was in full swing, and wealth poured in for the colonizers and enterprisers.

Dr. J. L. M. Curry and Alexander Stephens stated the case when they said:

> . . . there was with us no such a thing as "slavery" in the true and proper sense of that word. No people ever lived more devoted to the principles of liberty, secured by free democratic institutions, than were the people of the South. None had ever given stronger proofs of this than they had done. What was called "slavery" amongst us was but a legal subordination of the African to the Caucasian race. This relation was so regulated by law as to promote, according to the intent and design

> of the system, the best interests of both races, the black as well as the white, the inferior as well as the superior. Both had rights secured and both had duties imposed. . . . It was a system of reciprocal service and mutual bonds.

And this was so, as we readily see on defining the term or word "slave" and applying to the American South. A slave is one over whose life, liberty, and property another has unlimited control. The *jus vitae et necis* is included in pure or absolute slavery. Such a power has no foundation in natural law, and hence the Justinian Code declared it *contra naturam esse* (*Inst.* 1. 4. 2). Every limit placed by law upon this absolute control modifies, and to that extent it changes, the condition of the "slave."

In every "slaveholding" state of the United States the life and limbs of a slave were protected from violence. The civil-law rule, *partus sequitur ventrem* was adopted in the American states, the status of the mother at the time of birth deciding the status of the issue. Numerous court decisions affirm this.

The general, world-wide provisions covering ordinary slavery were much modified in the United States, especially in the South, where it was a subordination only of the African black to the Caucasian white, in a capital-labor arrangement satisfactory on the whole to both races in hot climates. The alternative would have been a barren, wasted, rotted wilderness instead of a prosperous, civilized, beneficial, and humane setup, and the South's investment in the labor of this class of her population exceeded $3,000,000,000, all of which became an impoverishing total loss by 1865.

Under the American poor laws, manumission varied with the different states, from the requirement of a certificate of merit, or good conduct, from the master, to his posting a bond ($100 to $1,000), in some of payment for return to Africa and in others the requirement that the freedman leave the state, even the country, within a year after manumission. In Virginia were thousands of known cases in which the requirement for leaving the state was ignored by masters and by authorities, and by the former slaves, who knew well that under Virginia law they made themselves liable to being sold back into "slavery" for not leaving—an indication of the affection in which many of the former slaves were held.

In leaving the United States Senate, 1861, Jefferson Davis cited the conviction of a pressing necessity, a belief, that the southern states were "to be deprived of the rights which our fathers had bequeathed. . . . There had been proclaimed the theory that all men had been created equal, and this made the basis of an attack on the region's social institutions; The Declaration of Independence had been invoked to maintain the position of the equality of the races." But that Declaration was to be construed by the circumstances and purposes for which it had been made, "the men" were *the men of the political community,* not everybody, regardless; it was to be taken that there was no divine right to rule; no man inherited the right to govern; there were no classes by which power and place descended to families, but all stations were equally within the grasp of each member of *the body politic.* That body did not include the African Negro "slaves" and, in that day, hardly could have meant to. The Dred Scott decision by the Supreme Court in 1857 went into that.

CHAPTER 13

Texts of the Declaration, the Articles and the Two Constitutions

BEFORE DISCUSSING FURTHER the revised constitutional provisions reflected in the Confederate Constitution, we would best reread the basic documents of the federal, constitutional American Union—the Declaration of Independence and the instrument of organic law *in toto* (including the pre-Civil-War amendments). In this chapter therefore are reprinted, first, the Declaration, then the Articles, then the United States and Confederate Constitutions side by side in parallel columns and so spaced as to be compared paragraph by paragraph, together with a brief note on the Articles of Confederation.

The Declaration of Independence was adopted by the Continental Congress at Philadelphia on July 4, 1776, and was signed by John Hancock as President and by Charles Thomson as Secretary. It was first published on July 6 in the *Pennsylvania Evening Post.* A copy of the Declaration, engrossed on parchment, was signed by members of the Congress on and after August 2, 1776.

THE DECLARATION OF INDEPENDENCE

When, in the Course of human events, it becomes necessary for one people to dissolve the political bands which have connected them with another, and to assume among the powers of the earth, the separate and equal station to which the Laws of Nature and of Nature's God entitle them, a decent respect to the opinions of mankind requires that they should declare the causes which impel them to the separation.

We hold these truths to be self-evident, that all *men* are created equal, that they are endowed by their Creator with certain unalienable Rights, that among these are Life, Liberty and the pursuit of Happiness. That to secure these rights, Governments are instituted among Men, deriving their just powers from the consent of the governed. That whenever any Form of Government becomes destructive of these ends, it is the Right of the People to alter or to abolish it, and to institute new Government, laying its foundation on such principles and organizing its powers in such form, as to them shall seem most likely to effect their Safety and Happiness. Prudence, indeed, will dictate that Governments long established should not be changed for light and transient causes; and accordingly all experience hath shewn, that mankind are more disposed to suffer, while evils are sufferable, than to right themselves by abolishing the forms to which they are accustomed. But when a long train of abuses and usurpations, pursuing invariably the same object, evinces a design to reduce them under absolute Despotism, it is their right, it is their duty, to throw off such Government, and to provide new Guards for their future security. Such has been the patient sufferance of these Colonies; and such is now the necessity which constrains them to alter their former Systems of Government. The history of the present King of Great Britain is a history of repeated injuries and usurpations, all having in direct object the establishment of an absolute Tyranny over these States. To prove this, let Facts be submitted to a candid world.

He has refused his Assent to Laws, the most wholesome and necessary for the public good.

He has forbidden his Governors to pass Laws of immediate and pressing importance, unless suspended in their operation till his Assent should be obtained, and when so suspended, he has utterly neglected to attend to them.

He has refused to pass other Laws for the accommodation of large districts of people, unless those people would relinquish the right of Representation in the Legislature, a right inestimable to them and formidable to tyrants only.

He has called together legislative bodies at places, unusual, uncomfortable, and distant from the depository of their public Records, for the sole purpose of fatiguing them into compliance with his measures.

He has dissolved Representative Houses repeatedly, for opposing with manly firmness his invasions on the rights of the people.

He has refused for a long time, after such dissolutions, to cause others to be elected; whereby the Legislative powers, incapable of Annihilation, have returned to the People at large for their exercise; the State remaining in the meantime exposed to all the dangers of invasion from without, and convulsions within.

He has endeavored to prevent the population of these States; for that purpose obstructing the Laws of Naturalization of Foreigners; refusing to pass others to encourage their migrations hither, and raising the conditions of new Appropriations of Lands.

He has obstructed the Administration of Justice, by refusing his Assent to Laws for establishing Judiciary powers.

He has made Judges dependent on his Will alone, for the tenure of their offices, and the amount and payment of their salaries.

He has erected a multitude of New Offices, and sent hither swarms of Officers to harass our people, and eat out their substance.

He has kept among us, in times of peace, Standing Armies, without the Consent of our legislatures.

He has affected to render the Military independent of and superior to the Civil power.

He has combined with others to subject us to a jurisdiction foreign to our constitution and unacknowledged by our laws; giving his Assent to their Acts of pretended Legislation: For quartering large bodies of armed troops among us: For protecting them by a mock Trial from punishment for any Murders which they should commit on the Inhabitants of these States: For cutting off our Trade with all parts of the world: For imposing Taxes on us without our Consent: For depriving us in many cases of the benefits of Trial by Jury: For transporting us beyond Seas to be tried for pretended offenses: For abolishing the free System of English Laws in a neighbouring Province, establishing therein an Arbitrary government, and enlarging its Boundaries so as to render it at once an example and fit instrument for introducing the same absolute rule into these Colonies: For taking away our Charters, abolishing our most valuable Laws and altering fundamentally the Forms of our Governments: For suspending our own Legislatures and declaring themselves invested with power to legislate for us in all cases whatsoever.

He has abdicated Government here by declaring us out of his Protection and waging War against us.

He has plundered our seas, ravished our Coasts, burnt our towns, and destroyed the lives of our people.

He is at this time transporting large Armies of foreign Mercenaries to complete the works of death, desolation and tyranny, already begun with circumstances of cruelty and perfidy scarcely paralleled in the most barbarous ages, and totally unworthy the Head of a civilized nation.

He has constrained our fellow Citizens taken Captive on the high Seas to bear Arms against their Country, to become the executioners of their friends and Brethren, or to fall themselves by their Hands.

He has excited domestic insurrections amongst us, and has endeavoured to bring on the inhabitants of our frontiers, the merciless Indian Savages, whose known rule of warfare is an undistinguished destruction of all ages, sexes and conditions. In every stage of these Oppressions We have Petitioned for Redress in the most humble terms. Our repeated Petitions have been answered only by repeated injury. A Prince, whose character is thus marked by every act which may define a Tyrant, is unfit to be the ruler of a free people. Nor have We been wanting in attentions to our British brethren. We have warned them from time to time of attempts by their legislature to extend an unwarrantable jurisdiction over us. We have reminded them of the circumstances of our emigration and settlement here. We have appealed to their native justice and magnanimity, and we have conjured them by the ties of our common kindred to disavow these usurpations, which would inevitably interrupt our connections and correspondence. They too have been deaf to the voice of justice and of consanguinity.

We must, therefore, acquiesce in the necessity, which denounces our Separation, and hold them, as we hold the rest of mankind, Enemies in War, in Peace Friends.

We, therefore, the Representatives of the United States of America, in General Congress, Assembled, appealing to the Supreme Judge of the world for the rectitude of our intentions do, in the Name, and by authority of the good people of these Colonies, solemnly publish and declare, That these United Colonies are, and of Right ought to be, Free and Independent States; that they are Absolved from all Allegiance to the British Crown, and that all political connection between them and the State of Great Britain is and ought to be totally dissolved; and that as Free and Independent States, they have full Power to levy War, conclude Peace, contract Alliances, establish Commerce, and to do all other Acts and Things which Independent States may of right do. And for the support of this Declaration, with a firm reliance on the protection of Divine Providence, we mutually pledge to each other our Lives, our Fortunes, and our sacred Honor.

This Declaration was signed by fifty-six men, representatives of the thirteen states. Their names are known to all Americans and can be found in all the history texts. A reproduction in facsimile was made in 1823 by John Q. Adams, then Secretary of State, for the original signers and their families, and was struck from a copperplate. The original document, now greatly deteriorated in the parchment and faded in the text, rests in the State Department, Washington, D.C.

President Wilson in a speech delivered July 4, 1914, at Independence Hall in Philadelphia on the Declaration of Independence, said that the signers "attached their signatures to that significant document knowing that if they failed it was certain that every one of them would hang for the failure. . . . They were committing treason in the interest of the liberty of 3,000,000 people in America. All the rest of the world was against them and smiled with cynical incredulity at the audacious undertaking. . . . Do you think if they could see this great nation now they would regret anything that they then did to draw the gaze of a hostile world upon them? Every idea must be started by somebody and it is a lonely thing to start any thing. . . ."

Our country was founded on the right of revolution, the right to change a form of government the people no longer felt was one that fitted them. The South as a people in 1861 felt that there was no longer safety, security, prosperity, for them within the frame of the old Union, where party sectionalism was working a tyranny upon the less strong states, penalizing the agricultural South to aggrandize and build up other sections of the nation at their expense. They decided, therefore, to get out of a Union which was detrimental to them and to form another more to their interests, security, safety, prosperity.

Appendix A-1

THE ARTICLES OF CONFEDERATION

Between the *Declaration of Independence* and the *Constitution of the United States of America* is found the first attempt to form a Union of the thirteen colonies along the Atlantic coast of America.

These colonies formed a league, to be known as the United States of America. John Dickinson, in 1776, drafted the *Articles of Confederation.* The States concerned engaged in a treaty of alliance and friendship, for mutual protection, agreeing to assist each other when or if aid were needed. In this agreement each State was empowered to regulate its own internal affairs, but should not receive or send separate embassies or contract engagements of alliance, conclude treaties, or carry on any negotiations with any foreign power without the consent of the general body. No public officer was to be allowed to accept any office or title, emoluments or presents, from any foreign State. Neither had Congress nor the separate State governments the power to confer any title of nobility, nor could the States form alliances among themselves without Congressional consent; they could not levy duties contrary to those enacted by Congress, nor could any State keep a standing army or navy in time of peace beyond the limits put upon it by Congress. The States raised troops for the common defence and appointed all officers of the rank of colonel and below by the State legislatures, the superior officers to be appointed by Congress. All war expenses were to be paid out of the public treasury. Congress alone could coin money. A neighbor to the North (Canada) might be admitted to the Confederacy were she disposed to apply for admission. There were other clauses, as will be seen in the study of the *Articles,* next given, dealing with the powers of certain governmental operations.

Submitted to the several State legislatures, the *Articles* were ratified by eleven States in 1778, by Delaware in 1779, and by Maryland in 1781; they remained in force until the United States Constitution was adopted in 1789.

When Richard Henry Lee of Virginia presented his *Resolution* for independence on June 7, 1776, he also proposed that a plan of confederation be prepared and transmitted to the respective colonies "for consideration and approbation," for which Congress had appointed, on June 12, the committee headed by Dickinson, who reported and presented to Congress on July 12 what they had done. Out of this came the *Articles,* which were debated intermittently for over a year, until a vote was taken, October 7, 1777, one vote for each State, and acceptances were secured.

As will be seen by the student in his study of the *Articles,* along with the two accompanying Constitutions, they simply defined the relations of the States to the Confederation as they had already shaped themselves. The Revolutionary War was fought on them, though they failed to create a federal government endowed with any real sovereignty and had to be replaced.

The Preamble of the Confederate and of the United States Constitutions should be compared with Articles 1, 2, and 3 of the *Articles of Confederation.*

Articles of Confederation and Perpetual Union between the States of New Hampshire, Massachusetts Bay, Rhode Island and Providence Plantations, Connecticut, New York, New Jersey, Pennsylvania, Delaware, Maryland, Virginia, North Carolina, South Carolina, and Georgia.

ARTICLE I. — The style of this Confederacy shall be, "The United States of America."

ARTICLE II. — Each State retains its sovereignty, freedom, and independence, and every power, jurisdiction, and right, which is not by this Confederation expressly delegated to the United States in Congress assembled.

ARTICLE III. — The said States hereby severally enter into a firm league of friendship with each other, for their common defence, the security of their liberties, and their mutual and general welfare, binding themselves to assist each other against all force offered to, or attacks made upon them, or any of them, on account of religion, sovereignty, trade, or any other pretence whatever.

ARTICLE IV. — The better to secure and perpetuate mutual friendship and intercourse among the people of the different States in this Union, the free inhabitants of each of these States, paupers, vagabonds, and fugitives from justice excepted, shall be entitled to all privileges and immunities of free citizens in the several States; and the people of each State shall have free ingress and egress to and from any other State, and shall enjoy therein all the privileges of trade and commerce subject to the same duties, impositions, and restrictions as the inhabitants thereof respectively; provided that such restrictions shall not extend so far as to prevent the removal of property imported into any State to any other State of which the owner is an inhabitant; provided also, that no imposition, duties, or restriction shall be laid by any State on the property of the United States or either of them. If any person guilty of, or charged with, treason, felony, or other high misdemeanour in any State shall flee from justice and be found in any of the United States, he shall, upon demand of the governor or executive power of the State from which he fled, be delivered up and removed to the State having jurisdiction of his offense. Full faith and credit shall be given in each of these States to the records, acts, and judicial proceedings of the courts and magistrates of every other State.

ARTICLE V. — For the more convenient management of the general interests of the United States, delegates shall be annually appointed in such manner as the Legislature of each State shall direct, to meet in Congress on the first Monday in November, in every year, with a power reserved to each State to recall its delegates, or any of them, at any time within the year, and to send others in their stead for the remainder of the year. No State shall be represented in Congress by less than two, nor by more than seven members; and no person shall be capable of being a delegate for more than three years in any term of six years; nor shall any person, being a delegate, be capable of holding any office under the United States for which he, or another for his benefit, receives any salary, fees, or emolument of any kind. Each State shall maintain its own delegates in any meeting of the States and while they act as members of the Committee of the States. In determining questions in the United States, in Congress assembled, each State shall have one vote. Freedom of speech and debate in Congress shall not be impeached or questioned in any court or place out of Congress; and the members of Congress shall be protected in their persons from arrests and imprisonment during the time of their going to and from, and attendance on, Congress, except for treason, felony, or breach of the peace.

ARTICLE VI. — No State, without the consent of the United States, in Congress assembled, shall send any embassy to, or receive any embassy from, or enter into any conference, agreement, alliance, or treaty with any king, prince, or state; nor shall any person holding any office of profit or trust under the United States, or any of them, accept of any present, emolument, office, or title of any kind whatever from any king, prince, or foreign state; nor shall the United States, in Congress assembled, or any of them, grant any title of nobility.

No two or more States shall enter into any treaty, confederation, or alliance whatever between them, without the consent of the United States, in Congress assembled, specifying accurately the purposes for which the same is to be entered into, and how long it shall continue.

No State shall lay any imposts or duties which may interfere with any stipulations in treaties entered into by the United States, in Congress assembled, with any king, prince, or state, in pursuance of any treaties already proposed by Congress to the courts of France and Spain.

No vessel of war shall be kept up in time of peace by any State, except such number only as shall be deemed necessary by the United States, in Congress assembled, for the defence of such State or its trade, nor shall any body of forces be kept up by any State in time of peace, except such number only as, in the judgment of the United States, in Congress assembled, shall be deemed requisite to garrison the forts necessary for the defence of such State; but every State shall always keep up a well-regulated and disciplined militia, sufficiently armed and accoutred, and shall provide and constantly have ready for use in public stores a due number of field-pieces and tents, and a proper quantity of arms, ammunition, and camp equipage.

No State shall engage in any war without the consent of the United States, in Congress assembled, unless such State be actually invaded by enemies, or shall have received certain advice of a resolution being formed by some nation of Indians to invade such State, and the danger is so imminent as not to admit of a delay till the United States, in Congress assembled, can be consulted; nor shall any State grant commissions to any ships or vessels of war, nor letters of marque or reprisal, except it be after a declaration of war by the United States, in Congress assembled, and then only against the kingdom or state, and the subjects thereof, against which war has been so declared, and under such regulations as shall be established by the United States, in Congress assembled, unless such State be infested by pirates, in which case vessels of war may be fitted out for that occasion, and kept so long as the danger shall continue, or until the United States, in Congress assembled, shall determine otherwise.

Article VII. — When land forces are raised by any State for the common defence, all officers of or under the rank of Colonel shall be appointed by the Legislature of each State respectively by whom such forces shall be raised, or in such manner as such State shall direct, and all vacancies shall be filled up by the State which first made the appointment.

Article VIII. — All charges of war, and all other expenses

that shall be incurred for the common defence, or general welfare, and allowed by the United States, in Congress assembled, shall be defrayed out of a common treasury, which shall be supplied by the several States in proportion to the value of all land within each State, granted to, or surveyed for, any person, as such land and the buildings and improvements thereon shall be estimated, according to such mode as the United States, in Congress assembled, shall, from time to time, direct and appoint. The taxes for paying that proportion shall be laid and levied by the authority and direction of the Legislatures of the several States, within the time agreed upon by the United States, in Congress assembled.

ARTICLE IX. – The United States, in Congress assembled, shall have the sole and exclusive right and power of determining on peace and war, except in the cases mentioned in the sixth Article; of sending and receiving ambassadors; entering into treaties and alliances, provided that no treaty of commerce shall be made, whereby the legislative power of the respective States shall be restrained from imposing such imposts and duties on foreigners as their own people are subjected to, or from prohibiting the exportation or importation of any species of goods or commodities whatever; of establishing rules for deciding, in all cases, what captures on land and water shall be legal, and in what manner prizes taken by land or naval forces in the service of the United States shall be divided or appropriated; of granting letters of marque and reprisal in times of peace; appointing courts for the trial of piracies and felonies committed on the high seas; and establishing courts for receiving and determining finally appeals in all cases of captures; provided that no member of Congress shall be appointed a judge of any of the said courts.

The United States, in Congress assembled, shall also be the last resort on appeal in all disputes and differences now subsisting, or that hereafter may arise between two or more States concerning boundary jurisdiction, or any other cause whatever; which authority shall always be exercised in the manner following: Whenever the legislative or executive authority, or lawful agent of any State in controversy with another, shall present a petition to Congress, stating the matter in question, and praying for a hearing, notice thereof shall be given by order of Congress to the legislative or executive authority of the other State in controversy, and a day assigned for the appearance of the parties by their lawful agents, who shall then be directed to appoint, by joint consent, commissioners or judges to constitute a court for hearing and determining the matter in question; but if they cannot agree, Congress shall name three persons out of each of the United States, and from the list of such persons each party shall alternately strike out one, the petitioners beginning, until the number shall be reduced to thirteen; and from that number not less than seven nor more than nine names, as Congress shall direct, shall, in the presence of Congress, be drawn out by lot; and the persons whose names shall be so drawn, or any five of them, shall be commissioners or judges, to hear and finally determine the controversy, so always as a major part of the judges who shall hear the cause shall agree in the determination; and if either party shall neglect to attend at the day appointed, without showing reasons which Congress shall judge sufficient, or being present, shall refuse to strike, the Congress shall proceed to nominate three persons out of each State, and the secretary of Congress shall strike in behalf of such party absent or refusing; and the judgment and sentence of the court, to be appointed in the manner before prescribed, shall be final and conclusive; and if any of the parties shall refuse to submit to the authority of such court, or to appear or defend their claim or cause, the court shall nevertheless proceed to pronounce sentence or judgment, which shall in like manner be final and decisive; the judgment or sentence and other proceedings being in either case transmitted to Congress, and lodged among the acts of Congress for the security of the parties concerned; provided, that every commissioner, before he sits in judgment, shall take an oath, to be administered by one of the judges of the supreme or superior court of the State where the cause shall be tried, "well and truly to hear and determine the matter in question, according to the best of his judgment, without favour, affection, or hope of reward." Provided, also, that no State shall be deprived of territory for the benefit of the United States.

All controversies concerning the private right of soil claimed under different grants of two or more States, whose jurisdictions, as they may respect such lands, and the States which passed such grants are adjusted, the said grants or either of them being at the same time claimed to have originated antecedent to such settlement of jurisdiction, shall, on the petition of either party to the Congress of the United States, be finally determined, as near as may be, in the same manner as is before prescribed for deciding disputes respecting territorial jurisdiction between different States.

The United States, in Congress assembled, shall also have the sole and exclusive right and power of regulating the alloy and value of coin struck by their own authority, or by that of the respective States; fixing the standard of weights and measures throughout the United States; regulating the trade and managing all affairs with the Indians, not members of any of the States; provided that the legislative right of any State, within its own limits, be not infringed or violated; establishing and regulating post-offices from one State to another, throughout all the United States, and exacting such postage on the papers passing through the same as may be requisite to defray the expenses of the said office; appointing all officers of the land forces in the service of the United States, excepting regimental officers; appointing all the officers of the naval forces, and commissioning all officers whatever in the service of the United States; making rules for the government and regulation of the said land and naval forces, and directing their operations.

The United States, in Congress assembled, shall have authority to appoint a committee, to sit in the recess of Congress, to be denominated "A Committee of the States," and to consist of one delegate from each State, and to appoint such other committees and civil officers as may be necessary for managing the general affairs of the United States under their direction; to appoint one of their number to preside; provided that no person be allowed to serve in the office of president more than one year in any term of three years; to ascertain the necessary sums of money to be raised for the service of the United States, and to appropriate and apply the same for defraying the public expenses; to borrow money or emit bills on the credit of the

United States, transmitting every half year to the respective States an account of the sums of money so borrowed or emitted; to build and equip a navy; to agree upon the number of land forces, and to make requisitions from each State for its quota, in proportion to the number of white inhabitants in such State, which requisition shall be binding; and thereupon the Legislature of each State shall appoint the regimental officers, raise the men, and clothe, arm, and equip them in a soldier-like manner, at the expense of the United States; and the officers and men so clothed, armed, and equipped shall march to the place appointed, and within the time agreed on by the United States, in Congress assembled; but if the United States, in Congress assembled, shall, on consideration of circumstances, judge proper that any State should not raise men, or should raise a smaller number than its quota, and that any other State should raise a greater number of men than the quota thereof, such extra number shall be raised, officered, clothed, armed, and equipped in the same manner as the quota of such State, unless the Legislature of such State shall judge that such extra number cannot be safely spared out of the same, in which case they shall raise, officer, clothe, arm, and equip as many of such extra number as they judge can be safely spared, and the officers and men so clothed, armed, and equipped shall march to the place appointed, and within the time agreed on by the United States, in Congress assembled.

The United States, in Congress assembled, shall never engage in a war, nor grant letters of marque and reprisal in time of peace, nor enter into any treaties or alliances, nor coin money, nor regulate the value thereof, nor ascertain the sums and expenses necessary for the defense and welfare of the United States, or any of them, nor emit bills, nor borrow money on the credit of the United States, nor appropriate money, nor agree upon the number of vessels of war to be built or purchased, or the number of land or sea forces to be raised, nor appoint a commander-in-chief of the army or navy, unless nine States assent to the same, nor shall a question on any other point, except for adjourning from day to day, be determined, unless by the votes of a majority of the United States, in Congress assembled.

The Congress of the United States shall have power to adjourn to any time within the year, and to any place within the United States, so that no period of adjournment be for a longer duration than the space of six months, and shall publish the journal of their proceedings monthly, except such parts thereof relating to treaties, alliances, or military operations as in their judgment require secrecy; and the yeas and nays of the delegates of each State, on any question, shall be entered on the journal when it is desired by any delegate; and the delegates of a State, or any of them, at his or their request, shall be furnished with a transcript of the said journal except such parts as are above excepted, to lay before the Legislatures of the several States.

ARTICLE X. – The Committee of the States, or any nine of them, shall be authorized to execute, in the recess of Congress, such of the powers of Congress as the United States, in Congress assembled, by the consent of nine States, shall, from time to time, think expedient to vest them with; provided that no power be delegated to the said Committee, for the exercise of which, by the Articles of Confederation, the voice of nine States in the Congress of the United States assembled is requisite.

ARTICLE XI. – Canada, acceding to this Confederation, and joining in the measures of the United States, shall be admitted into, and entitled to all the advantages of this Union; but no other colony shall be admitted into the same, unless such admission be agreed to by nine States.

ARTICLE XII. – All bills of credit emitted, moneys borrowed, and debts contracted by or under the authority of Congress, before the assembling of the United States, in pursuance of the present Confederation, shall be deemed and considered as a charge against the United States, for payment and satisfaction whereof the said United States and the public faith are hereby solemnly pledged.

ARTICLE XIII. – Every State shall abide by the determinations of the United States, in Congress assembled, on all questions which by this Confederation are submitted to them. And the Articles of this Confederation shall be inviolably observed by every State, and the Union shall be perpetual; nor shall any alteration at any time hereafter be made in any of them, unless such alteration be agreed to in a Congress of the United States, and be afterwards confirmed by the Legislatures of every State.

AND WHEREAS it hath pleased the great Governor of the world to incline the hearts of the Legislatures we respectively represent in Congress to approve of, and to authorize us to ratify, the said Articles of Confederation and perpetual Union, know ye, that we, the undersigned delegates, by virtue of the power and authority to us given for that purpose, do, by these presents, in the name and in behalf of our respective constituents, fully and entirely ratify and confirm each and every of the said Articles of Confederation and perpetual Union, and all and singular the matters and things therein contained. And we do further solemnly plight and engage the faith of our respective constituents, that they shall abide by the determinations of the United States, in Congress assembled, on all questions which by the said Confederation are submitted to them; and that the Articles thereof shall be inviolably observed by the States we respectively represent, and that the Union shall be perpetual.

> In Witness whereof we have hereunto set our hands in Congress. Done at Philadelphia in the State of Pennsylvania the ninth day of July in the year of our Lord one thousand seven hundred and seventy-eight, and in the third year of the independence of America.

(Then followed the signatures of the Delegates, by virtue of the power and authority given for the purpose, in the name and in behalf of their respective constituents.)

Note the great effort to bring the sovereign States into an effective and perpetual union; the many repetitions of the phrase "the United States, in Congress assembled." The intent was a federal Union, the style of the Confederacy to be, as Article 1 gives it, "The United States of America." With Article 2 comes the emphatic declaration that each State would retain "its sovereignty, freedom, and independence, and every power, jurisdiction, and right, which is not by this Confederation expressly delegated to the United States, in Congress assembled."

From the time of the assembling of the first Continental Congress in 1774 a genuine, though loose, union had existed between the thirteen colonies. By declaring their freedom, each had become an independent, sovereign state, surrendering a specific part of sovereignty to strengthen the whole, and for the sake of the common welfare. This we have seen was a fact, historically true, though many orators, from Webster to Lincoln, and many "historians" have made other claims, most of which were meant to be justifications for a cruel, needless, Civil War. Save for such functions facing *without*—better performed as a unit before the world—each State was sovereign over its own internal affairs, so much so that *that* was the prime reason the *Articles of Confederation* failed, necessitating the creation of a stronger bond than the "League of Friendship" made possible; and the result was the present United States Constitution.

To sketch the faults and shortcomings of the Articles in full would carry us needlessly beyond the scope of this work, but a resumé of some, it is thought, will better point up the gravity of the situation the new nation found itself in at the close of the war for independence and the imperative need for the new charter to stave off inevitable chaos.

The Continental Congress of the years 1774 to 1781 was one of the most remarkable bodies of a revolutionary kind that was ever known to history; only the Long Parliament possibly was to be compared to it. Assembled at the beginning to meet what was thought to be a temporary emergency, it continued for seven years before its powers were ever clearly defined, while it performed sovereign functions, declared the colonies to be each free and independent, contracted an alliance with France, raised and organized a Continental army, built a navy, granted letters of marque and reprisal, borrowed large sums of money, pledging to the lenders the national credit for their repayment, issued inconvertible paper money, and performed much else, all upon the authority of the general acquiescence in the purposes for which it acted. While in the very nature of the Articles later defining the purposes, its functions were to be but inefficiently, even wretchedly, performed; for eight more years this Congress staggered along getting weaker and weaker, until a more efficient instrument of government replaced the *Articles.*

Under the *Articles,* the freemen of each State were entitled to all the privileges and immunities of freemen in all the other States, with mutual extradition of criminals and fugitives; and in each, full faith and credit were to be given the records, acts, and judicial proceedings of every other State, and this universal intercitizenship gave reality to the feeble new "Union." In all the common relations of life a New Englander could deal with a Virginian on an equal footing before the law.

But here the cohesive provisions came to an end, and by the language of the rest of the *Articles,* the whole sovereignty of the States was reconciled with the fact of their being now merged to some extent in the larger political body. The delegates were paid by their States; each State had one vote regardless of population; important measures could only be carried by consent of at least nine states.

Between such a Congress and the government of the States, sovereignty was so shared that a maximum effort was required to produce even a minimum of result. While some essential attributes of sovereignty were withheld the States, the Congress was without power to enforce its own enactments. There was no President, no Supreme Court; the executive departments of war and finance were at first entrusted to committees. The Congress itself had a president, and representing as he did the dignity of the United States of America, he was like a modern president in a sense, but his powers were only those of any other delegate. Some fourteen of these "presidents" were in office between 1774 and 1789, of whom perhaps Randolph, Hancock, Laurens are best known in that capacity; Jay, St. Clair, Mifflin, Lee are remembered for other things, while Boudinot, Hanson, Griffin, are unknown to any but research students of American history.

As will be readily seen in an examination of the *Articles,* they failed to create a federal government endowed with sufficient sovereign powers to be able to look without, or within, effectively;

or to give confidence to foreign nations of the family of civilized nations, to secure us respect or standing. A change was imperative.

Money to run the government had to come from the several States, each of whom had their own debts, and some had made application to foreign countries for loans; there was no surplus to be found for the use of Congress. The public credit sank at home and abroad; neither an end nor a remedy appeared in sight. While British redcoats were still in New York, the disbanding of the Continental army, still unpaid, was proposed, so fearful was Congress of what these men might do on provocation. It was here that there occurred an incident little known to Americans, and perhaps best described in John Fiske's *Critical Period,* published in 1888, and which I sketch here.

Peace had been officially made, and Hamilton, with Livingston, urged that the army be held intact until the evacuation of the western frontier posts in addition to New York. But Congress could not pay the troopers and was in fear of them. Not only the soldiers, but officers too were gravely discontented. Washington had urged some fair compensation measures upon Congress for his men, but the collapse of paper money, along with the military disasters at Camden, and Charleston, and Benedict Arnold's treason, brought a general depression in which it came to be widespread thought the army would lose whatever its chief had already procured for them. The States too under Samuel Adams's opposition, were hostile to "half-pay" promises; popular clamor was against it; and the army felt it was being betrayed after its great efforts to win freedom for the country.

It all came from "republican" government; "too many cooks" were stirring the pot; a dozen heads were worse than no head at all, there being no one to be trusted; but a monarchy with a good King whom all knew and all could trust . . . ah, here was a solution which could salve the injuries and solve the problems. It is not necessary to give the names of the Continental officers who were involved, all are not known, and those who are were all able, brave and faithful men who had served the new country superbly and now faced a bleak future not unlike that of the plundering bands of ex-soldiers who wandered over Europe, banding together in desperate, robbing groups, terrorizing the countryside. Was that to be the sequel of seven long years of sacrifice, toil, and death? A letter was written to Washington setting forth the sorry story, asking him to come forward, be the savior of the society, and accept the crown at the hands of his trusting troopers. It was one of those great moments, too often afterwards hidden from the pen of history. Washington at once declined, telling his urgers that they could not have found a man to whom such a plan would have been more odious than to himself. Knowing the feelings of the country towards the army, however, Washington kept the matter confidential, lest it becoming known, the incident would enhance the distrust felt by the States. This was in 1782. The outcry against the "half-pay" ideas grew, and the men and officers continued to brood over the wrongs done them. One general asserted that "the army was verging to that state which we are told will make a wise man mad." Whispers of other public creditors were to the point that "if the army did but take a firm stand the States would be prevailed upon to a grant of funds to Congress to liquidate all the public debts, the troopers' included." Prominent public men felt the same, among them Robert Morris, Gouverneur Morris and General Greene. The latter's discreet letter to the South Carolina legislature brought an enraged reply to the effect that they would stand for "no dictation by any Cromwell." It was an eye-opener, at least to Nathanael Greene, of the dangers of the slightest appearance of military intervention in the civil affairs of the States. Right after this came almost open mutiny among the troops stationed at Newburgh, New York. An inflammatory, anonymous appeal was made to the soldiers.

"My friends, after seven long years your suffering and courage has conducted the USA through a doubtful and bloody war; and the peace returns to bless—whom? A country willing to redress your wrongs, cherish your worth, and reward your services? Or is it rather a country that tramples upon your rights, disdains your cries, and insults your distresses? If such be your treatment while the swords you wear are necessary for the defence of America, what have you to expect when those very swords, the instruments and companions of your glory, shall be taken from your sides, and no mark of military distinction left but your wants, infirmities, and scars? If you have sense enough to discover, and spirit enough to oppose tyranny, whatever garb it may assume, *awake* to your situation. If the present moment be lost, your threats hereafter will be as empty as your entreaties now. Appeal from the justice to the fears of government, and suspect the man who would advise to more moderation and longer forbearance."

This last sentence was aimed at George Washington; he rose to the occasion, the next day promulgating an official military order, noting the Manifesto, and setting the meeting called for at a later day, with Gates, the senior army general, present to preside at it. Now, Gates may have been at the bottom of the scheme; at any rate, Washington had called his hand. That order could not be disregarded, and, at the meeting, Washington appeared and spoke with great feeling in a desire to "arrest the feet that stood wavering on a precipice." He was mindful of their sufferings and claims, but reminded them also of the terrific difficulties Congress labored under, and of the folly of putting themselves in wrong; "forbearance was still the greatest of victories." He had himself refused all pay, while enduring more than any other before him in that room. His hearers listened in shamed and uneasy silence, and there shortly came a mighty revulsion of feelings, as he read to them a letter from a member of the Congress indicative of its good faith. He then left them to deliberate, and the outcome was a motion to report their "unshaken confidence in the Congress," adding that they "viewed with abhorrence and rejected with disdain the infamous proposals of a late anonymous suggestion addressed to the American army." Gates as chairman now could only put the question and report it unanimously carried. Out of it came two things, the 6% discharge certificates, and the formation of one of the most exclusive societies of men in the world, and today probably the oldest still in existence, the Society of the Cincinnati, with Washington its first President-General.

Appendix B

THE CONSTITUTIONS OF THE UNITED STATES OF AMERICA AND THE CONFEDERATE STATES OF AMERICA

Before examining the two Constitutions which follow, it may perhaps be of help or guidance to note just what the "South" consisted of in American history, as well as to define the "North." Two English attempts at settlements upon the seacoasts of North America were made in 1607. One, an expedition to the Kennebec River in what is now the state of Maine, failed. The other, to the James River in Virginia, after much suffering and travail, succeeded. A successful permanent colonization North did not emerge until 1620 at Plymouth. We see that all the *Mayflower* claims, great and noble as they doubtless are, must take second place to the Virginian settlement. Here was the first genuine and permanent English settlement in America. This "South" came to include what is now Maryland, Delaware, Virginia, and south to the present Georgia, later including also Florida, the far western wildernesses of North and South Carolina, and claims which became the states of Alabama and Mississippi (once called the "Southwest Territories"). Virginia then extended to the Father of Waters, the Mississippi River, and included what is now the States of West Virginia, Kentucky, Ohio, Indiana, Illinois, Michigan, Wisconsin, and a part of Minnesota. It was the largest by far of all the thirteen colonies, and by 1776, with Massachusetts, the most important of them.

Charles II, in 1663, cut off the southern sections of Virginia and formed a new province of Carolina, which extended also westward to the Mississippi. (The Western part of North Carolina became Tennessee.) Florida belonged to Spain by the

Treaty of Versailles, 1783. It was ceded to the United States in 1819, as a territory, receiving its State Constitution in 1833, and was admitted as a state in 1845.

From the great Louisiana Purchase, made by Thomas Jefferson, many more States were carved, the Southern ones being Arkansas and Louisiana; later came Texas; and still later Oklahoma, which was first known as the Indian Territory. Properly, Arizona, New Mexico, and the southern part of California would be "Southern" States; and at the hour of the Civil War, Missouri, too, was included. In the war, Maryland, Delaware, Kentucky, and Missouri were described as "border States." West Virginia, not wholly sympathetic with the Southern cause, was allowed, unconstitutionally, to be torn from her mother State in 1863, in violation of Article 4, Section 3.

In an early day, however, the "South" was Virginia, North and South Carolina, and Georgia; together with their western sections extending to the Mississippi River . . . the southern "zones." Spain held south, France west, of them.

The "North," or "northern zones" were Massachusetts (which included Maine), New Hampshire, Rhode Island, Connecticut. The Dutch, between 1614 and 1621, founded New Netherlands (New York State), then consisting of the lands between the Hudson and Delaware rivers. The Swedes colonized what is now the northern part of Delaware in 1638, only to lose it to the Dutch in 1655. In 1664 the British succeeded to the Dutch possessions, and the King, Charles II, gave the province to his brother, the Duke of York, who, in turn, granted portions to his friends Carteret and Berkley, thus marking off what became New Jersey. The year 1681 saw Quaker William Penn given the region west of the present state of New Jersey, with what is now Delaware. In this way, the present States of New York, New Jersey, Pennsylvania, Maryland, Delaware came to constitute the "Middle zones." A "plantation" in those days meant a "settlement"; there were Northern plantations as well as Southern ones.

While somewhat apart from this study, the student would

do well and profit by including in his reading, John Fiske's *Civil Government in the United States*: the chapters describing colonial governments, the State and federal governments, and the origins of the Union, with some "words about politics."

Turning to the two Constitutions, we shall note immediately the improvements made by the United States Constitution upon the *Articles*; and then the improvements by the Confederacy's Constitution upon the United States one. The latter is readily seen in comparisons of them shown in the parallel columns. Shortly, and speaking in general, slavery was caused by the inevitable results of "climăte." Except for the insane, unending, insulting, agitations of the Abolitionists there should never, under the United States Constitution, have been brought on a fraternal war. The institution of slavery, so called, would have been eradicated in a satisfactory manner by lawful, gradual means, and probably with a return to Africa of a majority of the blacks. Some of the slave States' laws required it upon manumission. Poet Lowell, with no knowledge of slavery himself, would yet advise, as in his *Stanzas on Freedom* (such drummers-up of hate and half truths, and they were legion in that curious day, played no small part in grave responsibility for a needless war):

> They are slaves who fear to speak,
> For the fallen and the weak.
> They are slaves who will not choose
> Hatred, scoffing, and abuse.

So ready, on half-knowledge, to condemn, but unwilling to share in the results of what he so glibly advocated, he would pour forth the "Anti-Texas," "Captured Fugitives," "Present Crisis," etc., to stir to fury the brew of the witches' cauldron. The unscrupulous, venomous, insulting nature of the anti-slavery propaganda carried on North finally led to a break in the Democratic Party ranks, allowing induction to political office of a new party, and the election of a president whom the majority of the American voters did not want. That president, unfortunately for his country, determined to maintain and perpetuate his hold upon the electorate and the office; and by violation of his oath, and a raw seizure of dictatorial powers, forced a civil strife upon the country lasting four direful years, and ended in his own assassination, destruction of a highly prosperous half of the land, with precipitation of an ugly race problem upon the Southern people. Today, all is "justified" in slanted, distorted, often wholly false "history" and in countless works eulogizing Lincoln as a martyr and a saint, at the same time vilifying a great section of America whose only great "crime" was an insistence upon the observation of the United States Constitution as the bond of the Union.

In the study of the two instruments of the basic American law which follow, sight should not be lost of another basic fact. It is that the Constitution is *not* what the president, *not* what the Congress, *not* what the Supreme Court, say it is, but what *the people*—the people in three-fourths of the States voting thereon by the methods provided in Article 5 of the Constitution itself—*say it is*. The student should study Article 5, noting the wording "shall be *valid*" and "oaths of office," finally considering the Fourteenth Amendment and its "ratification." What has sometimes been called the "elastic" clause of the Constitution, the last paragraph of Article 1, section 8—"to make all laws which shall be necessary and proper for carrying into execution the foregoing powers, and all other powers vested by this Constitution in the government of the United States, or in any department or officer thereof"—has, from time to time, undergone considerable "stretching" for one purpose or another; the disagreement in interpretation of this clause divided our people, after 1789, into two great political parties.

The patriotic men who framed the Constitution did not intend it to be as democratic as it has since been made. Some of them felt too much democracy might lead to mob rule, and hostility to unlimited democracy was every bit as great as opposition to unlimited monarchy. What they had tried to invent was a system that would not give too much power to any one man, to any one assembly, to any one class, or to any one region.

Certainly, the federal government was not to have absolute authority over the States, nor were the States to be absolutely independent. Each federal branch—President, Congress, the judiciary—was to be more or less independent of the others, and its powers were carefully defined . . . a separation of powers. Each branch was to be checked and balanced by the others, making the new government undemocratic at the start; the "checks and balances" system was designed to check the will of the common people as well as to safeguard against autocracy. We note the Senate was elected by State legislatures themselves undemocratic since only the wealthier citizens were eligible, as a rule, to the State legislatures. Only about half of the white men, and none of the Negro slaves were entitled to vote for members of the House of Representatives, each State decided on the qualifications of its own voters. All the early leaders were men aristocratic in spirit; they distrusted the common people. The first president, great man that he was, was essentially an aristocrat. Adams, the next President, had fears of an unlimited democracy, and had quite frankly admitted to "a fondness for the natural aristocracy of wealth, birth, and education."

It was not until Thomas Jefferson's times that a democratic spirit began more and more to assert itself. The third President, from 1801 to 1809, he believed that the only true aristocracy was one of virtue and ability and that the best way to select men of these exceptional traits was by democratic elections, with more people given the right to vote. Negro slavery he considered wrong; the Constitution should be revised every nineteen years, so that each generation might have the right to choose its own form of government, for "the Earth belonged to the living, who ought not to be forced to obey the laws of the dead." While his ideas, to any very great extent, were not carried out, his theories slowly gained momentum, and he was the father of America's greatest political party, once called, strangely enough, Republican, ultimately emerging as the Democratic Party. We shall come upon more Jeffersonian theory later.

In the following pages, note the variations (they are not too many) of the Confederate from the United States Constitution, and ask yourself *why* they were made.

Under the provisional Confederate government the South lost no time in framing and adopting the Constitution of the Confederate States of America. It was, as indicated before, modeled closely on the United States Constitution, even to vocabulary and sentence structure. In fact, it so closely reproduces the provisions of the original that every change in wording, every omission, every addition, is significant and can be explained in terms of the southern framers' efforts to make more explicit the provisions and spirit of the original that they were determined to preserve and faithfully to observe in their new nation.

Omission of words or phrases *within paragraphs* are not indicated here; but all changes of wording and all additional words, phrases, and sentences in the Confederate Constitution (in the right-hand columns below) have been printed *in italics* to facilitate quick identification of those changes.

*The Constitution of the United States of America**	*The Constitution of the Confederate States of America*
WE the People of the United States, in order to form a more perfect Union, establish Justice, insure domestic Tranquility, provide for the common defence, promote the general Welfare, and secure the Blessings of Liberty to ourselves and our Posterity, do ordain and establish this CONSTITUTION for the United States of America.	WE, the People of *the Confederate States, each State acting in its sovereign and independent character,* in order to form *a permanent Federal Government,* establish justice, insure domestic tranquility, and secure the blessings of liberty to ourselves and our posterity—*invoking the favor and guidance of Almighty God*—do ordain and establish this CONSTITUTION for the *Confederate* States of America.

* This is an exact reprint of the original in punctuation, spelling, capitals, etc.

ARTICLE I

SECTION 1. All legislative Powers herein granted shall be vested in a Congress of the United States, which shall consist of a Senate and House of Representatives.

SECTION 1. All legislative powers herein *delegated* shall be vested in a Congress of *the Confederate States,* which shall consist of a Senate and House of Representatives.

SECTION 2. The House of Representatives shall be composed of Members chosen every second Year by the People of the several States, and the Electors in each State shall have the Qualifications requisite for Electors of the most numerous Branch of the State Legislature.

SECTION 2. The House of Representatives shall be composed of members chosen every second year by the people of the several States; and the electors in each State shall *be citizens of the Confederate States, and* have the qualifications requisite for electors of the most numerous branch of the State Legislature; *but no person of foreign birth, not a citizen of the Confederate States, shall be allowed to vote for any officer, civil or political, State or Federal.*

No Person shall be a Representative who shall not have attained to the Age of twenty-five Years, and been seven Years a Citizen of the United States, and who shall not, when elected, be an Inhabitant of that State in which he shall be chosen.

No person shall be a Representative who shall not have attained the age of twenty-five years, and *be a citizen of the Confederate States,* and who shall not, when elected, be an inhabitant of that State in which he shall be chosen.

Representatives and direct Taxes shall be apportioned among the several States which may be included within this Union, according to their respective Number,* which shall

Representatives and direct taxes shall be apportioned among the several States, which may be included within this *Confederacy,* according to their respective numbers, which shall

* Under the census of 1860 one representative is allowed for every 127,381 persons.

be determined by adding to the whole Number of free Persons, including those bound to Service for a term of Years, and excluding Indians not taxed, three-fifths of all other Persons.† The actual Enumeration shall be made within three Years after the first meeting of the Congress of the United States, and within every subsequent Term of ten Years, in such Manner as they shall by Law direct. The Number of Representatives shall not exceed one for every thirty Thousand, but each State shall have at Least one Representative; and until such enumeration shall be made, the State of New Hampshire shall be entitled to chuse three, Massachusetts eight, Rhode-Island and Providence Plantations one, Connecticut five, New York six, New Jersey four, Pennsylvania eight, Deleware one, Maryland six, Virginia ten, North Carolina five, South Carolina five, and Georgia three.

When vacancies happen in the Representation from any State, the Executive Authority thereof shall issue Writs of Election to fill such Vacancies.

be determined by adding to the whole number of free persons, including those bound to service for a term of years, and excluding Indians not taxed, three fifths of all *slaves.* The actual enumeration shall be made within three years after the first meeting of the Congress of *the Confederate States,* and within every subsequent term of ten years, in such manner as they shall by law direct. The number of Representatives shall not exceed one for every *fifty thousand,* but each State shall have at least one Representative; and until such enumeration shall be made, *the State of South Carolina shall be entitled to choose six, the State of Georgia ten, the State of Alabama nine, the State of Florida two, the State of Mississippi seven, the State of Louisiana six, and the State of Texas six.*‡

When vacancies happen in the representation from any State, the Executive authority thereof shall issue writs of election to fill such vacancies.

† "Other persons" refer to slaves. See Amendments, Article XIV, Sections 1 and 2.

‡ Other states, Virginia, Arkansas, North Carolina, and Tennessee, joined the Confederacy *after* the day the Constitution was adopted—March 11, 1861.

The House of Representatives shall chuse their Speaker and other officers;* and shall have the sole Power of Impeachment.	The House of Representatives shall choose their Speaker and other officers; and shall have the sole power of impeachment, *except that any judicial or other Federal officer, resident and acting solely within the limits of any State, may be impeached by a vote of two thirds of both branches of the Legislature thereof.*
SECTION 3. The Senate of the United States shall be composed of two Senators from each State, chosen by the Legislature thereof, for six Years; and each Senator shall have one Vote.	SECTION 3. The Senate of *the Confederate States* shall be composed of two Senators from each State, chosen for six years by the Legislature thereof, *at the regular session next immediately preceding the commencement of the term of service;* and each Senator shall have one vote.
Immediately after they shall be assembled in Consequence of the first Election, they shall be divided as equally as may be into three Classes. The Seats of the Senators of the first Class shall be vacated at the Expiration of the second Year, of the second Class at the Expiration of the fourth Year, and of the third class at the Expiration of the sixth Year, so that one-third may be chosen every second year; and if Vacancies happen by Resignation, or otherwise, during the Recess of the Legis-	Immediately after they shall be assembled, in consequence of the first election, they shall be divided as equally as may be into three classes. The seats of the Senators of the first class shall be vacated at the expiration of the second year; of the second class at the expiration of the fourth year; and of the third class at the expiration of the sixth year; so that one third may be chosen every second year; and if vacancies happen by resignation or otherwise, during the recess of the Legislature

* The principal of these are clerk, sergeant-at-arms, doorkeeper, and postmaster.

lature of any State, the Executive thereof may make temporary Appointments until the next Meeting of the Legislature which shall then fill such Vacancies.

of any State, the Executive thereof may make temporary appointments until the next meeting of the Legislature, which shall then fill such vacancies.

No person shall be a Senator who shall not have attained to the Age of thirty Years, and been nine Years a Citizen of the United States, and who shall not when elected, be an Inhabitant of that State for which he shall be chosen.

No person shall be a Senator who shall not have attained the age of thirty years, and *be a citizen of the Confederate States;* and who shall not, when elected, be an inhabitant of the State for which he shall be chosen.

The Vice President of the United States shall be President of the Senate, but shall have no vote, unless they be equally divided.

The Vice-President of *the Confederate States* shall be President of the Senate, but shall have no vote unless they be equally divided.

The Senate shall chuse their other Officers, and also a President pro tempore, in the absence of the Vice President, or when he shall exercise the Office of President of the United States.

The Senate shall choose their other officers; and also a President *pro tempore* in the absence of the Vice-President, or when he shall exercise the office of President of *the Confederate States.*

The Senate shall have the sole Power to try all Impeachments. When sitting for that Purpose, they shall be on Oath or Affirmation. When the President of the United States is tried, the Chief Justice shall preside: And no Person shall be convicted without the Concurrence of two-thirds of the Members present.

The Senate shall have the sole power to try all impeachments. When sitting for that purpose, they shall be on oath or affirmation. When the President of *the Confederate States* is tried, the Chief-Justice shall preside; and no person shall be convicted without the concurrence of two thirds of the members present.

Judgment in Cases of Impeachment shall not extend further than to removal from

Judgment in cases of impeachment shall not extend further than to removal from

Office, and Disqualification to hold and enjoy an Office of Honour, Trust or Profit under the United States: but the Party convicted shall nevertheless be liable and subject to Indictment, Trial, Judgment and Punishment, according to Law.

SECTION 4. The Times, Places and Manner of holding Elections for Senators and Representatives, shall be prescribed in each State by the Legislature thereof: but the Congress may at any time by Law make or alter such Regulations, except as to the places of chusing Senators.

The Congress shall assemble at least once in every Year, and such Meeting shall be on the first Monday in December, unless they shall by Law appoint a different Day.

SECTION 5. Each House shall be the Judge of the Elections, Returns and Qualifications of its own Members, and a Majority of each shall constitute a Quorum to do Business; but a smaller Number may adjourn from day to day, and may be authorized to compel the Attendance of absent Members, in such Manner, and under such Penalties as each House may provide.

Each House may determine

office, and disqualification to hold and enjoy any office of honor, trust, or profit, under *the Confederate States;* but the party convicted shall, nevertheless, be liable and subject to indictment, trial, judgment, and punishment according to law.

SECTION 4. The times, place, and manner of holding elections for Senators and Representatives, shall be prescribed in each State by the Legislature thereof, *subject to the provisions of this Constitution;* but the Congress may, at any time, by law, make or alter such regulations, except as to the *times and* places of choosing Senators.

The Congress shall assemble at least once in every year; and such meeting shall be on the first Monday in December, unless they shall, by law, appoint a different day.

SECTION 5. Each House shall be the judge of the elections, returns, and qualifications of its own members, and a majority of each shall constitute a quorum to do business; but a smaller number may adjourn from day to day, and may be authorized to compel the attendance of absent members, in such manner and under such penalties as each house may provide.

Each House may determine

the Rules of its Proceedings, punish its Members for disorderly Behaviour, and, with the Concurrence of two-thirds, expel a Member.

Each House shall keep a Journal of its Proceedings, and from time to time publish the same, excepting such Parts as may in their Judgment require Secrecy; and the Yeas and Nays of the Members of either House on any question shall, at the Desire of one-fifth of those present, be entered on the Journal.

Neither House, during the Session of Congress, shall, without the Consent of the other, adjourn for more than three days, nor to any other Place than that in which the two Houses shall be sitting.

SECTION 6. The Senators and Representatives shall receive a Compensation for their Services, to be ascertained by Law, and paid out of the Treasury of the United States. They shall in all Cases, except Treason, Felony and Breach of the Peace, be privileged from Arrest during their Attendance at the Session of their respective Houses, and in going to and returning from the same, and for any Speech or Debate in either House, they shall not be questioned in any other Place.

the rules of its proceedings, punish its members for disorderly behavior, and, with the concurrence of two thirds *of the whole number,* expel a member.

Each House shall keep a journal of its proceedings, and from time to time publish the same, excepting such parts as may in their judgment require secrecy; and the yeas and nays of the members of either House, on any question, shall, at the desire of one fifth of those present, be entered on the journal.

Neither House, during the session of Congress, shall, without the consent of the other, adjourn for more than three days, nor to any other place than that in which the two Houses shall be sitting.

SECTION 6. The Senators and Representatives shall receive a compensation for their services, to be ascertained by law, and paid out of the Treasury of *the Confederate States.* They shall, in all cases, except treason, felony, and breach of the peace, be privileged from arrest during their attendance at the session of their respective Houses, and in going to and returning from the same; and for any speech or debate in either House, they shall not be questioned in any other place.

No Senator or Representative shall, during the time for which he was elected, be appointed to any civil Office under the Authority of the United States, which shall have been created, or the Emoluments whereof shall have been increased during such time; and no Person holding any Office under the United States, shall be a Member of either House during his Continuance in Office.

No Senator or Representative shall, during the time for which he was elected, be appointed to any civil office under the authority of *the Confederate States,* which shall have been created, or the emoluments whereof shall have been increased during such time; and no person holding any office under *the Confederate States* shall be a member of either House during his continuance in office. *But Congress may, by law, grant to the principal officer in each of the executive departments a seat upon the floor of either House, with the privilege of discussing any measures appertaining to his department.*

SECTION 7. All Bills for raising Revenue shall originate in the House of Representatives; but the Senate may propose or concur with Amendments as on other Bills.

Every Bill which shall have passed the House of Representatives and the Senate, shall, before it become a Law, be presented to the President of the United States; If he approve he shall sign it, but if not he shall return it, with his Objections to that House in which it shall have originated, who shall enter the Objections at large on their Journal, and

SECTION 7. All bills for raising the revenue shall originate in the House of Representatives; but the Senate may propose or concur with amendments, as on other bills.

Every bill which shall have passed *both Houses,* shall, before it becomes a law, be presented to the President of *the Confederate States;* if he approve, he shall sign it; but if not, he shall return it, with his objections, to that House in which it shall have originated, who shall enter the objections at large on their journal, and proceed to reconsider it. If, after such recon-

proceed to reconsider it. If after such Reconsideration two-thirds of that House shall agree to pass the Bill, it shall be sent, together with the Objections, to the other House, by which it shall likewise be reconsidered, and if approved by two-thirds of that House, it shall become a Law. But in all such Cases the Votes of Both Houses shall be determined by Yeas and Neys, and the Names of the Persons voting for and against the Bill shall be entered on the Journal of each House respectively. If any Bill shall not be returned by the President within ten Days (Sundays excepted) after it shall have been presented to him, the Same shall be a law, in like Manner as if he had signed it, unless the Congress by their Adjournment prevent its Return, in which Case it shall not be a Law.

sideration, two thirds of that House shall agree to pass the bill, it shall be sent, together with the objections, to the other House, by which it shall likewise be reconsidered, and, if approved by two thirds of that House, it shall become a law. But, in all such cases, the votes of both Houses shall be determined by yeas and neys, and the names of the persons voting for and against the bill shall be entered on the journal of each House, respectively. If any bill shall not be returned by the President within ten days (Sundays excepted) after it shall have been presented to him, the same shall be a law, in like manner as if he had signed it, unless the Congress, by their adjournment, prevent its return; in which case it shall not be a law. *The President may approve any appropriation and disapprove any other appropriation in the same bill. In such case he shall, in signing the bill, designate the appropriations disapproved; and shall return a copy of such appropriations, with his objections, to the House in which the bill shall have originated; and the same proceedings shall then be had as in case of other bills disapproved by the President.*

Every Order, Resolution, or Vote, to which the Concurrence

Every order, resolution, or vote, to which the concurrence

of the Senate and House of Representatives may be necessary (except on a question of Adjournment) shall be presented to the President of the United States; and before the Same shall take Effect, shall be approved by him, or being disapproved by him, shall be repassed by two-thirds of the Senate and House of Representatives, according to the Rules and Limitations prescribed in the Case of a Bill.

of *both Houses* may be necessary (except on a question of adjournment), shall be presented to the President of *the Confederate States;* and, before the same shall take effect, shall be approved by him; or, being disapproved, shall be repassed by two thirds of *both Houses,* according to the rules and limitations prescribed in the case of a bill.

SECTION 8. The Congress shall have Power

To lay and collect Taxes, Duties, Imposts and Excises, to pay the Debts and provide for the common Defence and general Welfare of the United States; but all Duties, Imposts and Excise shall be uniform throughout the United States;

To borrow Money on the credit of the United States;

To regulate Commerce with foreign Nations, and among the several States, and with the Indian Tribes;

SECTION 8. The Congress shall have power—

To lay and collect taxes, duties, imposts, and excises, *for revenue necessary* to pay the debts, provide for the common defense, *and carry on the Government of the Confederate States; but no bounties shall be granted from the Treasury; nor shall any duties or taxes on importations from foreign nations be laid to promote or foster any branch of industry; and* all duties, imposts, and excises shall be uniform throughout *the Confederate States:*

To borrow money on the credit of *the Confederate States:*

To regulate commerce with foreign nations, and among the several States, and with the Indian tribes; *but neither this, nor any other clause contained in the Constitution, shall ever be construed to delegate the power to Congress to appropriate money for any internal improvement intended to facilitate commerce; except for the purpose of furnishing lights, beacons, and buoys, and other aid to navigation upon the coasts, and the improvement of harbors and the removing of obstructions in river navigation, in all which cases, such duties shall be laid on the navigation facilitated thereby, as may be necessary to pay the costs and expenses thereof:*

To establish an uniform Rule of Naturalization, and uniform Laws on the subject of Bankruptcies throughout the United States;

To establish *uniform laws* of naturalization, and uniform laws on the subject of bankruptcies, throughout *the Confederate States; but no law of Congress shall discharge any debt contracted before the passage of the same:*

To coin Money, regulate the Value thereof, and of foreign Coin, and fix the Standard of Weights and Measures;

To coin money, regulate the value thereof, and of foreign coin, and fix the standard of weights and measures:

To provide for the Punishment of counterfeiting the Securities and current Coin of the United States;

To provide for the punishment of counterfeiting the securities and current coin of *the Confederate States:*

To establish Post Offices and post Roads;

To establish post-offices and post *routes; but the expenses of the Post-Office Department, after the first day of March, in the year of our Lord eighteen hundred and sixty-three, shall be paid out of its own revenue:*

To promote the progress of Science and useful Arts, by securing for limited Times to Authors and Inventors the exclusive Right to their respective Writings and Discoveries;

To constitute Tribunals inferior to the supreme Court;

To define and punish Piracies and Felonies committed on the high Seas, and Offences against the Law of Nations;

To declare War, grant Letters of Marque and Reprisal, and make Rules concerning Captures on Land and Water;

To raise and support Armies, but no Appropriation of Money to that Use shall be for a longer Term than two Years;

To provide and maintain a Navy;

To make Rules for the Government and Regulation of the land and naval Forces;

To provide for calling forth the Militia to execute the Laws of the Union, suppress Insurrections and repel Invasions;

To provide for organizing, arming, and disciplining, the Militia, and for governing such Part of them as may be employed in the Service of the United States, reserving to the States respectively, the Appointment of the Officers, and the Authority of training the Militia

To promote the progress of science and useful arts, by securing for limited times to authors and inventors the exclusive right to their respective writings and discoveries:

To constitute tribunals inferior to the Supreme Court:

To define and punish piracies and felonies committed on the high-seas, and offenses against the law of nations:

To declare war, grant letters of marque and reprisal, and make rules concerning captures on land and on water:

To raise and support armies, but no appropriation of money to that use shall be for a longer term than two years:

To provide and maintain a navy:

To make rules for the government and regulation of the land and naval forces:

To provide for calling forth the militia to execute the laws of *the Confederate States,* suppress insurrections, and repel invasions:

To provide for organizing, arming, and disciplining the militia, and for governing such part of them as may be employed by *the Confederate States* reserving to the States, respectively, the appointment of the officers and the authority of training the militia according to according to the Discipline prescribed by Congress;

To exercise exclusive Legislation in all Cases whatsoever, over such District (not exceeding ten Miles square) as may, by Cession of particular States, and the Acceptance of Congress, become the Seat of the Government of the United States, and to exercise like Authority over all Places purchased by the Consent of the Legislature of the State in which the Same shall be, for the Erection of Forts, Magazines, Arsenals, Dock-Yards, and other needful Buildings;—And

To make all Laws which shall be necessary and proper for carrying into Execution the foregoing Powers, and all other Powers vested by this Constitution in the Government of the United States, or in any Department or Officer thereof.

SECTION 9. The Migration or Importation of such Persons as any of the States now existing shall think proper to admit, shall not be prohibited by the Congress prior to the Year one thousand eight hundred and eight, but a Tax or Duty may be imposed on such Importation, not exceeding ten dollars for each Person.

the discipline prescribed by Congress;

To exercise exclusive legislation in all cases whatsoever, over such district (not exceeding ten miles square) as may, by cession of *one or more* States, and the acceptance of Congress, become the seat of the Government of *the Confederate States,* and to exercise like authority over all places purchased by the consent of the Legislature of the State in which the same shall be, for the erection of forts, magazines, arsenals, dock-yards, and other needful buildings; and

To make all laws which shall be necessary and proper for carrying into execution the foregoing powers, and all other powers vested by this Constitution in the Government of *the Confederate States,* or in any department or officer thereof.

SECTION 9. The importation of *negroes of the African race, from any foreign country other than the slave-holding States or Territories of the United States of America, is hereby forbidden; and Congress is required to pass such laws as shall effectually prevent the same.*

Congress shall also have power to prohibit the introduction of slaves from any State not a

The Privilege of the Writ of Habeas Corpus shall not be suspended, unless when in Cases of Rebellion or invasion the public Safety may require it.

No Bill of Attainer or ex post facto Law shall be passed.

No Capitation, or other direct, Tax shall be laid, unless in Proportion to the Census or Enumeration herein before directed to be taken.

No Tax or Duty shall be laid on Articles exported from any State.

No Preference shall be given by any Regulation of Commerce or Revenue to the Ports of one State over those of another; nor shall Vessels bound to, or from, one State, be obliged to enter, clear, or pay Duties in another.

No Money shall be drawn from the Treasury, but in Consequence of Appropriations made by Law; and a regular Statement and Account of the Receipts and Expenditures of all public Money shall be published from time to time.

member of, or Territory not belonging to, this Confederacy.

The privilege of the writ of habeas corpus shall not be suspended, unless when, in case of rebellion or invasion, the public safety may require it.

No bill of attainer, ex post facto law, *or law denying or impairing the right of property in negro slaves* shall be passed.

No capitation or other direct tax shall be laid, unless in proportion to the census or enumeration hereinbefore directed to be taken.

No tax or duty shall be laid on articles exported from any State *except by a vote of two thirds of both Houses.*

No preference shall be given by any regulation of commerce or revenue to the ports of one State over those of another.

No money shall be drawn from the Treasury, but in consequence of appropriations made by law; and a regular statement and account of the receipts and expenditures of all public money shall be published from time to time.

Congress shall appropriate no money from the Treasury, except by a vote of two thirds of both Houses, taken by yeas and nays, unless it be asked and estimated for by some one of the heads of departments, and submitted to Congress by the President; or for the purpose of paying its own expenses and contingencies; or for the payment of claims against the Confederate States, the justice of which shall have been judicially declared by a tribunal for the investigation of claims against the Government, which it is hereby made the duty of Congress to establish.

All bills appropriating money shall specify, in Federal currency, the exact amount of each appropriation, and the purposes for which it is made; and Congress shall grant no extra compensation to any public contractor, officer, agent, or servant, after such contract shall have been made or such service rendered.

No Title of Nobility shall be granted by the United States; And no Person holding any Office of Profit or Trust under them, shall, without the Consent of the Congress, accept of any present, Emolument, Office, or Title, of any kind whatever, from any King, Prince, or foreign State.

[See Articles of Amendment I–VIII, below.]

No title of nobility shall be granted by the *Confederate States;* and no person holding any office of profit or trust under them shall, without the consent of the Congress, accept of any present, emolument, office, or title of any kind whatever, from any king, prince, or foreign state.

Congress shall make no law respecting an establishment of religion, or prohibiting the free exercise thereof; or abridging the freedom of speech, or of the press; or the right of the people peaceably to assemble and petition the Government for a redress of grievances.

A well-regulated militia being necessary to the security of a free state, the right of the people to keep and bear arms shall not be infringed.

No soldier shall, in time of peace, be quartered in any house without the consent of the owner; nor in time of war, but in a manner to be prescribed by law.

The right of the people to be secure in their persons, houses, papers, and effects, against unreasonable searches and seizures, shall not be violated; and no warrants shall issue but upon probable cause, supported by oath or affirmation, and particularly describing the place to be searched, and the persons or things to be seized.

No person shall be held to answer for a capital or otherwise infamous crime unless on a presentment or indictment of a grand jury, except in cases arising in the land or naval forces, or in the militia, when in actual service in time of war or public danger; nor shall any person be subject, for the same offense, to be twice put in jeopardy of life or limb; nor be compelled, in any criminal case, to be a witness against himself; nor be deprived of life, liberty, or property, without due process of law; nor shall private property be taken for public use without just compensation.

In all criminal prosecutions, the accused shall enjoy the right to a speedy and public trial, by an impartial jury of the State and district wherein the crime shall have been committed, which district shall have been previously ascertained by law, and to be informed of the nature and cause of the accusation; to be confronted with the witnesses against him; to have compulsory process for obtaining witnesses in his favor; and to have the assistance of counsel for his defense.

In suits at common law, where the value in controversy shall exceed twenty dollars, the right of trial by jury shall be preserved; and no fact *so* tried by a jury shall be otherwise re-examined in any court of *the Confederacy,* than according to the rules of the common law.

Excessive bail shall not be required, nor excessive fines imposed, nor cruel and unusual punishment inflicted.

Every law, or resolution hav-

ing the force of law, shall relate to but one subject, and that shall be expressed in the title.

SECTION 10. No State shall enter into any Treaty, Alliance, or Confederation; grant Letters of Marque and Reprisal; coin Money; emit Bills of Credit; make any Thing but gold and silver Coin a Tender in Payment of Debts; pass any Bill of Attainer, ex post facto Law, or Law impairing the Obligation of Contracts, or grant any Title of Nobility.

No State shall, without the consent of the Congress, lay any Imposts or Duties on Imports or Exports, except what may be absolutely necessary for executing its inspection Laws; and the net Produce of all Duties and Imposts, laid by any State on Imports or Exports, shall be for the Use of the Treasury of the United States; and all such Laws shall be subject to the Revision and Controul of the Congress.

No State shall, without the Consent of Congress, lay any Duty of Tonnage, keep Troops, or Ships of War in time of Peace, enter into any Agreement or Compact with another State, or with a foreign Power, or engage in War, unless actually

SECTION 10. No State shall enter into any treaty, alliance, or confederation; grant letters of marque and reprisal; coin money; make anything but gold and silver coin a tender in payment of debts; pass any bill of attainer, or ex post facto law, or law impairing the obligation of contracts, or grant any title of nobility.

No State shall, without the consent of the Congress, lay any imposts or duties on imports or exports, except what may be absolutely necessary for executing its inspection laws; and the net produce of all duties and imposts, laid by any State on imports or exports, shall be for the use of the Treasury of *the Confederate States;* and all such laws shall be subject to the revision and control of Congress.

No State shall, without the consent of Congress, lay any duty *on* tonnage, *except on seagoing vessels for the improvement of its rivers and harbors navigated by the said vessels; but such duties shall not conflict with any treaties of the Con-*

invaded, or in such imminent Danger as will not admit of Delay.

federate States with foreign nations. And any surplus revenue thus derived shall, after making such improvement, be paid into the common Treasury; nor shall any State keep troops or ships of war in time of peace, enter into any agreement or compact with another State, or with a foreign power, or engage in war unless actually invaded, or in such imminent danger as will not admit of delay. *But when any river divides or flows through two or more States, they may enter into compacts with each other to improve the navigation thereof.*

ARTICLE II

SECTION 1. The Executive Power shall be vested in a President of the United States of America. He shall hold his Office during the Term of four Years, and, together with the Vice President, chosen for the same Term, be elected, as follows:

Each State shall appoint, in such Manner as the Legislature thereof may direct, a Number of Electors, equal to the whole Number of Senators and Representatives to which the State may be entitled in the Congress:

SECTION 1. The Executive power shall be vested in a President of *the Confederate States of America.* He *and the Vice-President shall hold their offices for* the term of *six* years; *but the President shall not be re-eligible. The President and the Vice-President shall* be elected as follows:

Each State shall appoint, in such manner as the Legislature thereof may direct, a number of electors, equal to the whole number of Senators and Representatives to which the State may be entitled in the Congress;

but no Senator or Representative, or Person holding an Office or Trust or Profit under the United States, shall be appointed an Elector.

* The Electors shall meet in their respective States, and vote by Ballot for two Persons, of whom one at least shall not be an Inhabitant of the same State with themselves. And they shall make a List of all the Persons voted for, and of the Number of Votes for each; which List they shall sign and certify, and transmit sealed to the Seat of the Government of the United States, directed to the President of the Senate. The President of the Senate shall, in the Presence of the Senate and House of Representatives, open all the Certificates, and the Votes shall then be counted. The Person having the greatest Number of Votes shall be the President, if such Number be a Majority of the whole Number of Electors appointed; and if there be more than one who have such Majority and have an equal Number of Votes, then the House of Representatives shall immediately chuse by Ballot one of them for President; and if no Person have a Majority, then from the five highest on the List

but no Senator or Representative, or person holding an office of trust or profit under *the Confederate States,* shall be appointed an elector.

† The electors shall meet in their respective States and vote by ballot for President and Vice-President, one of whom, at least, shall not be an inhabitant of the same State with themselves; they shall name in their ballots the person voted for as President, and in distinct ballots the person voted for as Vice-President, and they shall make distinct lists of all persons voted for as President, and all persons voted for as Vice-President, and of the number of votes for each, which list they shall sign and certify, and transmit sealed to the seat of the Government of *the Confederate States,* directed to the President of the Senate. The President of the Senate shall, in the presence of the Senate and House of Representatives, open all the certificates, and the votes shall then be counted. The person having the greatest number of votes for President shall be the President, if such number be a majority of the whole number of electors appointed; and if no person have such a majority, then from

* Superseded by the Twelfth Amendment.

† See Article of Amendment XII, below.

the said House shall in like Manner chuse the President. But in chusing the President, the Votes shall be taken by States, the Representation from each State having one Vote; a Quorum for this Purpose shall consist of a Member or Members from two-thirds of the States, and a Majority of all the States shall be necessary to a Choice. In every Case, after the Choice of the President, the Person having the greatest Number of Votes of the Electors shall be the Vice-President. But if there should remain two or more who have equal Votes, the Senate shall chuse from them by Ballot the Vice-President.

the persons having the highest numbers not exceeding three on the list of those voted for as President, the House of Representatives shall choose immediately, by ballot, the President. But in choosing the President, the votes shall be taken by States, the representation from each State having one vote; a quorum for this purpose shall consist of a member or members from two-thirds of the States, and a majority of all the States, shall be necessary to a choice. And if the House of Representatives shall not choose a President whenever the right of choice shall devolve upon them, before the fourth day of March next following, then the Vice-President shall act as President, as in the case of the death or other constitutional disability of the President.

The person having the greatest number of votes as Vice-President, shall be the Vice-President, if such number be a majority of the whole number of electors appointed; and if no person have a majority, then from the two highest numbers on the list the Senate shall choose the Vice-President. A quorum for the purpose shall consist of two-thirds of the whole number of Senators, and a majority of the whole number shall be necessary to a choice.

But no person constitutionally ineligible to the office of President shall be eligible to that of Vice-President of *the Confederate States.*

The Congress may determine the Time of chusing the Electors, and the Day on which they shall give their Vote; which Day shall be the same throughout the United States.

The Congress may determine the time of choosing the electors, and the day on which they shall give their votes; which day shall be the same throughout *the Confederate States.*

No Person except a natural born Citizen, or a Citizen of the United States, at the time of the Adoption of this Constitution, shall be eligible to the Office of President; neither shall any Person be eligible to that Office who shall not have attained to the Age of thirty-five Years, and been fourteen Years a Resident within the United States.

No person except a natural born citizen of *the Confederate States,* or a citizen thereof at the time of the adoption of this Constitution, *or a citizen thereof born in the United States prior to the 20th of December, 1860,* shall be eligible to the office of President; neither shall any person be eligible to that office who shall not have attained the age of thirty-five years, and been fourteen years a resident within *the limits of the Confederate States, as they may exist at the time of his election.*

In Case of the Removal of the President from Office, or of his Death, Resignation, or Inability to discharge the Powers and Duties of the said office, the same shall devolve on the Vice President, and the Congress may by Law provide for the Case of Removal, Death, Resig-

In case of the removal of the President from office, or of his death, resignation, or inability to discharge the powers and duties of the said office, the same shall devolve on the Vice-President; and the Congress may, by law, provide for the case of removal, death, resignation, or

nation, or Inability, both of the President and Vice President, declaring what Officer shall then act as President, and such Officer shall act accordingly, until the Disability be removed, or a President shall be elected.

The President shall, at stated Times, receive for his Services, a Compensation, which shall neither be encreased nor diminished during the Period for which he shall have been elected, and he shall not receive within that Period any other Emolument from the United States, or any of them.

Before he enter on the Execution of his Office, he shall take the following Oath or Affirmation:

"I do solemnly swear (or "affirm) that I will faithfully "execute the Office of President "of the United States, and will "to the best of my Ability, pre-"serve, protect and defend the "Constitution of the United "States."

SECTION 2. The President shall be Commander in Chief of the Army and Navy of the United States, and of the Militia of the several States, when called into the actual Service of the United States; he may require the Opinion, in writing, of the principal Officer in each

inability, both of the President and Vice-President, declaring what officer shall then act as President; and such officer shall act accordingly, until the disability be removed or a President shall be elected.

The President shall, at stated times, receive for his services a compensation, which shall neither be increased nor diminished during the period for which he shall have been elected; and he shall not receive within that period any other emolument from *the Confederate States,* or any of them.

Before he enters on the execution of his office, he shall take the following oath or affirmation:

"I do solemnly swear (or affirm) that I will faithfully execute the office of President of *the Confederate States of America,* and will to the best of my ability, preserve, protect, and defend the Constitution *thereof.*"

SECTION 2. The President shall be Commander-in-Chief of the Army and Navy of *the Confederate States,* and of the militia of the several States, when called into the actual service of *the Confederate States;* he may require the opinion, in writing, of the principal officer in each of of the executive Departments, upon any Subject relating to the Duties of their respective Offices, and he shall have Power to grant Reprieves and Pardons for Offences against the United States, except in Cases of Impeachment.

He shall have Power, by and with the Advice and Consent of the Senate, to make Treaties, provided two-thirds of the Senators present concur; and he shall nominate, and by and with the Advice and Consent of the Senate, shall appoint Ambassadors, other public Ministers and Consuls, Judges of the supreme Court, and all other Officers of the United States, whose Appointments are not herein otherwise provided for, and which shall be established by Law; but the Congress may by Law vest the Appointment of such inferior officers as they think proper, in the President alone, in the Courts of Law, or in the Heads of Departments.

the executive departments, upon any subject relating to the duties of their respective offices, and he shall have power to grant reprieves and pardons for offenses against *the Confederacy,* except in cases of impeachment.

He shall have power, by and with the advice and consent of the Senate, to make treaties, provided two thirds of the Senators present concur; and he shall nominate, and by and with the advice and consent of the Senate shall appoint ambassadors, other public ministers and consuls, Judges of the Supreme Court and all other officers of *the Confederate States,* whose appointments are not herein otherwise provided for, and which shall be established by law; but the Congress may by law vest the appointment of such inferior officers, as they think proper, in the President alone, in the courts of law, or in the heads of departments.

The principal officer in each of the executive departments, and all persons connected with the diplomatic service, may be removed from office at the pleasure of the President. All other civil officers of the executive department may be removed at any time by the President, or other appointing power, when

their services are unnecessary, or for dishonesty, incapacity, inefficiency, misconduct, or neglect of duty; and, when so removed, the removal shall be reported to the Senate, together with the reasons therefor.
But no person rejected by the Senate shall be reappointed to the same office during their ensuing recess.

The President shall have Power to fill all Vacancies that may happen during the Recess of the Senate, by granting Commissions which shall expire at the End of their next Session.

The President shall have power to fill all vacancies that may happen during the recess of the Senate, by granting commissions which shall expire at the end of their next session.

SECTION 3. He shall from time to time give to the Congress Information of the State of the Union, and recommend to their Consideration such Measures as he shall judge necessary and expedient; he may, on extraordinary Occasions, convene both Houses, or either of them, and in Case of Disagreement between them, with Respect to the time of Adjournment, he may adjourn them to such Time as he shall think proper; he shall receive Ambassadors and other public Ministers; he shall take Care that the Laws be faithfully executed, and shall Commission all the officers of the United States.

SECTION 3. *The President* shall from time to time give to the Congress information of the state of *the Confederacy,* and recommend to their consideration such measures as he shall judge necessary and expedient; he may on extraordinary occasions convent both Houses, or either of them; and in case of disagreement between them, with respect to the time of adjournment, he may adjourn them to such time as he shall think proper; he shall receive ambassadors and other public ministers; he shall take care that the laws be faithfully executed, and shall commission all the officers of *the Confederate States.*

SECTION 4. The President, Vice President and all civil Officers of the United States, shall be removed from Office on Impeachment for, and Conviction of, Treason, Bribery, or other high Crimes and Misdemeanors.

SECTION 4. The President, Vice-President, and all civil officers of *the Confederate States* shall be removed from office on impeachment for and conviction of treason, bribery, or other high crimes and misdemeanors.

ARTICLE III

SECTION 1. The Judicial Power of the United States, shall be vested in one supreme Court, and in such inferior Courts as the Congress may from time to time ordain and establish. The Judges, both of the supreme and inferior Courts, shall hold their Offices during good Behavior, and shall, at stated times, receive for their Services, a Compensation which shall not be diminished during their Continuance in Office.

SECTION 1. The judicial power of *the Confederate States* shall be vested in one Supreme Court, and in such inferior courts as the Congress may from time to time ordain and establish. The Judges, both of the Supreme and inferior Courts, shall hold their offices during good behavior, and shall at stated times, receive for their services a compensation, which shall not be diminished during their continuance in office.

SECTION 2. The judicial Power shall extend to all Cases, in Law and Equity, arising under this Constitution, the Laws of the United States, and Treaties made, or which shall be made, under their Authority;—to all Cases affecting Ambassadors, other public Ministers and Consuls;—to all Cases of admiralty and maritime Jurisdiction;—to Controversies to which the

SECTION 2. The judicial power shall extend to all cases arising under this Constitution, the laws of *the Confederate States,* and treaties made, or which shall be made, under their authority; to all cases affecting ambassadors, other public ministers, and consuls; to all cases of admiralty and maritime jurisdiction; to controversities to which *the Confederate States* shall be a party;

United States shall be a party; to Controversies between two or more States;—between a State and Citizens of another State;—between Citizens of different States,—between Citizens of the same State claiming Lands under Grants of different States, and between a State, or the Citizens thereof, and foreign States, Citizens or Subjects.

In all Cases affecting Ambassadors, other public Ministers and Consuls, and those in which a State shall be Party, the supreme Court shall have original Jurisdiction. In all the other Cases before mentioned, the supreme Court shall have appellate Jurisdiction, both as to Law and Fact, with such Exceptions, and under such Regulations as the Congress shall make.

The Trial of all Crimes, except Cases of Impeachment, shall be by Jury; and such Trial shall be held in the State where the said Crimes shall have been committed; but when not committed within any State, the Trial shall be at such Place or Places as the Congress may by Law have directed.

SECTION 3. Treason against the United States, shall consist only in levying War against them, or in adhering to their Enemies, giving them Aid and

to controversies between two or more States; between a State and citizens of another State, *where the State is plaintiff;* between citizens claiming lands under grants of different States, and between a State or the citizens thereof, and foreign states, citizens, or subjects. *But no State shall be sued by a citizen or subject of any foreign state.*

In all cases affecting ambassadors, other public ministers and consuls, and those in which a State shall be party, the Supreme Court shall have original jurisdiction. In all the other cases before mentioned, the Supreme Court shall have appellate jurisdiction, both as to law and fact, with such exceptions and under such regulations as the Congress shall make.

The trial of all crimes, except in cases of impeachment, shall be by jury, and such trial shall be held in the State where the said crimes shall have been committed; but when not committed within any State the trial shall be at such place or places as the Congress may by law have directed.

SECTION 3. Treason against *the Confederate States* shall consist only in levying war against them, or in adhering to their enemies, giving them aid and

Comfort. No Person shall be convicted of Treason unless on the Testimony of two Witnesses to the same overt Act, or on Confession in open Court.

The Congress shall have Power to declare the Punishment of Treason; but no Attainder of Treason shall work Corruption of Blood, or Forfeiture except during the Life of the Person attainted.

comfort. No person shall be convicted of treason unless on the testimony of two witnesses to the same overt act, or on confession in open court.

The Congress shall have power to declare the punishment of treason; but no attainer of treason shall work corruption of blood, or forfeiture, except during the life of the person attainted.

ARTICLE IV

Section 1. Full Faith and Credit shall be given in each State to the public Acts, Records, and judicial Proceedings of every other State. And the Congress may by general Laws prescribe the Manner in which such Acts, Records and Proceedings shall be proved, and the Effect thereof.

Section 1. Full faith and credit shall be given in each State to the public acts, records, and judicial proceedings of every other State. And the Congress may, by general laws, prescribe the manner in which such acts, records, and proceedings shall be proved, and the effect thereof.

Section 2. The Citizens of each State shall be entitled to all Privileges and Immunities of Citizens in the several States.

Section 2. The citizens of each State shall be entitled to all *the* privileges and immunities of citizens in the several States, *and shall have the right of transit and sojourn in any State of this Confederacy, with their slaves and other property; and the right of property in said slaves shall not be thereby impaired.*

A Person charged in any State with Treason, Felony, or other Crime, who shall flee from Justice, and be found in another State, shall on Demand of the executive Authority of the State from which he fled, be delivered up, to be removed to the State having Jurisdiction of the Crime.

No Person held to Service or Labour in one State, under the Laws thereof, escaping into another, shall, in Consequence of any Law or Regulation therein, be discharged from such Service or Labour, but shall be delivered up on Claim of the Party to whom such Service or Labour may be due.

SECTION 3. New States may be admitted by the Congress into this Union; but no new State shall be formed or erected within the Jurisdiction of any other State; nor any State be formed by the Junction of two or more States, or Parts of States, without the Consent of the Legislature of the States concerned as well as of the Congress.

A person charged in any State with treason, felony, or other crime *against the laws of such State,* who shall flee from justice, and be found in another State, shall, on demand of the Executive authority of the State from which he fled, be delivered up, to be removed to the State having jurisdiction of the crime.

No *slave or other* person held to service or labor *in any State or Territory of the Confederate States,* under the laws thereof, escaping *or lawfully carried* into another, shall, in consequence of any law or regulation therein, be discharged from such service or labor; but shall be delivered up on claim of the party *to whom such slave belongs, or* to whom such service or labor may be due.

SECTION 3. *Other States* may be admitted *into this Confederacy by a vote of two thirds of the whole House of Representatives and two thirds of the Senate, the Senate voting by States;* but no new State shall be formed or erected within the jurisdiction of any other State; nor any State be formed by the junction of two or more States, or parts of States, without the consent of the Legislature of the States concerned as well as of the Congress.

The Congress shall have power to dispose of and make all needful Rules and Regulations respecting the Territory or other Property belonging to the United States; and nothing in this Constitution shall be so construed as to Prejudice any Claims of the United States, or of any particular State.

The Congress shall have power to dispose of and make all needful rules and regulations *concerning the property of the Confederate States, including the lands thereof.*

The Confederate States may acquire new territory; and Congress shall have power to legislate and provide governments for the inhabitants of all territory belonging to the Confederate States, lying without the limits of the several States; and may permit them, at such times and in such manner as it may by law provide, to form States to be admitted into the Confederacy. In all such territory, the institution of negro slavery, as it now exists in the Confederate States, shall be recognized and protected by Congress and by the territorial government; and the inhabitants of the several Confederate States and Territories shall have the right to take to such Territory any slaves lawfully held by them in any of the States or Territories of the Confederate States.

SECTION 4. The United States shall guarantee to every State in this Union a Republican Form of Government, and shall protect each of them against Invasion, and on Application of the Legislature, or of the Executive (when the Legislature

The Confederate States shall guarantee to every State *that now is, or hereafter may become, a member of this Confederacy,* a republican form of government; and shall protect each of them against invasion; and on application of the Legislature (or of

cannot be convened) against domestic Violence.

the Executive when the Legislature *is not in session*), against domestic violence.

ARTICLE V

THE Congress, whenever two-thirds of both Houses shall deem it necessary, shall propose Amendments to this Constitution. or, on the application of the Legislatures of two-thirds of the several States, shall call a Convention for proposing Amendments, which, in either Case, shall be valid to all Intents and Purposes, as Part of this Constitution, when ratified by the Legislatures of three-fourths of the several States, or by Conventions in three-fourths thereof, as the one or the other Mode of Ratification may be proposed by the Congress: Provided that no Amendment which may be made prior to the Year one thousand eight hundred and eight shall in any Manner affect the first and fourth Clauses in the Ninth Section of the first Article; and that no State, without its Consent, shall be deprived of its equal Suffrage in the Senate.

Upon the demand of any three States, legally assembled in their several conventions the Congress shall summon a Convention of all the States, to take into consideration such amendments to the Constitution as the said States shall concur in suggesting at the time when the said demand is made; and should any of the proposed amendments to the Constitution be agreed on by the said Convention—voting by States—and the same be ratified by the Legislatures of two thirds of the several States, or by conventions in two thirds thereof—as the one or the other mode of ratification may be proposed by *the general Convention—they shall thenceforward form a part of this Constitution. But* no State shall, without its consent, be deprived of its equal *representation* in the Senate.

ARTICLE VI

The Government established by this Constitution is the successor of the Provisional Government of the Confederate States of America, and all the laws passed by the latter shall continue in force until the same shall be repealed or modified; and all the officers appointed by the same shall remain in office until their successors are appointed and qualified, or the offices abolished.

ALL Debts contracted and Engagements entered into, before the Adoption of this Constitution, shall be as valid against the United States under this Constitution, as under the Confederation.

This Constitution, and the Laws of the United States which shall be made in Pursuance thereof; and all Treaties made, or which shall be made, under the authority of the United States, shall be the supreme Law of the Land; and the Judges in every State shall be bound thereby, any Thing in the Constitution or Laws of any State to the Contrary notwithstanding.

The Senators and Representatives before mentioned, and the

All debts contracted and engagements entered into before the adoption of this Constitution shall be as valid against *the Confederate States* under this Constitution as under *the Provisional Government.*

This Constitution, and the laws of *the Confederate States* made in pursuance thereof, and all treaties made or which shall be made under the authority of *the Confederate States,* shall be the supreme law of the land; and the Judges in every State shall be bound thereby, anything in the Constitution or laws of any State to the contrary notwithstanding.

The Senators and Representatives before mentioned, and the

Members of the several State Legislatures, and all executive and judicial Officers, both of the United States and of the several States, shall be bound by Oath or Affirmation to support this Constitution; but no religious Test shall ever be required as a Qualification to any Office or public Trust under the United States.

[See Articles of Amendment IX and X, below.]

members of the several State Legislatures, and all executive and judicial officers, both of *the Confederate States* and of the several States, shall be bound by oath or affirmation to support this Constitution; but no religious test shall ever be required as a qualification to any office or public trust under *the Confederate States.*

The enumeration in the Constitution, of certain rights, shall not be construed to deny or disparage others retained by the people *of the several States.*

The powers not delegated to *the Confederate States* by the Constitution, nor prohibited by it to the States, are reserved to the States, respectively, or to the people *thereof.*

ARTICLE VII

THE Ratification of the Conventions of nine States, shall be sufficient for the Establishment of this Constitution between the States so ratifying the Same.

THE ratification of the Conventions of *five* States shall be sufficient for the establishment of this Constitution between the States so ratifying the same.

When five States shall have ratified this Constitution, in the manner before specified, the Congress under the Provisional Constitution shall prescribe the time for holding the election of President and Vice-President, and for the meeting of the elec-

toral college, and for counting the votes, and inaugurating the President. They shall also prescribe the time for holding the first election of members of Congress under this Constitution, and the time for assembling the same. Until the assembling of such Congress, the Congress under the Provisional Constitution shall continue to exercise the legislative powers granted them; not extending beyond the time limited by the Constitution of the Provisional Government.

Following Article VII of the Confederate Constitution is the announcement:

ADOPTED unanimously by the Congress of the Confederate States of South Carolina, Georgia, Florida, Alabama, Mississippi, Louisiana, and Texas, sitting in Convention at the capitol, in the city of Montgomery, Alabama, on the 11th day of March, in the year Eighteen Hundred and Sixty-One.

HOWELL COBB
President of the Congress

The signers, the seven states, are given:

South Carolina
R. BARNWELL RHETT
C. G. MEMMINGER
WM. PORCHER MILES
JAS. CHESNUT, JR.
R. W. BARNWELL
WM. W. BOYCE
LAWRANCE M. KEITT
T. J. WITHERS

Georgia
FRANCIS S. BARTOW
MARTIN J. CRAWFORD
BENJ. H. HILL
THOS. R. R. COBB

Florida
JACKSON MORTON
J. PATTON ANDERSON
JAMES B. OWENS

Alabama

RICHD. W. WALKER
ROBT. H. SMITH
THOS. FEARNS
COLIN J. MC RAE
J. L. M. CURRY
WM. P. CHILTON
STEPHEN F. HALE
DAVID P. LEWIS
JOHN GILL SHORTER

Mississippi

ALEX M. CLAYTON
JAMES T. HARRISON
WM. W. BARRY
W. S. WILSON
WALKER BROOKE
W. P. HARRIS
J. A. P. CAMPBELL

Louisiana

ALEX. DE CLOUET
C. M. CONRAD
DUNCAN F. KENNER
HENRY MARSHALL

Texas

JOHN HEMPHILL
THOMAS N. WAUL
JOHN H. REAGAN
WILLIAMSON S. OLDHAM
LOUIS T. WIGFALL
JOHN GREGG
WM. BECK OCHILTREE

J. J. HOOPER
Secretary of the Congress

Prefixed to the first ten amendments to the Constitution of the United States of America is the following:

CONGRESS OF THE UNITED STATES,

Begun and held at the city of New York, on Wednesday, the fourth of March, one thousand seven hundred and eighty nine.

The Conventions of a number of the States, having at the time of their adopting the Constitution, expressed a desire, in order to prevent misconstruction or abuse of its powers, that further declaratory and restrictive clauses should be added; And as extending the ground of public confidence in the Government, will best insure the beneficent ends of its institution;

Resolved by the Senate and House of Representatives of the United States of America, in Congress assembled, two-thirds of both Houses concurring, That the following Articles be proposed to the Legislatures of the several States, as amendments to the Constitution of the United States, all, or any of which articles, when ratified by three-fourths of the said Legislatures, to be valid to all intents and purposes, as part of the said Constitution; viz.

Articles in Addition to, and Amendment of, the Constitution of the United States of America. Proposed by Congress, and ratified by the Legislatures of the several States, pursuant to the fifth article of the original Constitution.

ARTICLE I

Congress shall make no law respecting an establishment of religion, or prohibiting the free exercise thereof; or abridging the freedom of speech, or of the press; or the right of the people peaceably to assemble, and to petition the Government for a redress of grievances.

ARTICLE II

A well regulated Militia, being necessary to the security of a free State, the right of the people to keep and bear Arms, shall not be infringed.

ARTICLE III

No Soldier shall, in time of peace be quartered in any house, without the consent of the Owner, nor in time of war, but in a manner to be prescribed by law.

ARTICLE IV

The right of the people to be secure in their persons, houses, papers, and effects, against unreasonable searches and seizures, shall not be violated, and no Warrants shall issue, but upon probable cause, supported by Oath or affirmation, and particularly describing the place to be searched, and the persons or things to be seized.

ARTICLE V

No person shall be held to answer for a capital, or otherwise infamous crime, unless on a presentment or indictment of a Grand Jury, except in cases arising in the land or naval forces, or in the Militia, when in actual service in time of War or public danger; nor shall any person be subject for the same offence to be twice put in jeopardy of life or limb; nor shall be compelled in any Criminal Case to be a witness against himself, nor be deprived of life, liberty, or property, without due process of law; nor shall private property be taken for public use, without just compensation.

ARTICLE VI

In all criminal prosecutions, the accused shall enjoy the right to a speedy and public trial, by an impartial jury of the State and district wherein the crime shall have been committed, which district shall have been previously ascertained by law, and to be informed of the nature and cause of the accusation; to be confronted with the witnesses against him; to have Compulsory process for obtaining Witnesses in his favor, and to have the Assistance of Counsel for his defence.

ARTICLE VII

In Suits at common law, where the value in controversy shall exceed twenty dollars, the right of trial by jury shall be preserved, and no fact tried by a jury shall be otherwise reexamined in any Court of the United States, than according to the rules of the common law.

ARTICLE VIII

Excessive bail shall not be required, nor excessive fines imposed, nor cruel and unusual punishments inflicted.

ARTICLE IX

The enumeration in the Constitution of certain rights shall not be construed to deny or disparage others retained by the people.

ARTICLE X

The powers not delegated to the United States by the Constitution, nor prohibited by it to the States, are reserved to the States respectively, or to the people.

ARTICLE XII*

The Electors shall meet in their respective states, and vote by ballot for President and Vice President, one of whom, at

---

* This article is substituted for Article II, Section 1, Clause 3, and annuls it. It was declared adopted in 1804.

least, shall not be an inhabitant of the same state with themselves; they shall name in their ballots the person voted for as President, and in distinct ballots the person voted for as Vice President, and they shall make distinct lists of all persons voted for as President, and of all persons voted for as Vice President, and of the number of votes for each, which lists they shall sign and certify, and transmit sealed to the seat of the government of the United States, directed to the President of the Senate;—The President of the Senate shall, in presence of the Senate and House of Representatives, open all the certificates and the votes shall then be counted;—The person having the greatest number of votes for President, shall be the President, if such number be a majority of the whole number of Electors appointed; and if no person have such a majority, then from the persons having the highest numbers not exceeding three on the list of those voted for as President, the House of Representatives shall choose immediately, by ballot, the President. But in choosing the President, the votes shall be taken by states, the representation from each state having one vote; a quorum for this purpose shall consist of a member or members from two-thirds of the states, and a majority of all the states shall be necessary to a choice. And if the House of Representatives shall not choose a President whenever the right of choice shall devolve upon them, before the fourth day of March next following, then the Vice President shall act as President, as in the case of the death or other constitutional disability of the President.—The person having the greatest number of votes as Vice President, shall be the Vice President, if such number be a majority of the whole number of Electors appointed, and if no person have a majority, then from the two highest numbers on the list, the Senate shall choose the Vice President; a quorum for the purpose shall consist of two-thirds of the whole number of Senators, and a majority of the whole number shall be necessary to a choice. But no person constitutionally ineligible to the office of President shall be eligible to that of Vice President of the United States.

* * *

CHAPTER 14

The Two Constitutions Compared

HAVING READ AND STUDIED the two Constitutions, we are in a position to evaluate them and determine for ourselves the truth of the many assertions which have been made of the aims and objectives of the Confederacy in the attempted separation of the section from the original United States. Probably one of the best authorities, aside from the ex-President of the Confederacy himself, was Dr. J. L. M. Curry, LL.M., who was one of the framers of the Confederate States' organic law. He wrote:

> The provisional Constitution and government were temporary and tentative expedients to meet emergencies, and it was understood that a permanent government should supersede the temporary within a year or perhaps sooner. Time was taken from necessary legislation to devise, consider, discuss and adopt for State ratification a permanent Constitution. . . . This was a more serious matter than had been the transient and ephemeral scheme under which the Confederacy was bravely meeting heavy responsibilities.
>
> In the deliberations were exhibited the powers of the best minds, the learning of jurisconsults, the legislative experience of members, and the convictions of what the history of the United States had shown to be the weaknesses or failures in the old system. On the day the President and the Vice-President of the Confederacy were elected a committee for framing a constitution for a permanent government, composed of two members from each State, was appointed, with R. B. Rhett of South Carolina as chairman.

This committee was in permanent session and made its report on February 26, 1861. The final unanimous vote on adoption was taken on March 11 following.

The debates on the Constitution, frequent, sparkling, earnest, learned, Dr. Curry says, were

> . . . conducted in the best spirit, and there predominated the one controlling desire to devise a system which would stand the test of antagonism, and result in the welfare of the people and the safeguarding of human rights. It cannot be considered invidious, when, with due and strong acknowledgment of general and special merit, it is stated that Rhett, Cobb, Stephens, Toombs, Hill, Smith, Walker, Campbell, Conrad, Withers, were the men who did most towards suggesting and enforcing the changes which were adopted. The difficulties were much minimized by the attachment to the old Constitution, to which the South from the beginning of the government had given a consistent, cordial and loyal support. The South had relied on a faithful adherence to the Constitution as the surest security of the rights of the States, as the guardian of what she held most dear, and as the only bond and assurance of the Union as framed by the fathers.

The main features of the old Constitution were readopted, and only such changes made as were explanatory of the well-known intent of the authors. They were remedial of the evils which had provoked secession, purgative of the vicious interpretations of selfish majorities, made to secure the accomplishment of the true ends of the Confederacy.

To build up with greater security and permanence a constitutional Confederacy commanded the energies and patriotism of a body of men than whom Vice-President Alexander Stephens, with his large experience, said "he had never associated with an abler. . . . They were men of substance, of solid character, of moral worth, versed in the principles and practice of government, and some of them among the first men of the Continent."

Reformation of the Union was the cardinal object. Many of the changes were verbal, introduced for clearness, to prevent ambiguity and to settle controversy. The work of their hands refutes the common charges of unholy ambition, conspiracy, treason, preference for monarchy; and unprejudiced critics must accept it as a most trustworthy exposition of the opinions and principles of those who made it. The framework of government, adopted unanimously by the Congress on March 11, 1861, and ratified promptly by the seceding states, asserted the derivative character of the Confederacy, the equality and sovereignty of the states, the limitations upon the powers of the general government, and devised such restrictions as to make almost impossible future aggressions and usurpations.

These specific enumerations and reservations were made necessary by the action of the federal Executive and legislature, and have been justified by the claims put forth by writers on constitutional law. One of them even ventures the singular statement that the states had no existence anterior to the formation of the Constitution, apparently heedless or ignorant of the fact that the Declaration of Independence recognizes their sovereignty and independence, and that treaties with France, Holland, and Sweden during the Revolution, and with Great Britain at the close of that war, enumerated the states by name and treated with them as such.

So much misapprehension and misrepresentation becloud the American mind in reference to the Confederate Constitution that it may be well to present anew some of the more important changes. Some we have indicated in this comparison already. When such men as Edward Everett and Motley affirm that in the Constitution of the United States the states are not named, one can hardly be astonished at the gross ignorance about the Confederate Constitution. Can it be possible that the American people are often represented in the Congress by senators and by representatives *who do not know, have perhaps not even ever read,* that Constitution, under which they stand and to which they have solemnly sworn support? It is hardly believable; nevertheless, it would seem to be a fact. Ignorance like this, incredible as it might appear, helped to bring on the Civil War of 1861.

Dr. Curry in his work *The Southern States of the American Union* (pages 191–213) has given a full analysis of the two instruments, excerpts of which I have used here because of the clarity of his presentation.

The several sovereign states in 1787 had submitted to them for ratification the articles of Union known as the Constitution. These States had the power, as sovereigns, to accept or to reject. In the event that nine of them accepted, the compact was to be binding over those concurring, and the federal government, as the common agent, was to be invested with the *delegated* powers, and those only. Two of the states, North Carolina and Rhode Island, for some time declined to accede, and until after the inauguration of George Washington as President they continued to exercise the functions of separate, independent, sovereign states or nations. No one had the temerity to propose that they be coerced, forced, to join the Union of the federal government their neighboring sister states had set up. It was up to them alone, as sovereigns, to decide.

In the Constitution as ratified and made the supreme law of the land, certain duties were recognized as obligatory on the states, and the exercise of certain powers was restrained. That necessarily implied the continued existence of the states as retaining or reserving as sovereigns all the powers and the rights which they had not prohibited to themselves or delegated to the United States.

The federal Union became a government with defined objects and powers, limited to the express words of the grant, or what was a necessary implication. This left the residuary mass of powers in the hands of the states, or the people thereof—meaning the people of the different states separately, not the whole people, en masse, of the entire United States. There were thirteen peoples, as there were thirteen states. The states that ratified the Constitution formed the United *States* of America, not the *United People* of America; there is a vast difference, as we can see at once. Three-fourths of the whole people of the United States, living in the northeastern small section, might alter the organic law by their three-fourths vote, but when three-fourths of the *States* have to vote, it becomes a different matter.

The confusion should never arise. Take a dollar bill from your pocket, a postage stamp, and look at it; you will see that it mentions the United *States* of America on it, and there is nothing about a United *People* of America. So the states, and the peoples of those states, made the Constitution, and they alone can change it, and only in the manner provided in the instrument itself.

The residuary mass of powers in the hands of the people of the states rendered unnecessary any specifications of what was reserved. As it was well said, "there were no vagrant powers, no derelicts, subject of wind and wave seeking a resting place"; and in the Union, as creatures of the Constitution, were three divisions of powers:

1. A grant to the federal government;
2. Prohibitions on the exercise of certain powers by the federal government, by the states, or by both these agencies; and
3. The retention of the remaining mass of powers in the states, or in the people of the states.

Our Constitution with all its defects remains one of the most abiding monuments of human wisdom, and it has received a tribute to its general excellence such as no other political system was ever honored with. These are the words of English historian Freeman, who in 1863 left his *History of Federal Government From the Achaian League to the Disruption of the American Union* unfinished. It may have been his belief that the Confederacy would win in the strife, to justify a belief in the short lives of democracies as compared, say, with Britain. At any rate, the work ended about the time of the battle of Gettysburg, and he offered no excuse for the non-completion I know of. (English upper classes were for the South.)

Macaulay had predicted that the Constitution ". . . would prove all sail and no anchor." And George III predicted return to the British Empire.

The copying by the Confederate framers of one Constitution from the other was none the less an honor, but the more so because the contention was that the United States Constitution had not been observed and its guarantees and provisions had been disregarded for selfish sectional purposes by northern majorities. The States which had seceded were not dissatisfied with the Constitution, but with its administration, and their avowed and manifest purpose was to restore its integrity and to secure in the future its faithful observance. The permanent Constitution was framed on the states' rights, or Jeffersonian, school of politics, to take from a majority in Congress unlimited control, and to give effective assurances of purity and economy in all national legislation. Any careful examination will demonstrate that the seceding states were deeply attached to the plan and principles of the old Constitution, and southern statesmen often had eulogized it as the palladium of American liberties. The wisdom and conservatism of the Confederate framers will be amply vindicated by a consideration of the reforms which were attempted.

How to elect a President was one of the perplexing problems the 1787 Constitutional Convention had run up against, as we see from the records of the proceedings which Madison and others kept. The discussions show there had been no clear convictions as to a best method of choosing an Executive; and the fears were of a monarchy. Election by Congress came very near adoption, and other plans found only partial favor. When finally a plan was adopted, it was a compromise all around, and more or less tentative, in a spirit of compromise from the contrariety of the views expressed and from the apparent impossibility of any general harmonious agreement.

Such was the experience of the Confederate framers, as of the earlier ones, and no proposal of change in the organic law excited more argument and discussion than what came up on the floor as suggestions in reference to the election of a President.

What is now in force in our country in this matter had very few friends in the early day. An electoral college was provided, as we know, each state choosing as many electors as it had representatives in Congress. It was hoped that these would be an independent reality, exercising an unbiased judgment in selecting the best man with an eye only to the public interest. The electors stood between the office of the Presidency and the people, to study and to select in accordance with fitness.

Many think that while the letter of the law remains, the intent has been entirely frustrated, as the intermediate electors have no independent opinions and are pledged agents to vote for a chosen candidate on a prescribed political "platform" the party has proposed. What was meant as a restraint, a check, upon party excess and control has become its most efficient instrument. No elector would dare to disregard the will of his party that has been expressed in national caucus.

Dispensing with the intermediary agency and exalting the power and influence of a national caucus has made a presidential election the main object of political management; it has absorbed public opinion and dominates all other elections. An election has become a gigantic party struggle that never ceases, and determines in its result the policy of the administration and the distribution of the offices and the "plums."

Party organization is compact and despotic, heartless and resistless, and a few "bosses" by manipulation control it. A place as a delegate in a nominating caucus is sought for; a campaign fund sometimes running into millions of dollars, spent without accounting or audit of any kind, is secured by assessments or by voluntary contributions, which may be reimbursed by appointment to offices, ambassadorships, contracts, appropriations, or legislative discrimination and like skullduggery. Therefore, an American presidential election, instead of being what the founding fathers had sought to make of it, the choice of the best and the fittest by an intermediary group, is but the quadrennial political stirring of every neighborhood across the country.

The serious men who formed the committees to frame the Confederate Constitution saw themselves up against a system essentially vicious and of long operation. To reform it demanded serious effort. A number of proposals were made, debated, voted upon. All favored some change to get out from under the system the old method had degenerated to, but as it turned out they found it not possible to agree on any scheme that would be free from objection; all had faults of one kind or another. So the condemned mode was finally retained, with the hope that some of the evils might be remedied under more favorable conditions—that is, when the war had ended, successfully for their side, as they hoped.

Therefore, in the Executive Department of the Confederate government a radical change was made so that the country would not too soon be deprived of the experience, ability, and services of a President just when he would likely be most needed. The tenure of the presidential office was fixed at six years, with ineligibility for second terms. Some years after the Civil War an American President leaving office was asked to express what he would consider needed or improving changes in the Executive branch. President Rutherford B. Hayes gave only the two here made by the Confederates.

Our history and that of much of the so-called "free" world has shown that the great muniments of freedom, wrung from the grasp of tyrants, have been protests against the arbitrary exercise of Executive power. Our people sought protection against it in a written Constitution and in specific guarantees.

Under our system the President is, to all practical purposes, the appointee of irresponsible bodies of men. Any disinherited wanderer with a vote has a say in his elevation to the highest office. The triumph of a party is of more consequence than the public welfare. We have seen such an exhibition in the triumph of a so-called New Deal only recently, with all the shameful degradations it brought, the wars, the dishonest money, the infiltration of traitors into the very seats of government itself, the intellectual dishonesty of most of the politicians, from the President himself down to the lowest ward boss. Instead of a new "deal" it was simply an old "steal" wherein the thrifty and the provident are robbed for the benefit of the lesser of society's membership, in "humanity's" name, paraded as "the general welfare."

The patronage of a President is used as spoils of office for rewarding partisans, or for silencing free thought; the halls of the legislature become arenas for personal disputes and disgraceful strifes. To try to eliminate some of these evils the framing body at Montgomery, Alabama, decided it would be wise to make the change to six years and no second term for the Executive. When a President is a candidate to succeed himself, he may be tempted to use the immense patronage and influence of his high office to secure renomination and success at the polls. Nowhere has this been better seen in our country than in the record-breaking office tenure of Franklin D. Roosevelt, of two decades. We need but compare the national debt of our country when he went into office in 1933 with that debt when he left it to grasp at a glance what the office can hold for the nation. If the President wants to be re-elected, nearly everything is made to bend to that one ambition. The weaker or more pliable that President, the greater are the possibilities for evil. He may think of himself as the indispensable man—something no man is. He may forget the country's good in his desire for re-election and yield to the persuasions or motives which may make him the instrument of those who are ambitious, or designing, or self-seeking. One term, six years, for an Executive was one important change, worthy still of study today in the political realm of the United States.

Connected with federal legislation is the term "log-rolling." Bills are often loaded with objectionable items. Combinations of interested persons and interests succeed in fastening upon the Treasury bad schemes that could not singly pass either house of the Congress. Upon the Confederate Executive devolved the responsibility of estimating and asking for appropriations with a view to an economic administration and to a better guardianship of the Treasury. Congress could not make an appropriation except by a two-thirds vote of both houses, taken by the yeas and nays, unless asked for and estimated by the department heads through the President, but this did not apply for its own expenses and certain judicially determined claims. To obtain some security against extravagance, corrupt, or illegitimate expenditures, the President had power to veto particular clauses in an appropriation bill and to approve others.

Power and responsibility were lodged in the same hands by a number of devices. Initiative in disbursing was placed to a considerable degree in the President's hands. He became a sort of legislative committee, as in the English House of Commons, to watch receipts and expenditures, and to make suggestions for raising revenue or lowering taxation. Every law must relate to but one subject, which must be expressed in the title. At stated intervals the Treasury published its receipts and disbursements by items. These were all meant as precautionary measures to limit the power and objects of taxation, and to take scrupulous care of the public moneys. We must accord the southern men in the Congress the distinction that they were the most conservative of men, believing in economy and guarding against waste and corruption, and their long domination of the Congress was one of the little heeded or written-up goods that the nation early knew and benefited from.

The Confederate Constitution attempted to restrict Executive powers. The officers of the Cabinet, or those in diplomatic service, could be removed by the President at his discretion, but in all other cases removal could only be made for cause, and that had to be reported to the Confederate Senate. No one nominated for civil office and rejected by the Senate could be reappointed in the interim of Congress.

In England the Crown is exempt from all political or personal responsibility, and instead, the Ministry takes this over. Their recommendations and acts can be discussed in Parliament and a vote of censure, or disapproval, may result in a change of the Ministry or government. A large part of the power is transferred to a Cabinet or Ministry, each member of which must be a Parliament member with the right of duty and the initiative even of management of the legislation, and to appear and be heard in defense or otherwise, under the British system.

It is often different in Washington, D.C. Under some administrations there, it has been seen there is an injurious lack of sympathetic intercourse between the Congress and the White House, and between Cabinet members and the various committees of Congress concerned in matters of mutual interest. Recall the Hoover administration, 1929–33.

Ease of communication makes for better working of the government. So, as far as the wide difference between a presidential (as ours) and a cabinet (as in Britain) government, there was put in the Confederate government in modified form an imitation of an essential feature of the British Constitution, to allow the President to be heard on the floor of the two houses through his constitutional advisers. A member of the Cabinet could not be a member of Congress as a member of the British Cabinet must be a member of Parliament, but the Confederate Congress was authorized by law to grant to the principal officer in each Executive department a seat upon the floor of either house, with the privilege of discussing any matters appertaining to his department.

The provision for the appropriation of money upon the estimates of the Executive, so making him responsible to the Congress for an economical administration, combined with some other advantages which the British system enjoys, caused the adoption of this experiment; but because of the many intervening and imperative exigencies of the war, the legislation necessary to put this judicious reform into execution was left undone. The occasional appearance of Cabinet officers before the Congress to participate in debates appeared to work beneficially and demonstrated the importance of enlarging the privilege.

The words "general welfare" appear in both the body and the preamble of the United States Constitution; it will be noted it is not in the Confederate version (Art. I, § 8). Now, it has never been seriously contended that the framing fathers intended to grant to Congress a blanket, separate power, unrestricted, to provide for the general welfare, yet it was a clause used to hurt the South seriously as a region. Hamilton and Madison in the *Federalist* gave interpretations. Madison noted that the phrase, whose breadth was questioned, was to be limited by the succeeding clauses, "immediately following . . . not even separated by a longer pause than a semi-colon. . . . For what purposes could the enumeration of particular powers be inserted, if these, and all others were meant to be included in the preceding general power?" To Jefferson it was a qualification of the power to lay taxes:

> Congress are not to lay taxes *ad libitum,* for any purpose they please; but only to pay the debts, or provide for the welfare of the Union. . . . In like manner they are not to do anything they please to provide for the general welfare, but only to lay taxes for that purpose. To consider the latter phrase not as describing the purpose of the first, but to give a distinct and independent power to do any act they please which might be for the good of the Union, would render all the preceding and subsequent enumerations of power completely useless. It would reduce the whole instrument to a single phrase, that of instituting a Congress with power to do whatever would be for the good of the United States; and, as they would be the sole judges of the good or evil, it would also be a power to do whatever evil they pleased. . . . It is an established rule of construction, where a phrase will bear either of two meanings, to give that which will allow some meaning to the other parts of the instrument, and not that which would render all the others useless. . . . Certainly, no such power of universality was meant to be given here to Congress. It was intended to lace them up strictly within the enumerated powers, and those without which, as means, those powers could not be carried into effect. . . . [Bank opinion, Feb. 15, 1791.]

Opposed therefore to the United States Constitution, Article I, Section 8, the Confederate wording was, "The Congress shall have power—To lay and collect taxes, duties, imposts, and excises, for revenue necessary to pay the debts, provide for the common defense, and carry on the government of the Confederate States; but no bounties shall be granted from the Treasury; nor shall any duties or taxes on importations from foreign nations be laid to promote or foster any branch of industry; and all duties, imposts, and excises shall be uniform throughout the Confederate States. . . ."

Commodore Maury, "the pathfinder," wrote on the inequities which had been practiced against the South—wrongs and injustices a politically stronger North had imposed. He had made his protest, setting forth many instances where the "general welfare" clause had brought about inequities, always against the South, so that when the South decided to go its own way it was careful to make specific provisions in its own version of the Constitution; it followed the founding fathers' intent in that respect.

Hamilton's interpretation, as given in the *Federalist* and other writings, was that Congress may not legislate generally with respect to any matter which concerns the general welfare; it may appropriate money for any purpose concerning the general welfare. But Madison's was a narrower view. The first clause of Article I, Section 8, of the United States Constitution is coextensive with and limited by the powers expressly conferred on Congress in the remaining clauses of Section 8. Under his interpretation Congress can appropriate money for the general welfare only insofar as the appropriation may be incidental to other expressly delegated powers, such as the power to regulate commerce and the power to establish post offices and post roads. His claim was that where general words or phrases are followed by special words or phrases, the general words are limited by the special words—an argument which is analogous to the legal principle of *ejusdem generis* (Latin, "of the same kind"), under which in the construction of laws, wills, and other legal instruments it commonly is held that where the general words follow words of a particular and specific meaning, such general words are not to be construed in their widest extent but are held to be limited to persons or things of the same general kind or class as those specifically mentioned.

Madison's argument, that there would have been no purpose in inserting the subsequent enumerated powers in the Section 8 if a general power to legislate for the general welfare was intended, is of very great force. It was always insisted upon by the southerners, because it is obvious that the Constitution was not framed to contain useless surplusage. So it has become accepted today that Clause 1 gives the Congress only a limited power to appropriate money for the general welfare, and that, so limited, delegation of other powers in Section 8 was both necessary and purposeful.

The main controversy remaining concerned the permissible purposes for which money was to be appropriated. The Confederates had suffered long from political opponents on the matter, and they now were taking care to put, in positive ways which there could be no question about, limits as to money expenditures.

There were certain legislative restrictions connected with the Executive. As we know, a bulging Treasury is a usual source of corruption, legislative favoritism, unrepublican paternalism, and we note that some of the wisest of American statesmen have made it a maxim of prime importance to keep the government poor. The vague clause of the U. S. Constitution—of "the general welfare"—has been used for party and personal advantage and a sectional use not fair to all. Such unjust discrimination aroused the bitterest discontent and hostility, and in the final analysis, it was this which brought on the Civil War. This, not the absurd idea that the North was crusading to "free the Negro slaves of the South from a degrading bondage" . . . that is laughable.

Subsidies, bounties, partnerships in trusts, corporations, "vast plutonic combinations of incorporated wealth," as it was sometimes referred to, the fostering of favored branches of industry by taxing with import duties the southern planter to enrich by high wages and profits the northern manufacturer and his wage-slave employee . . . here is another cause of the Civil War.

It is, in fact, possible to trace to the collection and the disbursement of tax money by the general government anarchy, communism, labor trouble, corrupt politics; and they were among the chief causes of the South's discontent and the real reason for the break with the North, in effort to find *outside* the Union the safety, the prosperity, the rights and security, it no longer could find, even hope for, *within* the Union. With this the Negro had nothing whatever to do, and was merely dragged in by the feet and set up as a "humanitarian" excuse to justify the carrying of fire and sword into the southern regions by the Lincoln administration. Lincoln's expressions throughout are blunt proofs and corroborations of it. The Emancipation itself was an Executive act done towards prosecution of the war to try to hasten its end, and it was admitted humorously by Thaddeus Stevens and Lincoln himself (that occasion privately) that it "freed not one slave in all the South."

The Confederate Constitution forbade the levying and collection of taxes, imposts, duties, excises, except for the discharge of debts and carrying on the government. Connected with this was the establishment of courts to adjudicate claims, the power of Congress over which was strictly limited (Art. I, § 9).

Once we were a government of economy and frugality, in better days of the republic, only slowly to lapse into billion-dollar extravagant expenditures for the paternalism of the government in "class" legislation, pork-barrel appropriations. It would seem that, however wide the differences with administrations or party on the questions of great moment, they are secondary to, or subordinated to, personal benefits of protection. History has justified the precautions taken against the governmental wrongs. Error and falsehood and corruption and wrong die but slowly when they have fastened themselves upon and draw vitality from governments, as we have seen in the abuses of olden times inseparable from alliance of the State and the Church. Any government partnerships in business either direct or by legislative fostering become evils in the federal and the municipal governments, and the general government becomes impeded by private cupidity. To protect a favorite interest makes all other issues sink to insignificance, if an election is involved.

Facilities granted in one place give preferences and advantages and consequent disadvantages. Therefore the Confederate Congress was denied the right to make appropriations for internal improvements, even for the facilitation of commerce, except the usual costs for lights, beacons, aids to navigation, harbor and river improvement, and here the costs and expenses had to be borne by duties on the facilities aided. But under certain conditions a state could accomplish the work within her boundaries by levy of a duty on the seagoing tonnage participating in the trade on the rivers or in the harbors improved. Any two or more states were constitutionally authorized to enter into agreements with one another for improvements of navigation of the rivers between them or flowing through them.

The Confederate Post Office, after March 1, 1863, was to be required to pay its own expenses out of its own revenues—this to do away with the abuse so widely made of federal franking privileges, and was a constitutional provision. Congress could not change it.

The methods of amendment to the Confederate Constitution had some changes recommended from the method of the other instrument, and changes also were had in the admission of new states, in bankruptcy laws, the jurisdiction of suits between citizens of different states being withheld in federal courts and territories, to correct abuses and to give greater clearness. To prevent alien suffrage, voters were required to be citizens, and senators were to be chosen at the session next immediately preceding the beginning of the term of service. We have mentioned the slavery matter.

It had been affirmed that the reopening of the slave trade was a recognized feature of the scheme of the leaders of the Confederacy. What was in the minds of the leaders, "unavowed and as yet carefully disavowed," as was falsely spread about, no one could say or guess at the fantasy. At that date a number of slavers had been fitted out in New York, supposedly to engage in bringing slaves into Cuba, and such vessels had been permitted to depart without molestation, according to historian Rhodes (*History of the United States,* Vol. II, page 369). Some lawless adventurers during 1859 and 1860 had attempted to bring some Africans into southern ports, or land them on the coasts in violation of law. The southerners looked upon these as semi-piratical efforts, and severely punished those who fell under the toils of the law. Such attempts had no standing.

Certainly no provision was ever made in the Confederate Congress to connive at the opening of such trade, and certainly there was no sympathy for it, and no favor for the scheme to be found in the government, whatever might or might not have existed among a few individuals of the South or the North. When Section 9 of Article I was up for adoption, there was not a dissenting vote. So the fantastic statements could only have been propaganda and lies to injure and prejudice against the South. That there were "conspirators overthrowing the Constitution of the United States and erecting a great slavery oligarchy" was a lie out of whole cloth, and but part of the long list of misrepresentations and distortions spread to disparage the South.

Conclusion

A STUDY of the Constitution of the Confederacy shows that every possible infringement upon popular liberty, or upon states' rights, every oppression or sectional use of the taxing power, was most carefully guarded against; civil-service reform was made easy and practicable. Stubborn and corrupting controversies about tariff, post office, river improvements, harbor improvements, subsidies, extra pay, etc., were avoided; the taxing power was placed under salutary restrictions, and responsibility more clearly fixed. The money of the Treasury was protected against purchasable majorities and wicked combinations; there were adequate powers for a frugal and just administration granted to the general government. The states maintained their autonomy and were not reduced to petty corporations, or counties, or dependencies.

A vast accumulation of power at Washington, D.C., a supposedly necessary supremacy of the central government, was a wide departure from the founding fathers' theories and principles and had fearful import. If it continued, the southerners felt, the country would drift away from the purposes and the hopes of their ancestors. Expansion, militarism, the extension of laws and administration without constitutional grants, and inhibitions over territory and people acquired by purchase and conquest and treaty had become of vast concern, and the best minds of the nation were required to handle the unprecedented comings with wisdom and integrity.

In that day the Confederate Constitution was subjected to a blast of condemnation and disparagement not at all warranted by facts and the truth. One northern source, however—the New York *Herald*—on March 19, 1861, printed these editorial considerations and recommendations:

> The ultimatum of the seceded States is now before the Government in Washington, in this new Constitution adopted by the Congress at Montgomery, Alabama. Heretofore even our

best-disposed Northern conservatives have been perplexed how to move, and what to propose to reconcile the Cotton States to the Union. Now, however, with their ultimatum before us there can be no longer any doubt upon the subject. In their unrestricted discretion to shape a Federal Constitution for themselves, the seceded States have unquestionably provided these securities, checks, and balances which they regard as essential for the maintenance of their peculiar institutions. Thus our Northern politicians and the administration at Washington are furnished the conditions upon which the Union may be re-established, without war and without trouble.

The new Southern Constitution is the Constitution of the United States with various modifications and some very important and most desirable improvements. . . .

Such are the provisions of this Southern Constitution which we may accept as the ultimatum of the seceded States on the subject of slavery. Upon some other questions however there are certain stringent provisions which it would be extremely difficult to persuade our Northern fishermen, manufacturers, and lobby corruptionists to swallow even to re-establish the Union. . . . [They include:]

(1) The absolute prohibition of all bounties from the Federal Treasury, and all duties or taxes on imported goods intended to promote or foster any branch of home industry.
(2) A positive prohibition of Federal appropriations for internal improvements and substitution of local tonnage dues for such improvements.
(3) The restriction of Congress by a majority vote to such appropriations as may be recommended by the President or some Executive department. All other appropriations requiring a two-thirds vote.
(4) A holding of contractors to the strict letter of their contract.
(5) That the Post Office Department shall pay its own expenses.

These are excellent constitutional amendments. If they had been in force in Washington during the last ten years they would have prevented the wasteful squandering in swindling

> lobby jobs, contracts, etc., of three, four, or five hundred million dollars of public money and public property that have been squandered to the enriching of the lobby jobbers, and the general demoralization of our Northern political parties and politicians to the lowest level of debasement and corruption. The two classes of amendments upon slavery and upon other important subjects comprehend the peace offerings of the seceding States to the border States. They are radical propositions of change and reform. . . . We are free to say, also, that the invaluable reforms enumerated should be adopted by the United States, with or without a reunion of the seceded States, and as soon as possible. But why not accept them with the propositions of the Confederate States on slavery as a basis of reunion? Practically to the North these slavery abstractions amount to nothing, while the reforms indicated are indispensable to the existence of our government for any length of time, with or without the seceded States. Let President Lincoln then call Congress together, and let him lay before it this new Constitution of the seceded States and the peace propositions of their treaty commissioners, and perhaps there may be wisdom enough in the two houses to provide ways and means for peace, and the purification of the Government at Washington, even if there be no way to absorb the government at Montgomery, Alabama. . . .

That was published in mid-March, 1861. But President Lincoln did not call the Congress into special session, as he should have at so grave an hour. It was set to meet July next. Meanwhile, the President seized power, and thrust the Constitution underfoot.

Bibliography

Adams, James T. *Epic of America.*
Alfriend. *Life of Jefferson Davis.*
Black. *On Constitutional Law* (4th ed.).
Bowers. *The Tragic Era;* others in MS.
Curry, Dr. J. L. M. *Confederate States Constitution and Government; History of the Government of the Confederate States; Personal Reminiscences; Southern States of the American Union.*
Calhoun, John C. *Works.*
Calhoun & McAlarney. *Readings in American Literature.*
Chase, Samuel P. *Diaries.*
Davis, Jefferson. *Rise and Fall of the Confederate Government,* 2 vols.
Davis, Varina (Mrs. J.). *Biography of Ex-President Davis of the Confederate States of America,* 2 vols.
Evans. *Cases on Constitutional Law.*
Federalist Papers, The (various numbers).
Fiske, John. *Critical Period of American History.*
—*Civil Government in the United States.*
Grant, U. S. *Memoirs,* 2 vols.
Henry, R. S. *Story of the Confederacy.*
Hoover, Herbert. *Addresses on the American Road; Challenge to Liberty.*
Hughes, Charles E. *Supreme Court of the United States* (Columbia University lectures, 1927).
Johnson. *Government in the United States* (2d [Crowell] ed., 1937).
Jones, Daniel, *et al. Memorials of the Confederacy* (monographs).
Norton. *Constitution of the United States of America.*
Pollard. *Secret History of the Confederacy.*
Quynn, R. H. *Jefferson Davis, Confederate President.*
Robinson. *Elementary Law.*
Rhodes. *History of the United States From the Compromise of 1850.*
U.S. District Courts, Miscellaneous Reports of the.
Wilson, Woodrow. *History of the American People; Works.*
Woodward. *New History.*
Zane. *Law.*

In addition, there was frequent use of various reference works, among them the *Encyclopaedia Britannica,* the *Cyclopedic Law Dictionary,* and the *Funk and Wagnalls Encyclopedia*; to printed and MS. holdings of the American Archives (Washington, D.C.), the Law and Rare Book Sections of the Library of Congress (Washington), the Confederate Soldiers' Home at Pikesville, Maryland, and the Southern Historical Society; to various magazine and newspaper articles and reports from the period 1830–73; and to *Reminiscences* of many of the nineteenth century, including Campbell, Dr. Curry, Daniel, Mr. Davis, FitzLee, Garland, Gordon, Hoge, Johnson, Jones, Lawton, Marshall, Minnigerode, Reagan, Tucker, Vest, Wallis, and numerous others, prominent men, officials and soldiers, who served the Confederacy.

Index

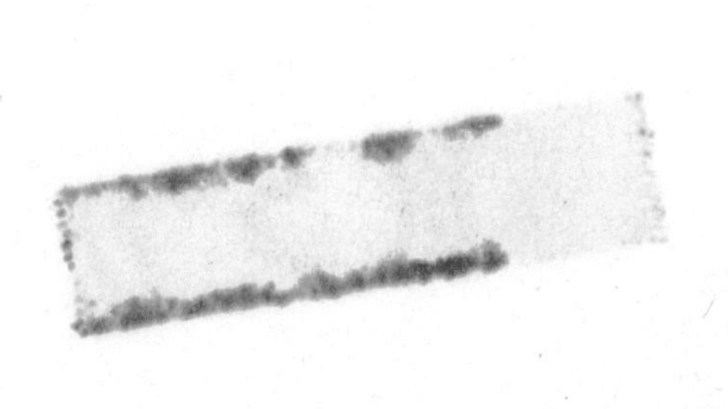